K. MARX
AND
F. ENGELS

THE HOLY FAMILY
OR
CRITIQUE OF CRITICAL CRITIQUE

*

FOREIGN LANGUAGES PUBLISHING HOUSE

Moscow 1956

The Holy Family

Marx and Engels

FROM THE INSTITUTE OF MARXISM-LENINISM

The Holy Family, or Critique of Critical Critique. Against Bruno Bauer and Co. is the first joint work of Karl Marx and Frederick Engels. At the end of August 1844 Marx and Engels met in Paris and their meeting was the beginning of their joint creative work in all fields of theoretical and practical revolutionary activity. By this time Marx and Engels had completed the transition from idealism to materialism and from revolutionary democratism to communism. The polemic *The Holy Family* was written in Paris in autumn 1844. It reflects the progress in the formation of Marx and Engels's revolutionary materialistic world outlook.

In *The Holy Family* Marx and Engels give a devastating criticism of the subjectivist views of the Young Hegelians from the position of militant materialists. They also criticize Hegel's own idealistic philosophy: giving credit for the rational element in his dialectics, they criticize the mystic side of it.

The Holy Family formulates a number of fundamental theses of dialectical and historical materialism. In it Marx already approaches the basic idea of historical materialism —the decisive role of the mode of production in the development of society. Refuting the idealistic views of history which had dominated up to that time, Marx and Engels prove that of themselves progressive ideas can lead society only beyond the ideas of the old system and that "in order to carry out ideas men are needed who dispose of a certain practical force." (See p. 160 of the present edition.) The proposition put forward in the book that the mass, the people, is the real maker of the history of mankind is of paramount importance. Marx and Engels show that the wider and the more profound a change taking place in society is, the more numerous the mass effecting that change will be. Lenin especially stressed the importance of this thought and described it as one of the most profound and most important theses of historical materialism.

The Holy Family contains the almost mature view of the historic role of the proletariat as the class which, by virtue of its position in capitalism, "can and must free itself" and at the same time abolish all the inhuman conditions of life of bourgeois society, for "not in vain does" the proletariat "go through the stern but steeling school of *labour*. The question is not what this or that proletarian, or even the whole of the proletariat at the moment *considers* as its aim. The question is *what the proletariat is*, and what, consequent on that *being*, it will be compelled to do." (Pp. 52-53.)

A section of great importance is "Critical Battle against French Materialism" in which Marx, briefly outlining the development of materialism in West-European philosophy, shows that communism is the logical conclusion of materialistic philosophy.

The Holy Family was written largely under the influence of the materialistic views of Ludwig Feuerbach, who was responsible to a great extent for Marx's and Engels's transition from idealism to materialism; the work also contains elements of the criticism of Feuerbach's metaphysical and contemplative materialism given by Marx in spring 1845 in his *Theses on Feuerbach*. Engels later defined the place of *The Holy Family* in the history of Marxism when he wrote: "The cult of abstract man, which formed the kernel of Feuerbach's new religion, had to be replaced by the science of real men and of their historical development. This further development of Feuerbach's standpoint beyond Feuerbach was inaugurated by Marx in 1845 in *The Holy Family*." (F. Engels, *Ludwig Feuerbach and the End of Classical German Philosophy*.)

The Holy Family formulates some of the basic principles of Marxist political economy. In contrast to the Utopian Socialists Marx bases the objective inevitability of the victory of communism on the fact that private property in its economic motion drives itself towards its downfall.

The Holy Family dates from a period when the process of the formation of Marxism was not yet completed. This is reflected in the terminology used by Marx and Engels. Marxist scientific terminology was gradually elaborated and defined by Marx and Engels as the formation and development of their teaching progressed.

Institute of Marxism-Leninism
of the C.C., C.P.S.U.

Die heilige Familie,

oder

Kritik

der

kritischen Kritik.

Gegen Bruno Bauer & Consorten.

Von

Friedrich Engels und Karl Marx.

Frankfurt a. M.

Literarische Anstalt

(J. Rütten.)

1 8 4 5.

Title page of the first edition of *The Holy Family*

FOREWORD

Real Humanism has no more dangerous enemy in Germany than *spiritualism* or *speculative idealism* which substitutes "*self-consciousness*" or the "*spirit*" for the *real individual man* and teaches with the evangelist "that the spirit quickeneth everything and that the flesh profiteth not." Needless to say, this fleshless spirit is spiritual only in his imagination. What we are combating in *Bauer's* criticism is *speculation* reproducing itself as a *caricature*. We see in it the most complete expression of the *Christian-Germanic* principle which, in a last effort, transforms "criticism" itself into a transcendent power.

Our exposition deals first and foremost with Bruno Bauer's *Allgemeine Literatur-Zeitung*[2] the first eight numbers are here before us—because in it Bauer's criticism, and with it the nonsense of *German speculation in general*, has reached its peak. The more completely Critical Criticism—the criticism of *Literatur-Zeitung*—distorts reality into an obvious comedy through philosophy, the more instructive it is. For examples see *Faucher* and *Szeliga*. *Literatur-Zeitung* offers material by which even the broad public can be enlightened on the illusions of speculative philosophy. That is the aim of this book.

Our exposition is naturally determined by its *subject*. Critical Criticism is in all respects *below* the level already attained by German theoretical development. The nature of our subjects therefore justifies our refraining from further *discussion* of that development itself *here*.

Critical Criticism makes it necessary, on the other hand, to assert in contrast to it the already achieved results *as such*.

We therefore give this polemic as a preliminary to the independent works in which we—each for himself, of course—shall present our positive view and thereby our positive attitude to more recent philosophical and social doctrines.

Paris, September 1844

ENGELS. MARX

CRITICAL CRITICISM AS A BOOKBINDER, OR CRITICAL CRITICISM IN THE PERSON OF HERR REICHARDT

Critical Criticism, however superior to the mass it deems itself, has infinitive pity for the mass. And therefore Criticism has so loved the mass that it sent it its only begotten son, that all who believe in him may not be lost, but that they may have Critical life. Criticism was made mass and dwelt amongst us and we beheld its glory, the glory of the only begotten of the father. In other words, Criticism becomes socialistic and speaks of "works on pauperism." It considers it not a crime to be equal to God but empties itself and takes the form of a bookbinder and humbles itself even to nonsense, yea, even to Critical nonsense in foreign languages. It, whose heavenly virginal purity shrank from contact with the sinful leprous mass, overcame itself to the extent of taking notice of *Boz* and "*all* original writers on pauperism" and "has for years been following the complaint of the century step by step"; it scorns writing for experts, it writes for the general public, banning all outlandish expressions, all "Latin intricacies, all professional cant." It bans all that from the works of *others*, for it would be too much to expect Criticism itself to submit to "that regulation." And yet it does partly, renouncing with astonishing ease if not the words themselves at least their content. And who will reproach it for using "the great number of unintelligible foreign words" when it repeatedly proves that it does not understand those words itself? Here are a few samples:

"That is why the *institutions of mendicity* inspire them with horror."

"A doctrine of responsibility in which every motion *of human thought becomes an image of Lot's wife.*"

"On the keystone of this really *profound edifice of art.*"

"This is the main content of Stein's political legacy, which the great statesman handed in before retiring from the active service of the government *and from all its actions.*"

"This people had *not yet any dimensions* at that time for such extensive freedom."

"*Conferring* with fair assurance at the end of his publicistic work that only confidence was still lacking."

"To a reason worthy of a state-elevating man, above routine and pusillanimous fear, reared on history and nurtured with a vivacious conception of foreign public and state system."

"The education of general national welfare."

"Freedom lay dead *in the breast of the Prussian national mission* under the control of the authorities."

"*Popular-organic* publicism."

"The people to whom even Herr Brüggemann delivers a *baptism certificate of majority.*"

"A fairly sharp antithesis of all the other *certitudes* which have been expressed in the work on professional capacities of the people."

"Pitiful self-interest quickly dispels all the *chimaeras of the national will.*"

"Passion for great gains, etc., was the spirit that pervaded the whole of the Restoration period and which, with a *fair quantity of indifference, adhered* to the new age."

"The vague idea of political significance noticeable in the *Prussian countrymanship nationality rests on the memory of a great history.*"

"The antipathy disappeared and turned into a completely exalted condition."

"In this wonderful transition each one in his own way still *held forth the prospect of* his own special *wish*."

"A catechism with unctuous Solomon-like language the words of which—chirp! chirp!—rise gently like a dove to the regions of pathos and *thunder-like aspects*."

"All the *dilettantism of thirty-five years of negligence*."

"The *too sharp thundering* at the citizens by one of their former town authorities could have been suffered with the calmness characteristic of our representatives if Benda's view of the Town Charter of 1808 had not laboured under a *Mussulman affectation of the concept* of the essence and the application of the Charter."

In Herr Reichardt, bold style always goes with bold thought. He makes transitions like the following:

"Herr Brüggemann ... 1843 ... state theory ... every outspoken man ... the great modesty of our socialists ... natural marvels ... demands to be made on Germany ... supernatural marvels ... Abraham ... Philadelphia ... manna ... baker ... but *as* we are speaking of *marvels, Napoleon* brought," etc.

After these samples it is no wonder that Critical Criticism gives us another "explanation" of a sentence which it describes as a "popular way of speaking," for it "arms its eyes with organic power to penetrate chaos." And here it must be said that even a "popular way of speaking" cannot remain unintelligible to Critical Criticism. It admits that the way of the writer must necessarily be a crooked one if the individual who sets out on it is not strong enough to make it straight; and therefore it naturally ascribes "mathematical operations" to the author.

It goes without saying—and history, which proves everything which goes without saying, also proves this—that Criticism does not become mass in order to remain mass, but to

2*

redeem the mass from its massy massiness, that is, to raise the popular way of speaking to the critical language of Critical Criticism. It is the lowest degree of humiliation for Criticism to learn the popular language of the mass and transfigure that vulgar jargon into the transcendent intricacy of the dialectics of Critical Criticism.

CHAPTER II

CRITICAL CRITICISM AS A MILL-OWNER,[3]
OR
CRITICAL CRITICISM IN THE PERSON OF HERR JULES FAUCHER

Having humbled itself to nonsense in foreign languages and thus rendered the most substantial services to self-consciousness, and at the same time freed the world from pauperism, Criticism humbles itself even to nonsense in *practice* and *history*. It masters "*English questions of the day*" and gives us a genuinely *critical Outline of the History of English Industry.*

Self-sufficient Criticism, complete and perfect in itself, naturally must not recognize history as it really took place, for that would mean recognizing the base mass in all its massy massiness, whereas the problem is to redeem the mass from massiness. History is therefore freed from its massiness, and Criticism, which has a *free* attitude to its object, calls to history, saying: "*You ought to have happened in such and such a way!*" All the laws of Criticism have *retroactive* force: history behaved quite differently *before* the decrees of Criticism than it did *after* them. Hence massy history, the so-called *real* history, deviates considerably from *Critical* history, as is the case in No. VII of *Literatur-Zeitung* from page 4 onwards.

In massy history there were *no industrial towns* before there were *factories*; but in Critical history, in which the son begets his father, as already in *Hegel, Manchester, Bolton* and *Preston* were flourishing industrial towns before factories were even thought of. In real history the *cotton in-*

dustry was founded on *Hargreaves's* jenny and *Arkwright's throstle, Crompton's mule* being only an improvement on the spinning jenny according to a new principle discovered by Arkwright. But Critical history knows how to distinguish between things: it scorns the one-sidedness of the jenny and the throstle and gives the crown to the mule as the speculative identity of the extremes. In reality, the invention of the throstle and the mule made possible the immediate *application* of *water power* to those machines, but Critical Criticism sorts out principles mixed up by vulgar history and makes this application come only later, as something quite special. In reality the invention of the steam-engine *preceded* all the above-mentioned inventions; according to Criticism it is the crowning of them all, the *last*.

In reality the *business ties* between Liverpool and Manchester in their present scope were the result of the export of English goods; according to Criticism they are the *cause* of the export and both are the result of the proximity of the two towns. In reality nearly all goods go from Manchester to the continent via *Hull*, according to Criticism via *Liverpool*.

In reality all *grades of wages* exist in English factories, from 1s 6d to 40s and more; but according to Criticism there is only *one rate*—11s. In reality the *machine* replaces *manual labour*; according to Criticism it replaces *thought*. In reality the *association* of workers for wage rises is allowed in *England*, but according to Criticism it is prohibited, for when the mass wants to allow itself anything it must first ask Criticism. In reality *factory work* is extremely *exhausting* and gives rise to peculiar diseases—there are even special medical works on them; according to Criticism "extreme exertion cannot hinder labour, for the power is provided by the machine." In reality the machine is a machine, according to Criticism it has a *will*, for as it does not rest, neither can the worker: He is subordinated to the will of another.

But all that is nothing. Criticism cannot be content with the *massy parties* in England: it creates new ones, including a *"Factory Party,"* for which history may be thankful to it. On the other hand, it throws together in *one* massy heap the manufacturers and the factory workers—why bother about such details!—and decrees that the factory workers refused to contribute to the Anti-Corn-Law League not out of ill-will or in support of Chartism, as the stupid factory-owners maintain, but solely because they were poor. It further decrees that with the repeal of the English Corn Laws agricultural labourers will have to put up with a drop in wages, to which, however, we must most submissively observe that that destitute class cannot be deprived of another penny without the risk of absolute starvation. It decrees that the working day in English factories is *sixteen* hours, although a silly un-Critical English law has fixed a maximum of twelve hours. It decrees that England is to become a huge workshop for the world, although the un-Critical massy Americans, Germans and Belgians are spoiling one market after another for the English through competition. Lastly, it decrees that neither the propertied nor the non-propertied classes in England are aware of the *centralization of property* and its consequences for the working classes, although the stupid Chartists think they are well aware of them, the *Socialists* maintain that they expounded those consequences in detail long ago, and Tories and Whigs like *Carlyle, Alison* and *Gaskell* have proved their knowledge in their books.

Criticism decrees that Lord *Ashley's Ten-Hour Bill*[4] is a half-hearted *juste milieu* measure and Lord Ashley himself "a true illustration of constitutional action," while the factory-owners, the Chartists, the estate-owners—in short all the massiness of England—have so far considered this measure as an expression, the mildest possible one admittedly, of a downright radical principle, as it would lay the axe at the root of foreign trade and thereby at the root of the factory system, and even chop deep into it. Critical Criticism knows better. It knows that the ten-hour question was discussed before a "commission" of the Lower House, although the un-Critical newspapers try to make us believe that the "commission" was the *House itself, "a committee of the whole House"*; but Criticism must needs do away with that eccentricity of the English Constitution.

Critical Criticism, which itself *begets* its *opposite, the stupidity of the mass,* also produces the stupidity of Sir James Graham: by a Critical understanding of the English language, it puts things in his mouth which the un-Critical Home Secretary never said, just to allow Critical wisdom to shine brighter in comparison with his stupidity. Graham, according to Criticism, says that the machines in the factories wear out in about twelve years whether they work ten hours a day or twelve, and that therefore a ten-hour bill would make it impossible for the capitalists to reproduce in twelve years through the work of their machines the capital laid out on them in that time. Criticism proves that it has thus put a false conclusion in the mouth of Sir James Graham, for a machine that works one-sixth of the time less every day will naturally remain longer in use.

However correct this observation of Critical Criticism against its own false conclusion, it must, on the other hand, be conceded that Sir James Graham said that under a ten-hour bill the machine would have to work all the quicker as its working time was reduced (Criticism itself quotes this in No. VIII, page 32) and that in that case the wearing-out time would be the same—twelve years. This must all the more be acknowledged as the acknowledgement contributes to the glory and exaltation "of Criticism"; for only Criticism both made the false conclusion and then refuted it. Criticism is just as magnanimous towards Lord *John Russel,* to whom it imputes the wish to change the state system and the electoral system. From this we must conclude either that Criti-

cism has an uncommonly powerful urge to produce stupidities
or that Lord John Russel must have become a Critical critic
within the past week.

But Criticism does not really become magnificent in its
fabrication of stupidities until it discovers that the English
workers—who in April and May held meeting after meeting,
drew up petition after petition, and all for the Ten-Hour Bill;
who showed more agitation up and down the factory district
than ever in the preceding two years—that those workers
take only a *"partial* interest" in this question, although it is
evident that "legislation shortening the working day has also
occupied their attention." Criticism is magnificent when it—
ultimately makes the great, the wonderful, the unheard-of
discovery that "the apparently more immediate help from the
repeal of the Corn Laws absorbs most of the wishes of the
workers and will do so until no longer doubtful realization of those wishes practically proves the futility of the
repeal"—proves it to workers who drag Anti-Corn-Law
agitators down from the rostrum at every public meeting,
who have seen to it that the Anti-Corn-Law League no longer dares to hold a public meeting in any industrial town,
who consider the League to be their only enemy and who,
during the debate of the Ten-Hour Bill—as nearly always before in similar matters—had the support of the Tories. Criticism is superb, too, when it discovers that "the workers still
let themselves be lured by the sweeping promises of the
Chartist movement," which is nothing but the political expression of public opinion among the workers; when it realizes, in the depths of its Absolute Spirit, that "the two party
groupings, the political one and that of the land and mill-
owners, *no longer* merge or wish to cover each other." It was
so far not known that the party grouping of the land and
mill-owners, because of the small number of members in each
class of owners and the equal political rights of each (with
the exception of the few peers) was so comprehensive that

it was completely identical with the political party groupings, not their most consistent expression, their peak. Criticism is splendid when it suggests that Anti-Corn-Law Leaguers do not know that, *caeteris paribus*, a drop in the price of bread must be followed by a drop in wages, so that all would remain as it was; whereas these people expect that, granted there is a drop in wages and a consequent lowering of production costs, the result will be an expansion of the market. This, they expect, would lead to a reduction of competition among the workers, and consequently wages would be kept a little higher in comparison with the price of bread than they are now.

Freely creating its opposite—nonsense—and moving in artistic rapture, Criticism, which only two years ago cried "Criticism speaks German, theology speaks Latin!"[5] has now learnt *English* and calls the estate owners. "*Landeigner,*" the factory owners "*Mühleigner,*" and the workers "*Hände.*" Instead of "*Einmischung*" it says "interference"; and in its infinite mercy for the English language, which is bloated with sinful massiness, it condescends to improve it by doing away with the pedantism with which the English place the title "Sir" before the *christian* name of knights and baronets, and where the mass says "Sir James Graham" it says "Sir Graham."

That Criticism reforms *English* history and the *English* language out of *principle* and not out of *levity* will presently be proved by the *thoroughness* with which it treats the *history of Herr Nauwerk.*

CHAPTER III

THE THOROUGHNESS OF CRITICAL CRITICISM,
OR
CRITICAL CRITICISM IN THE PERSON
OF HERR J. (JUNGNITZ?)[6]

Criticism cannot ignore Herr *Nauwerk's* infinitely important dispute with the Berlin Faculty of Philosophy. It has had similar experiences and it must take Herr Nauwerk's fate as a background to place its own *dismissal from Bonn*[7] in sharper relief. Being used to considering the Bonn affair as the event of the century, and having already written the *Philosophy of the Deposition of Criticism,* Criticism could be expected to give a similar detailed philosophical construction to the Berlin "collision." It proves *a priori* that everything had to happen in such a way and no other. It proves:

1) Why the Faculty of Philosophy was bound to come into "collision" with a philosopher of the state and not with a logician or metaphysician;

2) Why that collision could not be so sharp and decisive as Criticism's conflict with theology in Bonn;

3) Why that collision, properly speaking, was a stupid business, since Criticism had exhausted all possible principles and concentrated all its content in its Bonn collision, so that nothing remained for world history but to become the plagiarist of Criticism;

4) Why the Faculty of Philosophy considered attacks on the works of Herr Nauwerk as attacks on itself;

5) Why Herr N. could do nothing but retire of his own accord;

6) Why the Faculty had to take up Herr N.'s defence if it did not want to disavow itself;

7) Why the "inner split in the Faculty had to be presented in such a way" that the Faculty declared both N. and the government right and wrong at the same time;

8) Why the Faculty finds in N.'s works no reason for dismissing him;

9) In what respect the vagueness of the whole verdict is conditional;

10) Why the Faculty "deems itself (!) entitled (!) as a scientific authority (!) to make a thorough investigation of the case"; and finally,

11) Why, nevertheless, the Faculty will not write after the fashion of Herr N.

Criticism disposes of these important questions with rare thoroughness in four pages, showing by Hegel's logic why everything had to happen as it did and no god could have prevented it. In another place Criticism says that not a single epoch in history has yet been cognized; modesty prevents it from saying that it has fully cognized its own collision and Nauwerk's, which, although they are not epochs, appear to Criticism to be epoch-*making*.

Having "abolished" the "aspect" of *thoroughness* in itself, Critical Criticism becomes *"the calm of knowledge."*

Chapter IV

CRITICAL CRITICISM
AS THE CALM OF KNOWLEDGE,
OR
CRITICAL CRITICISM IN THE PERSON
OF HERR EDGAR

1) "Flora Tristan's *Union Ouvrière*"[8]

The French Socialists maintain that the worker makes everything, produces everything and yet has no rights, no possessions, in a word, nothing at all. Critical Criticism answers in the words of Herr *Edgar,* the personification of the *calm of knowledge:* "To be able to create everything, a stronger consciousness is needed than that of the worker; only the opposite of the above proposition would be true: the worker makes nothing, therefore he has nothing; but the reason why he makes nothing is that his work is always individual, having as its object his most personal needs, and everyday work."

Here Criticism reaches a height of abstraction in which it considers only the creations of its own thoughts and generalities which contradict all reality as "something," even as "*everything.*" The worker creates nothing because he creates only "individual," that is perceptible, palpable, spiritless and un-Critical objects, the sight of which horrifies pure Criticism. Everything that is real and living is un-Critical, massy, and therefore "nothing"; only the ideal, fantastic creatures of Critical Criticism are "*everything.*"

The worker creates nothing, because his work remains individual, having only his individual needs as its object, that is, because in the present world system the individual interconnected branches of labour are separated from, and even opposed to, one another; in short, because labour is not *organized*. Criticism's own proposition, if taken in the only reasonable sense it can possibly have, demands the organization of labour. Flora Tristan, in an assessment of whose work this great proposition appears, puts forward the same demand and is treated a *canaille** for her insolence in anticipating Critical Criticism. Anyhow, the proposition that the worker creates nothing is utter madness— except in the sense that the *individual* worker produces nothing *whole,* which is tautology. Critical Criticism creates nothing, the worker creates everything; and so much so that even his spiritual creations put the whole of Criticism to shame; the English and French workers provide proof of this. The worker creates even *man*; the critic will never be anything but sub-human *[ein Unmensch]*, but on the other hand he will have the satisfaction of being a Critical critic.

"Flora Tristan is an example of the feminine dogmatism which must have a formula and constructs it out of the categories of what exists."

Criticism does nothing but "construct formulae out of the categories of what exists," to be precise, out of the existing *Hegelian* philosophy and the existing social aspirations. Formulae, nothing but formulae. And despite all its invectives against dogmatism, it condemns itself to dogmatism and even to *feminine* dogmatism. It is and remains an old woman, faded, widowed *Hegelian* philosophy, which paints and adorns her wrinkled and repugnant abstraction of a body and ogles all over Germany in search of a wooer.

---

* Scoundrel.—*Ed.*

2) *Béraud on Prostitutes*

Herr Edgar, taking pity on social questions, interferes in
"Relations of Prostitution" too (No. V, p. 26).

He criticizes the Paris Police Commissioner Béraud's
book on prostitution because he is worried about the "point
of view" from which "Béraud considers the attitude of prostitutes to society." The "calm of knowledge" is surprised to
see that a policeman adopts the point of view of the police,
and it gives the mass to understand that that point of view
is quite wrong. But it does not reveal its own point of view.
Of course not! When Criticism plays about with prostitutes
it cannot be expected to do so in public.

3) *Love*

In order to complete its transformation into the "calm of
knowledge" Critical Criticism must first seek to dispose of
love. Love is a passion, and nothing is more dangerous for
the calm of knowledge than passion. That is why, speaking
of Madame von Palzow's novels, which, he assures us, he
has "thoroughly *studied,*" Herr Edgar is amazed at "*child-
ishness* like *so-called love.*" It is horror and abomination
and maketh Critical Criticism furious, stirreth up its bile
and almost driveth it insane.

"Love ... is a cruel goddess, and, like every deity, it
wishes to subjugate the whole of man; it is not satisfied
until he has surrendered to it not only his soul, but his
physical self. The worship of love is suffering, its peak
is self-immolation, suicide."

In order to change love into Moloch, a devil incarnate,
Herr Edgar first changes it into a goddess. When love has
become a goddess, i.e., a theological thing, it is naturally
an object of *theological criticism*; moreover, we know that
god and the devil are not far from each other. Herr Edgar

changes love into a "goddess," a "cruel goddess" at that,
by changing *man who loves*, the love *of man*, into a man
of love; by making *"love"* a being apart, separate from man
and as such endowed with independent being. By this simple process, by changing the predicate into the subject, all
the attributes and manifestations of human nature can be
Critically transformed into their opposite (*Unwesen*) and
estrangements. Thus, for example, Critical Criticism makes
out of criticism, as a predicate and activity of man, a subject apart, criticism referring itself to itself and therefore
Critical Criticism: a Moloch, the worship of which consists
in the self-immolation and suicide of man, and in particular of his *ability to think*.

"*Object*," exclaims the calm of knowledge, "object is the
right expression, for the beloved is important to the lover
(there is no feminine) only as *this external object* of the
emotion of his soul, as the object in which he wishes to
satisfy his selfish feeling."

Object! Horrid! There is nothing more damnable, more
profane, more massy than an *object*—down with the object!
How could absolute subjectivity, the *actus purus*, "pure"
Criticism, not see in love its *bête noire*,* that Satan incarnate, in love, which first really teaches man to believe in
the objective world outside himself, which not only makes
man an object, but the object a man!

Love, continues the calm of knowledge, beside itself, is
not even content with turning man into the *category* "Object" for another man, it even makes out of him a *definite,
real* object, this evil-individual (see Hegel's *Phenomenology* on the categories "This" and "That," where there is also
a polemic against the evil "*This*") *external* object which
does not remain internal, hidden in the brain, but is sen-
sually manifest.

---

* Black beast—object of horror.—*Ed.*

"Love

Lives not *only* in the *brain* immured."

No, the beloved is a *sensuous object*, and if Critical Criticism is to condescend to recognition of an object, it demands at the very least a *senseless* object. But love is an *un-Critical, unchristian materialist.*

Finally, love even makes one man "*this external object of the emotion of the soul*" of another man, the object in which the *selfish* feeling of the other man finds its satisfaction, a *selfish* feeling because it *looks for its own essence* in the other man, and that must not be. Critical Criticism is *so free* from all *selfishness* that for it the whole range of human essence is exhausted *by its own self.*

Herr Edgar naturally does not tell us in what way the beloved differs from the other "external objects of the emotion of the soul in which the selfish feelings of men find their satisfaction." The profound, sensitive, most expressive object of love means nothing to the calm of knowledge but the abstract formula: "this external object of the emotion of the soul," something in the way the comet means nothing to the speculative natural philosopher but "negativity." By making man the external object of the emotion of his soul, man does in fact attach "importance" to him, Critical Criticism itself admits, but only *objective importance*, so to speak, while the importance which Criticism attaches to objects is none other than that which it attaches to itself. Hence this importance lies not in the "evil *external being*," but in the "*Nothing*" of the Critically important object.

If the calm of knowledge has no *object* in real man, it has, on the other hand, a *cause* in *humanity*. Critical love "*is careful* above all not to forget the *cause* behind the personality, for that cause is none other than the cause of humanity." Un-Critical love does not separate humanity from the personal, individual man.

3—1192

"Love itself, as an *abstract* passion, which comes we know not whence and goes we know not whither, is incapable of an interest in *internal* development."

In the eyes of the calm of knowledge, love is an abstract passion according to the *speculative* terminology in which the concrete is called abstract and the abstract concrete.

> *The maid was not born in that valley,*
> *Whence she came no one knew.*
> *Not long did her memory tarry,*
> *When she had bidden adieu.*[9]

For abstraction, love is "the maid from abroad" who has no dialectical passport and is therefore expelled from the country by the Critical police.

The passion of love is incapable of any interest in *internal* development because it cannot be construed *a priori*, because its development is a real one which takes place in the world of the senses and among real individuals. The main interest of speculative construction, on the other hand, is the "Whence" and the "Whither." The "Whence" is the "*necessity* of a concept, its proof and deduction" (Hegel). The "Whither" is the determination "by which each separate link of the speculative circular motion, as the animated content of the method, is at the same time the beginning of a new link" (Hegel). Hence, only when its "Whence" and its "Whither" could be construed *a priori,* would love deserve the "interest" of speculative criticism.

Here Critical Criticism is not against love alone, but against everything living, everything which is immediate, every sensuous experience, any and every *real* experience the "Whence" and the "Whither" of which is not known beforehand.

By overcoming love, Herr Edgar has completely *asserted* himself as the "calm of knowledge." By his treatment of *Proudhon*, he can now show great virtuosity in knowledge, the *"object"* of which is no longer *"this external object,"* and a still greater *lack of love* for the French language.

4) *Proudhon*

It was not *Proudhon* himself, but "Proudhon's *point of view,"* Critical Criticism informs us, that wrote *Qu'est-ce que la propriété?"*[10]

"I begin my exposition of Proudhon's point of view by characterizing its (the point of view's) work, *What is property?"*

As only the works of the Critical point of view have a character of themselves, the Critical characteristic necessarily begins by giving Proudhon's work character. Herr Edgar gives this work a character by *translating* it. He naturally gives it a *bad* character, for he turns it into an *object* "of Criticism."

Proudhon's work is hence submitted to a double attack by Herr Edgar—*an unspoken* one in his characterizing translation and an *outspoken* one in his Critical glosses. We shall see that Herr Edgar is more devastating when he translates than when he glosses.

Characterizing Translation No. 1

"I do not wish (says the Critically translated Proudhon) to give any system of the new; all I want is the abolition of privilege, the abolition of slavery.... Justice, nothing but justice, that is what I think."

The characterized Proudhon confines himself to wishing and thinking, because "good will" and unscientific "thinking" are the characteristic attributes of the un-Critical mass. The characterized Proudhon shows a meekness which becomes the mass and subordinates what he wishes to what he does *not* wish. He does not presume to wish to give a system of the new, he wishes less, he even wishes *nothing* but the abolition of privilege, etc. Besides this Critical sub-ordination of the will he has to the will he has not, his very first word is marked by a characteristic lack of logic. A writer who begins his book by saying that he does not wish to give any system of the new, should then tell us what he does wish to give: whether it is a systematized old or unsystematized new. But does the characterized Proudhon, who does not wish to *give* any system of the new, wish to give the abolition of privilege? No. He just *wishes* it.

The *real* Proudhon says: "*je ne fais pas de système; je demande la fin du privilège, etc.*" (I do not make any system; I demand an end of privilege, etc.) This means that the real Proudhon declares that he does not pursue any abstract-scientific aims, but makes immediately practical demands on society. And the demand he makes is not an arbitrary one. It is motivated and justified by his whole argumentation and is the summary of that argumentation: for "*justice, rien que justice; tel est le resumé de mon discours.*" With his "Justice, nothing but justice, that is what I mean," the characterized Proudhon gets himself into a position which is all the more embarrassing as he means much more. According to Herr Edgar, for example, he "*thinks*" that philosophy has not been practical enough, he *thinks* of refuting *Charles Comte*, and so forth.

The Critical Proudhon asks: "Must *man* then always be unhappy?" In other words, he asks whether unhappiness is man's moral destiny. The real Proudhon is a light-minded Frenchman and he asks whether unhappiness is a material necessity, an *inevitability*. (*L'homme doit-il être éternellement malheureux?*)

The massy Proudhon says:

"*Et, sans m'arrêter aux explications à toute fin des entrepreneurs de réformes, accusant de la détresse générale, ceux-ci la lâcheté et l'impéritie du pouvoir, ceux-là les con-*

spirateurs et les émeutes, d'autres l'ignorance et la corruption générale," etc.*

The expression *"à toute fin"* being a bad massy expression that is not in the massy German dictionaries, the Critical Proudhon naturally omits this more exact definition of the "explanations." This term is taken from massy French jurisprudence, and *explications à toute fin* means explanations which preclude any objection. The Critical Proudhon attacks the *"reformists,"* a French Socialist party[11]; the massy Proudhon attacks the initiators of reforms. The massy Proudhon distinguishes various classes of *entrepreneurs de réformes.* These, *(ceux-ci)* say *one thing,* those, *(ceux-là)* say *another,* others, *(d'autres) a third.* The Critical Proudhon, on the other hand, makes *the same reformists* "accuse now one, then another, then a third," which in any case is proof of their inconstancy. The real Proudhon, who follows massy French practice, speaks of *"les conspirateurs et les émeutes,"* i.e., first of the conspirators and then of their activity, revolts. The Critical Proudhon, on the other hand, lumping together the various classes of reformists, classifies the rebels and hence says: the conspirators and the *rebels.* The massy Proudhon speaks of *ignorance* and *"general corruption."* The Critical Proudhon changes ignorance to stupidity, corruption to depravity, and finally, as a Critical critic, makes the stupidity *general.* He himself gives an immediate example of it by putting *générale* in the singular instead of the plural. He writes: *l'ignorance et la corruption générale* for general *stupidity and depravity.* According to un-Critical French grammar this should be: *l'ignorance et la corruption générales.*

---

* Without dwelling on the explanations precluding all objections given by the initiators of reforms, some of whom blame for the general distress the cowardice and incapacity of the government, others— conspirators and revolts, others again—ignorance and general corruption, etc.—*Ed.*

The characterized Proudhon, who speaks and thinks otherwise than the massy one, necessarily went through quite a different *course of education*. He "questioned the masters of science, read hundreds of volumes of philosophy and law, etc., and *at last*" he "realized that we have never yet grasped the meaning of the words 'Justice, Equity, Freedom.'" The real Proudhon thought he had realized *at first*, (*je crus d'abord reconnaitre*) what the Critical Proudhon realized only "*at last*." The Critical changing of *d'abord* (at first) into *enfin* (at last) is necessary because the mass may not think it realizes anything *at first*. The massy Proudhon tells explicitly how he was astounded by the unexpected result of his studies and was dubious of it. But he decided to carry out a "*counterproof*" and asked himself: "Is it possible that mankind has so long and so universally been mistaken in the application of the principles of moral? How and why was it mistaken? etc." He made the correctness of his observations dependent on the solution of these questions. He found that in moral, as in all other branches of knowledge, errors "*are the degrees of science.*" Contrariwise, the Critical Proudhon immediately trusted the first impression that his political-economic, law and similar studies made upon him. Needless to say, the mass may not proceed *with thoroughness*; it must raise the first results of its investigations to the level of indisputable truths. It has "reached the end before it has started, before it has measured itself with its opposite." Hence "it appears" later "that it has not yet started when it thinks it has reached the end."

The Critical Proudhon therefore continues his reasoning in the most groundless and incoherent way.

"Our knowledge of moral laws is not complete from the beginning; *hence* it can for some time suffice for social progress, but in the long run it will lead us the wrong way."

The Critical Proudhon does not give any reason why incomplete knowledge of moral laws can suffice for social

progress even for a day. The real Proudhon, having set
himself the question whether and why mankind could universally and so long have been mistaken, finds the solution
that all errors are degrees of science; that our most imperfect judgements contain a sum of truths sufficient for a certain number of inductions and for a certain circle of practical life, beyond which number and which circle they lead
theoretically to the absurd and practically to decay. Thus
he is in a position to say that even imperfect knowledge of
the moral laws can suffice for social progress for a time.

The Critical Proudhon says:

"As soon as new knowledge becomes necessary, a bitter
struggle arises between the old prejudices and the new
idea."

How can a struggle arise against an opponent who does
not yet exist? Admitted, the Critical Proudhon has told us
that a new idea has become necessary but he has not said
that it has already *come into existence.*

The massy Proudhon says:

"Once higher knowledge has become indispensable it *is
never lacking,*" it is therefore ready at hand. *"Then it is*
that the struggle begins."

The Critical Proudhon asserts: "It is man's destiny to
learn step by step," as though man had not a quite different
destiny, namely, that of being man, and as if that learning
"step by step" necessarily brought him a step farther. I can
go step by step and arrive at the very point from which I set
out. The un-Critical Proudhon speaks, not of destiny, but of
the *condition* (condition) for man to learn not *step by step*
(pas à pas), but by *degrees (par degrés).*

The Critical Proudhon says to himself:

"Among the principles upon which society rests there is
one which society does not understand, which is spoilt by
society's ignorance and is the cause of all evil. But all the
same man honours *this* principle and wills it, for otherwise

it would have no influence. Now this principle which is true
in *essence* but is false in the way we conceive it ... which
is it?"

In the first sentence the Critical Proudhon says that the
principle is spoilt, misconceived by society, hence that it is
correct in itself. In the second sentence he commits the tautology of stating that it is true in its essence. He nevertheless reproaches society with willing and honouring "this
principle." The massy Proudhon, on the other hand, reproaches society with willing and honouring not this principle, but this principle falsified by our ignorance ("*ce
principe ... tel que notre ignorance l'a fait, est honoré*").
The Critical Proudhon finds the *essence* of the principle in
its untrue form *true*. The massy Proudhon finds that the
essence of the falsified principle is our incorrect conception,
but that it is true in its *object* (*objet*), just as the essence of
alchemy and astrology is our imagination, but their objects
—the movement of the heavenly bodies and the chemical
properties of bodies—are true.

The Critical Proudhon pursues his monologue:

"The object of our investigation is the law, the definition
of the social principle. Now the politicians, i.e., the men of
social science, are a prey to complete vagueness; but as
there is a reality at the basis of every error, in their books
we shall find the truth, which they have brought into the
world without knowing it."

The Critical Proudhon has a most fantastic way of reasoning. From the fact that politicians are ignorant he goes
on in the most arbitrary fashion to say that a reality lies at
the basis of every error, which can all the less be doubted
as there is reality at the basis of every error—in the person
of its author. From the fact that a reality lies *at the basis* of
every error he goes on to conclude that truth is to be found
in the books of politicians. And finally he even makes the
politicians bring this truth into the *world*. Had they brought

it into the *world* we would not need to look for it in their
books.

The massy Proudhon says: "The politicians do not agree
among themselves (*ne s'entendent pas*); their error is therefore a subjective one, having its origin in them (*donc
c'est en eux qu'est l'erreur*)." Their disagreement proves
their one-sidedness. They confuse "their private opinion
with common sense," and "as," according to the previous
deduction, "every error has a true reality as *object*, their
books must contain the truth which they unconsciously put
there—i.e., in their books—but did not bring into the world"
(*dans leurs livres doit se trouver la vérité, qu'à leur insu ils
y auront mis*).

The Critical Proudhon asks himself: "What is justice,
what is its essence, its character, its meaning?" as if it had
some meaning apart from its essence and character. The
un-Critical Proudhon asks: What is its principle, its character and its formula (*formule*)? The formula is the principle as a principle of scientific reasoning. In the massy
French language there is a substantial difference between
formule and *signification*. In the Critical French language
there is none.

After his highly irrelevant disquisitions, the Critical
Proudhon pulls himself together and exclaims:

"Let us try to get somewhat nearer to our object."

The un-Critical Proudhon, who arrived at his object long
ago, tries, on the other hand, to attain more precise and positive definitions of his object (*d'arriver à quelque chose de
plus précis et de plus positif*).

For the Critical Proudhon "the law" is a "*definition* of
what is right," for the un-Critical it is a "*statement*" (*décla-
ration*) of it. The un-Critical Proudhon disputes the view
that right is made by law. But a "definition of the law" can
mean that the law is defined just as it can mean that it defines." The Critical Proudhon himself spoke about the defini-

tion of the social principle in this latter sense. Incidentally it does not become the massy Proudhon to make such nice distinctions.

Considering these differences between the Critically characterized Proudhon and the real Proudhon, it is no wonder that Proudhon No. 1 seeks to *prove* quite different things than Proudhon No. 2.

The Critical Proudhon "*seeks to prove* by the *experience of history*" that "if the idea that we have of just and right is false, *evidently*—(he tries to prove it in spite of its evidence)—all applications of it in law must be bad, all our institutions must be defective."

The massy Proudhon is far from wishing to prove what is evident. He says: "If the idea that we have of what is just and right were badly defined, if it were incomplete or even false, it is *evident* that all our legislative applications would be bad, etc."

What, then, does the un-Critical Proudhon wish to prove?

"This hypothesis," he continues, "of the perversion of justice in our understanding, and as a necessary consequence in our actions, would be an established fact if the opinions of men concerning the concept of justice and its applications had not remained constantly the same: if at different epochs they had undergone changes; in a word, if there had been progress in ideas."

And precisely that inconstancy, that change, that progress "is what *history* proves by the most striking testimonies." And the un-Critical Proudhon quotes these striking testimonies of history. His Critical duplicate, who proves a completely different proposition by the experience of history, also presents that experience in quite a different way.

According to the real Proudhon "the wise" (*les sages*) foresaw the fall of the Roman Empire; according to the Critical Proudhon "the philosophers" did. The Critical Proudhon can of course consider only philosophers to be wise men. According to the real Proudhon, Roman "right was consecrated by ten centuries of law practice or administration of justice" (*ces droits consacrés par une justice dix fois séculaire*); according to the Critical Proudhon Rome had "right consecrated by ten centuries of *justice.*"

According to the same Proudhon No. 1, the Romans reasoned as follows: "Rome ... was victorious through its policy and its gods; any reform in worship or public spirit would be stupidity and profanation (according to the Critical Proudhon *sacrilège* means not the profanation or desecration of a holy thing, as in the massy French language, but just profanation). Had it wished to free the peoples, it would thereby have renounced its right." "Rome had thus fact and right in its favour," Proudhon No. 1 adds.

According to the un-Critical Proudhon, the Romans reasoned much more logically. *Fact* was more defined:

"The slaves are the most fertile source of its wealth; the emancipation of the slaves would therefore be *the ruin of its finance.*"

And the massy Proudhon adds, referring to *law:* "Rome's claims were justified by the law of nations (*droit des gens*)." This way of proving the right of subjugation was completely in keeping with the Roman view on law. See the massy pandects: "*jure gentium servitus invasit*" (Fr. 4. D. I. I)*

According to the Critical Proudhon, "idolatry, slavery and softness" were "the basis of Roman institutions," of all its institutions without exception. The real Proudhon says: "Idolatry in religion, slavery in the state, and epicurism (épicurisme in the profane French language is not synonymous of *mollesse*, softness) in private life were the basis of the institutions." Within that Roman situation there "appeared," says the mystic Proudhon, "the Word of

_____

* "Slavery was established by the law of nations" *Digesta*, Book I. Part I. Fragment 4 —*Ed*

God," but according to the real rational Proudhon "a man who *called* himself the Word of God." In the real Proudhon that man calls the priests "vipers" (*vipères*): in the Critical Proudhon he speaks more courteously and calls them "serpents." In the former he speaks in the Roman way of "advocates" [*Advokaten*], in the latter in the German way of "lawyers" [*Rechtsgelehrte*].

The Critical Proudhon calls the spirit of the French Revolution a spirit of contradiction and then adds: "That is enough to realize that the new that replaced the old had on itself nothing methodical and considered." He cannot refrain from repeating the favourite categories of Critical Criticism, the "old" and the "new." He cannot refrain from the senseless demand that the "new" should have *on* itself [*an sich*] something methodical and considered as one has, say, a stain *on* oneself (*an sich*). The real Proudhon says: "That is enough to prove that the new order of things which was substituted for the old was *in* itself (*in sich*) without method or consideration."

Carried away by the memory of the French Revolution, the Critical Proudhon *revolutionizes* the French language so much that he translates *un fait physique** by "a fact of physics," and *un fait intellectuel*** by "a fact of the intellect." By this revolution in the French language the Critical Proudhon manages to put physics in possession of all the facts to be found in nature. Raising natural science unduly on one side, he debases it just as much on the other by depriving it of intellect and distinguishing between a fact of physics and a fact of the intellect. To the same extent he makes all further psychologic and logic investigation unnecessary by raising the intellectual fact directly to the level of a fact of the intellect.

---

* A physical fact.—*Ed.*
** An intellectual fact.—*Ed.*

As the Critical Proudhon, Proudhon No. 1, has not the slightest idea what the real Proudhon, Proudhon No. 2, wishes to prove by his historical deduction, neither accordingly does the real content of that deduction exist for him, namely, the proof of the change in the views on right and the continuous *implementation* of justice by the *negation* of historical positive law.

"Society was saved by *negation* of its principles ... and the *violation* of the most sacred *rights*," says the real Proudhon.

Thus he proves how the negation of Roman right led to the widening of right in the Christian *conception*, the nega- ✗ tion of the right of conquest to the right of the communes and the negation of the whole feudal law by the French Revolution to the present more comprehensive system of law.

Critical Criticism could not possibly leave Proudhon the glory of having discovered the law of the implementation of a principle by its negation. In this conscious conception that thought was a real revelation for the French.

Critical Gloss No. 1

As the first criticism of any science necessarily finds itself under the influence of the premises of the science it is fighting against, so Proudhon's treatise *Qu'est-ce que la proprié- té?* is the criticism of *political economy* from the standpoint of political economy.—We need go no deeper into the juridical part of the book, which criticizes law from the standpoint of law, for our main interest is the criticism of political economy.—Proudhon's treatise will therefore be outstripped by a criticism of *political economy*, including Proudhon's conception of political economy. This work became possible only after Proudhon's own work, just as Proudhon's criticism supposed the physiocrats' criticism of the mercantile system, Adam Smith's criticism of the physiocrats, Ricardo's criticism of Adam Smith and the works of Fourier and Saint Simon.

All treatises on political economy take *private property* for granted. This basic premise is for them an incontestable fact admitting of no further investigation, nay more, a fact which is spoken about only "accidentally," as *Say* naively admits. But Proudhon makes a critical investigation—the first resolute, pitiless, and at the same time scientific investigation—of the foundation of political economy, *private property*. This is the great scientific progress he made, a progress which revolutionizes political economy and first makes a real science of political economy possible. Proudhon's treatise *Qu'est-ce que la propriété?* is as important for modern political economy as Sieyes' work *Qu'est-ce que le tiers état?* for modern politics.

Proudhon does not consider the further forms of private property, e.g., wages, trade, value, price, money, etc., as forms of private property in themselves, as they are considered, for example, in *Deutsch-Französische Jahrbücher*[12] (see *Notes for a Critique of Political Economy*, by F. Engels), but uses these economic premises as an argument against economists; this is fully in keeping with his historically justified standpoint to which we referred above.

Accepting the relations of private property as human and reasonable, political economy moves in permanent contradiction to its basic premise, private property, a contradiction analogous to that of theology, which, continually giving a human interpretation to religious conceptions, is by the very fact in constant conflict with its basic premise, the superhuman character of religion. Thus, in political economy wages appear at the beginning as the proportional share of the product due to labour. Wages and profit on capital stand in a friendly, mutually favourable, apparently most human relationship to each other. Afterwards it turns out that they stand in the most hostile relationship, in *inverse* proportion to each other. Value is determined at the beginning in an apparently reasonable way by the cost of production of an object and its social usefulness. Later it turns out that value is determined quite fortuitously and that it does not need to bear any relation to cost of production or social usefulness. The magnitude of wages is determined at the beginning by *free* agreement between the free worker and the free capitalist. Later it turns out that the worker is compelled to allow the capitalist to determine it, just as the capitalist is compelled to fix it as low as possible. *Freedom* of the contracting parties has been supplanted by *compulsion*. The position is the same in trade and all other political-economic relations. The economists themselves occasionally feel these contradictions, the discussion of which is the main content of the struggle between them. When, however, the economists become conscious of these contradictions, *they themselves* attack *private property* in one of its particular forms as the falsifier of what is in itself (i.e., in their imagination) reasonable wages, in itself reasonable value, in itself reasonable trade. Adam Smith, for instance, occasionally polemizes against the capitalists, Destutt de Tracy against the bankers, Simonde de Sismondi against the factory system, Ricardo against landed property, and nearly all modern economists against the *non-industrial* capitalists, in whom property appears as a mere *consumer*.

Thus, as an exception—when they attack some special abuse—the economists occasionally stress the semblance of humanity in economic relations, while sometimes, and as often as not, they take these relations precisely in their marked *difference* from the human, in their strictly economic sense. They stagger about within that contradiction completely unaware of it.

Proudhon puts an end to this unconsciousness once for all. He takes the *human semblance* of the economic relations seriously and sharply opposes it to their *inhuman reality*.

He forces them to be in reality what they imagine themselves to be, or, to be more exact, to give up their own idea of themselves and confess their real inhumanity. He is therefore consistent when he represents as the falsifier of economic relations not this or that particular kind of private property as other economists do, but private property taken in its entirety. He does all that a criticism of political economy from the standpoint of political economy can do.

Herr Edgar, who wishes to *characterize* the *standpoint* of the treatise *Qu'est-ce que la propriété?*, naturally does not say a word of political economy or of the distinctive character of that treatise, which is precisely that it has made the *essence of private property* the vital question of political economy and jurisprudence. This is all self-evident for Critical Criticism. Proudhon, it says, has done nothing new by his negation of private property. He has only divulged one of Critical Criticism's close secrets.

"Proudhon," Herr Edgar continues immediately after his characterizing translation, "therefore finds something Absolute, an eternal foundation in history a god, that guides mankind—justice."

Proudhon's treatise, written in French in 1840, does not adopt the standpoint of German development in 1844. It is Proudhon's standpoint, a standpoint which is shared by countless diametrically opposed French writers and therefore gives Critical Criticism the advantage of having characterized the most contradictory standpoints with a single stroke of the pen. Incidentally, to settle with this Absolute in history one has only to apply logically the law formulated by Proudhon himself, that of the implementation of justice by its negation. If Proudhon does not carry logic that far, it is only because he had the misfortune of being born a Frenchman, not a German.

For Herr Edgar, Proudhon has become a *theological* object by his Absolute in history and his belief in justice; Critical Criticism, which is *ex professo* a criticism of theology, can now set to work on him in order to expatiate on "religious conceptions."

"It is a characteristic of every religious conception that it sets up as a dogma a situation in which at the end one of the opposites comes out victorious as the only truth."

We shall see how religious Critical Criticism sets up as a dogma a situation in which at the end one of the opposites, "*Criticism*," comes out victorious over the other, the "Mass," as the only truth. But Proudhon committed an all the greater injustice by seeing in massy justice an Absolute, a god of history as just Criticism had *explicitly* reserved for itself the role of that Absolute, that god in history.

Critical Gloss No. 2

"The fact of misery, poverty, makes Proudhon one-sided in his considerations; he sees in it a *contradiction* to equality and justice; it provides him with a weapon. Hence this fact becomes for him absolute and justified while the fact of property is unjustified."

The calm of knowledge tells us that Proudhon actually sees in the fact of misery a contradiction to justice and therefore finds it unjustified; yet in the same breath it assures us that this fact becomes for him absolute and justified.

Hitherto political economy proceeded from the *wealth* that the movement of private property was supposed to create for the *nations* to considerations which were an apology of private property. Proudhon proceeds from the opposite side, which political economy sophistically conceals, from the poverty bred by the movement of private property, to his considerations, which are a negation of private property. The first criticism of private property naturally proceeds from the fact in which its contradictory essence

4—1192

appears in the form that is most perceptible and most glaring and most directly arouses man's indignation—from the fact of poverty, of misery.

"Criticism, on the other hand, joins the two facts, poverty and property in a single unity, grasps the interior link between them and makes them a single whole, which it investigates as such to find the conditions for its existence."

Criticism, which has hitherto understood nothing of the facts of property and of poverty uses, "on the other hand," its imaginary accomplished fact as an argument against Proudhon's real fact. It unites the *two* facts in a *single* unity, and having made *one* out of *two*, grasps the interior link between the *two*. Criticism cannot deny that Proudhon too grasps an interior link between the facts of poverty and of property, since because of that very link he wants to abolish property in order to abolish poverty. Proudhon even did more. He proved in detail *how* the movement of capital produces poverty. But Critical Criticism does not bother with such trifles. It admits that poverty and private property are *opposites*—a rather widespread admission. It *makes* poverty and property a *single whole*, which it "investigates *as such* to find the conditions for its existence"; an investigation which is all the more superfluous as it has just *made* that "whole as such" and therefore its *making* is in itself the condition for its existence.

By investigating "the whole as such" to find the conditions for its existence, Critical Criticism is searching in the genuine theological manner, *outside* the whole, for the conditions for its existence. Critical speculation moves outside the object which it pretends to deal with. The *whole contradiction* is nothing but the *movement of both its sides*, and the condition for the existence of the whole lies in the very nature of the two sides. Critical Criticism dispenses with the study of this real movement which forms the whole in order to be able to declare that it. Critical Criticism as the calm of knowledge, is above both extremes of the contradiction, and that its activity, which has made the "whole as such," is now alone in a position to abolish the abstraction of which it is the maker.

Proletariat and wealth are opposites; as such they form a single whole. They are both forms of the world of private property. The question is what place each occupies in the antithesis. It is not sufficient to declare them two sides of a single whole.

Private property as private property, as wealth, is compelled to maintain *itself*, and thereby its opposite, the proletariat, in *existence*. That is the *positive* side of the contradiction, self-satisfied private property.

The proletariat, on the other hand, is compelled as proletariat to abolish itself and thereby its opposite, the condition for its existence, what makes it the proletariat, i.e., private property. That is the *negative* side of the contradiction, its restlessness within its very self, dissolved and self-dissolving private property.

The propertied class and the class of the proletariat present the same human self-alienation. But the former class finds in this self-alienation its confirmation and its good, *its own power*: it has in it a *semblance* of human existence. The class of the proletariat feels annihilated in its self-alienation; it sees in it its own powerlessness and the reality of an inhuman existence. In the words of Hegel, the class of the proletariat is in abasement *indignation* at that abasement, an indignation to which it is necessarily driven by the contradiction between its human *nature* and its condition of life, which is the outright, decisive and comprehensive negation of that nature.

Within this antithesis the private owner is therefore the *conservative* side, the proletarian, the *destructive* side. From the former arises the action of preserving the antithesis, from the latter, that of annihilating it.

Indeed private property, too, drives itself in its economic movement towards its own dissolution, only, however, through a development which does not depend on it, of which it is unconscious and which takes place against its will, through the very nature of things; only inasmuch as it produces the proletariat *as* proletariat, that misery conscious of its spiritual and physical misery, that dehumanization conscious of its dehumanization and therefore self-abolishing. The proletariat executes the sentence that private property pronounced on itself by begetting the proletariat, just as it carries out the sentence that wage-labour pronounced on itself by bringing forth wealth for others and misery for itself. When the proletariat is victorious, it by no means becomes the absolute side of society, for it is victorious only by abolishing itself and its opposite. Then the proletariat disappears as well as the opposite which determines it, private property.

When socialist writers ascribe this historic role to the proletariat, it is not, as Critical Criticism pretends to think, because they consider the proletarians as *gods*. Rather the contrary. Since the abstraction of all humanity, even of the *semblance* of humanity, is practically complete in the full-grown proletariat; since the conditions of life of the proletariat sum up all the conditions of life of society today in all their inhuman acuity; since man has lost himself in the proletariat, yet at the same time has not only gained theoretical consciousness of that loss, but through urgent, no longer disguisable, absolutely imperative *need*—that practical expression of *necessity*—is driven directly to revolt against that inhumanity; it follows that the proletariat can and must free itself. But it cannot free itself without abolishing the conditions of its own life. It cannot abolish the conditions of its own life without abolishing *all* the inhuman conditions of life of society today which are summed up in its own situation. Not in vain does it go through the stern but steeling school of *labour*. The question is not what this or that proletarian, or even the whole of the proletariat at the moment *considers* as its aim. The question is *what the proletariat is*, and what, consequent on that *being*, it will be compelled to do. Its aim and historical action is irrevocably and obviously demonstrated in its own life situation as well as in the whole organization of bourgeois society today. There is no need to dwell here upon the fact that a large part of the English and French proletariat is already *conscious* of its historic task and is constantly working to develop that consciousness into complete clarity.

"Critical Criticism" can all the less admit this as it has proclaimed itself the exclusive creative element in history. To it belong the historical contradictions, to it belongs the task of abolishing them. That is why it issues the following *notification* through its incarnation, Edgar:

"Education and lack of education, property and absence of property, these *opposites*, if they are not to be profaned, must *devolve wholly and entirely upon* Criticism."

Property and absence of property have received metaphysical consecration as Critical speculative opposites. That is why only the hand of Critical Criticism can touch them without committing a sacrilege. Capitalists and workers must not interfere in their mutual relations.

Far from the idea that his Critical conception of opposites could be touched, that this holy thing could be profaned, Herr Edgar lets his opponent make an objection that he alone could make to himself.

"Is it then possible," the imaginary opponent of Critical Criticism asks, "to make use of other concepts than those already existing—liberty, equality, etc.? I answer" (note Herr Edgar's answer) "that Greek and Latin perished as soon as the range of thoughts that they served to express was exhausted."

It is now clear why Critical Criticism does not give a

single thought in *German*. The language of its thoughts has not yet come, in spite of all Herr Reichardt by his Critical handling of foreign words, Herr Faucher, by his handling of English, and Herr Edgar, by his handling of French have done to prepare the *new Critical* language.

Characterizing Translation No. 2

The Critical Proudhon says: "The husbandmen divided the land among themselves; equality consecrated only possession; on this occasion it consecrated property." The Critical Proudhon makes landed property rise simultaneously with the division of the land. He effects the transition from possession to property by the expression "on this occasion."

The real Proudhon says: "Husbandry was the basis of *possession of the land*.... It was not enough to ensure for the tiller the fruit of his work without ensuring for him at the same time the instruments of production. To guard the weak against the encroachments of the strong ... it was felt necessary to establish permanent demarcation lines between owners."

"On this occasion," it is, therefore *possession* that **equality** consecrates in the first place.

"Every year saw the population increase and the greed of the settlers grow: it was thought ambition would be checked by new insuperable barriers against which it must be shattered. Thus the land was made property out of a need for equality ... doubtless the division was never geographically equal ... but the principle remained nevertheless the same: equality had consecrated possession, equality consecrated property."

According to the Critical Proudhon, "the ancient founders of property, absorbed with concern for their needs, overlooked the fact that to the right of property corresponded at the same time the right to alienate, to sell, to give away, to acquire and to lose, which destroyed the equality from which they proceeded."

According to the real Proudhon, it was not that the founders of property overlooked this course of its development in their concern for their own needs. It was rather that they did not foresee it; and even had they been able to foresee it, their actual need would have taken the upper hand. Besides, the real Proudhon is too massy to oppose the right to alienate, sell, etc. to the *"right of property,"* i.e., to oppose the varieties to the species. He opposes the "right to *keep* one's heritage" to the "right to *alienate* it, etc." which constitutes a real opposition and a real step forward.

Critical Gloss No. 3

"What does Proudhon base his proof of the impossibility of property on? Difficult as it is to believe it—on the same principle of equality!"

A short consideration would have been enough to arouse the belief of Herr Edgar. He must be aware that Herr Bruno Bauer based all his arguments on *"infinite* self-consciousness" and that he also saw in this principle the creative principle of the gospels, which, by their infinite unconsciousness, appear to be in direct contradiction to infinite self-consciousness. In the same way Proudhon considers equality as the creative principle of private property, which is in direct contradiction to equality. If Herr Edgar compares French *equality* with German "self-consciousness" for an instant, he will see that the latter principle expresses *in German*, i.e., in abstract thought, what the former says *in French*, that is, in the language of politics and of thoughtful observation. Self-consciousness is man's equality with himself in pure thought. Equality is man's consciousness of himself in the element of practice, i.e., therefore, man's consciousness of other men as his equals and man's rela

tion to other men as his equals. Equality is the French expression for the unity of human essence, for man's consciousness of his species and his attitude toward his species,
for the practical identity of man with man, i.e., for the social or human relation of man to man. As therefore destructive criticism in Germany, before progressing in *Feuerbach*
to the consideration of *real man*, tried to solve everything
definite and existing by the principle of *self-consciousness*,
destructive criticism in France tried to do the same by the
principle of *equality*.

"Proudhon is angry with philosophy, for which, in itself,
we cannot blame him. But why is he angry? Philosophy, he
maintains, has not yet shown itself practical enough; it has
mounted the high horse of *speculation*, and seen from up
there *human beings* have seemed too small. I think that
philosophy is over-practical, i.e., it has so far been nothing
but the abstract expression of the existing systems; it has
always been a prisoner of the premises of the systems which
it has accepted as absolute."

The opinion that philosophy is the abstract expression of the
existing situations does not belong originally to Herr Edgar.
It belongs to *Feuerbach*, who was the first to describe
philosophy as speculative and mystic empirics and proved
it to be so. But Herr Edgar manages to give this opinion an
original, Critical twist. While Feuerbach concludes that philosophy must come down from the heaven of speculation to
the depth of human misery, Herr Edgar, on the contrary,
teaches us that philosophy is over-practical. It rather seems,
however, that philosophy, precisely because it was only the
transcendent, abstract expression of the actual situation, by
reason of its transcendency and abstraction, by reason of
its *imaginary difference* from the world, must have imagined it had left the actual situation and real human beings
too far below it. On the other hand, it seems that because
philosophy is not really different from the world it could

not give any *real opinion* on it, it could not bring any real
differentiating force to act upon it and could therefore not
interfere *practically*, but had to be satisfied at the best with
a practice *in abstracto.* Philosophy was over-practical only
in the sense that it soared above practice. Critical Criticism
gives the most striking proof how small real human beings
seem to speculation by lumping humanity together in a spiritless mass. In this the old speculation agrees with Criticism, as the following sentence out of Hegel's *Rechtsphi-
losophie* shows:

"From the standpoint of needs the concrete of the idea is
what is called *man*; the question here, and *properly speaking
only* here, is therefore man in this sense."

In other cases in which speculation speaks of man it does
not mean the *concrete*, but the *abstract*, the *idea,* the *spirit,*
etc. The way in which philosophy expresses the actual situation is strikingly exemplified by Herr Faucher in connection
with the actual English situation and by Herr Edgar in connection with the actual situation of the French language.

"Thus Proudhon also is practical when he finds that the
concept of equality is the base of the proof of property, and
argues from the same concept against property."

Proudhon does exactly the same thing as the German critics who, basing the proofs of the existence of God on man,
argue from the idea of man against the existence of God.

"If the consequences of the principle of equality are more
powerful than equality itself, how does Proudhon intend to
help that principle to acquire its sudden power?"

Self-consciousness, according to Herr Bauer, is at the basis of all religious ideas. It is, he says, the creative principle
of the gospels. Why, then, were the consequences of the principle of self-consciousness more powerful than the principle
itself? Because, the answer comes after the German fashion,
self-consciousness is indeed the creative principle of religious ideas, but only taken outside itself, in contradiction to

itself, divested of itself and estranged. Self-consciousness
that has come to itself, that understands itself, that appre-
hends its essence, therefore governs the creatures of its self-
estrangement. Proudhon finds himself in the same case, naturally, with the difference that he speaks French whereas
we speak German, and he therefore expresses in a French
way what we express in a German way.

Proudhon asks himself why equality, although as the creative principle of reason it is the basis of the institution of
property and as the ultimate reasonable basis underlies every argument in favour of property, does not, however, exist,
while its negation, private property, does. He accordingly
considers the fact of property in itself. He proves "that, in
truth, property, as an institution and a principle, is *impossible*" (p. 34), i.e., *that it contradicts itself* and abolishes itself
in all points; that, to put it the German way, it is the existence of dispossessed, self-contradicting, self-estranged equality. The real conditions in France, like the recognition of this
estrangement, suggest correctly to Proudhon the necessity
of abolishing that estrangement.

While negating private property, Proudhon feels the need
to justify the existence of private property *historically*. His
argument, like all first arguments of this kind, is pragmatic,
i.e., he assumes that earlier generations wished consciously
and with reflexion to realize in their institutions that equality which for him represents the human essence.

"We always come back to the same thing.... Proudhon
writes in the interests of the proletarians."

. He does not write in the interests of self-sufficient Criticism or out of any abstract, self-made interests, but out of a
massy, real, historic interest, an interest that goes beyond
criticism, that will go as far as a *crisis*. Not only does Proudhon write in the interests of the proletarians, he is himself a
proletarian, *un ouvrier*.* His work is a scientific manifesto

* A workman.—*Ed.*

of the French proletariat and therefore has quite a different
historic significance than that of the literary bungling of a
Critical Critic.

"Proudhon writes in the interests of those who have nothing: to have and not to have are for him Absolute Categories.
To have is for him the highest, because at the same time not
to have is for him the highest object of thought. Every man
must have, but no more or less than another, Proudhon
thinks. But, then, of all I have only what I have exclusively,
what I have more of than the other, is interesting for me.
With equality, both to have and equality itself will be a matter of indifference to me."

According to Herr Edgar, *To Have* and *Not To Have* are
for Proudhon absolute *categories*. Critical Criticism sees
nothing but categories everywhere. Thus, according to Herr
Edgar, To Have and Not To Have, wages, salary, want and
need, and work to satisfy that need are nothing but categories.

If society had to free itself only from the *categories* To
Have and Not To Have, how easy every dialectician, were
he even weaker than Herr Edgar, would make it for it to
"overcome" and "abolish" these categories! Herr Edgar considers this too such a trifle that he does not think it worth
the trouble to give even an *explanation* of the categories To
Have and Not To Have as an argument against Proudhon.
But Not To Have is not a mere category, it is a most discon-
solate reality; today the man who has nothing is nothing, for
he is cut off from existence in general and still more from a
human existence; for the condition of having nothing is the
condition of complete separation of man from his objectivity.
And therefore Not To Have seems quite justified in being for
Proudhon the highest object of thought; all the more as so
little thought has been given to this subject before him
and the socialist writers in general. Not To Have is the most
desperate *spiritualism*, a complete unreality of the human, a

complete reality of the dehumanized, a very positive To
Have, a having of hunger, of cold, of disease, of crime, of
debasement, of all inhumanity and monstrosity. But every
object which for the first time is made the object of thought
with full consciousness of its importance is the *highest
object of thought.*

Proudhon's wish to abolish Not To Have and the old way
of To Have is quite identical with the wish to abolish the
practically estranged relation of man to his *objective essence*
and the *political-economic* expression of human self-
estrangement. But as his criticism of political economy is a
prisoner of the premises of political economy, he still understands the very re-appropriation of the objective world as the
political-economic form of *possession.*

Proudhon does not oppose To Have to Not To Have, as
Critical Criticism makes him do; he opposes *possession* to the
old way of To Have, to *private property.* He proclaims possession to be a *"social function."* What is "interesting" in a
function, however, is not to "exclude" the other, but to occupy and to realize the forces of my own being.

Proudhon did not succeed in giving this thought the appropriate development. The idea of *"equal* possession" is a political-economic one and therefore itself still an alienated expression for the principle that the *object* as *being for man,*
as the *objectified being of man,* is at the same time the existence *of man for other men,* his *human relation to other
men, the social relation of man to man.* Proudhon abolishes
political-economic estrangement *within* political-economic
estrangement.

Characterizing Translation No. 3

The Critical Proudhon has a *Critical owner* too, by whose
"own admission those who had to work for him lost what he
appropriated." The massy Proudhon says to the massy
owner: "You have worked! Would you never have had others

work for you? How, then, can they have lost, working for you, what you were able to acquire not working for them?"

By "natural wealth" the Critical Proudhon makes Say understand "natural *possessions*" although Say, to preclude all error, states explicitly in the Epitome to his *Traité d'Economie Politique* that by *richesse* he understands neither property nor possession, but a "sum of values." It is natural that the Critical Proudhon should reform Say just as he himself is reformed by Herr Edgar. He makes Say "infer immediately a right to take a field as his property" because land is easier to appropiate than air or water. But Say, far from inferring from the greater possibility of appropriating the land a property *right* to it, says quite explicitly: "The *rights* of landed proprietors are to be traced to *plunder*." (*Traité d'écon. polit.* édit. III. T. I. p. 136, Note.) That is why, in Say's opinion, there must be "a concurrence of legislation" and "positive right" to justify the *right* to landed property. The real Proudhon does not make Say "immediately" *infer* the right of landed property from the easier appropriation of land. He reproaches him with taking possibility *for* right and *confusing* a question of possibility with a question of right:

"Say takes possibility *for* right. The question is not why land has been appropriated rather than sea or air, but by what *right* man has appropriated that wealth."

The Critical Proudhon continues: "The *only* remark on this is that with the appropriation of a piece of land the other elements—air, water and fire—are also appropriated: *terra, aqua, aëra et igne interdicti sumus.*"

Far from making "*only*" this remark, the real Proudhon says, on the contrary, that he drew "attention" to the appropriation of air and water incidentally (*en passant*). The Critical Proudhon makes an unintelligible use of the Roman formula of exile. He forgets to say who the "*we*" are who have been banished. The real Proudhon addresses the non-proprietors: "Proletarians ... property *banishes us: terra, etc. inter-dicti sumus.*"

The Critical Proudhon polemizes against Charles Comte as follows:

"Charles Comte thinks that in order to live man needs air, food and clothing. Some of these things, like air and water, are inexhaustible and therefore remain common property; but others are available in smaller quantities and become private property. Charles Comte therefore bases his proof on the concepts of limitedness and unlimitedness; he might have come to a different conclusion had he made the concepts of dispensableness and indispensableness his main categories."

How childish the Critical Proudhon's polemic is! He expects Charles Comte to give up the categories he uses for his proof and to jump over to others so as to come, not to his own conclusions, but *"perhaps"* to those of the Critical Proudhon.

The real Proudhon does not make any such demand on Charles Comte; he does not appease him with a "perhaps," he defeats him with his own categories.

Charles Comte, Proudhon says, proceeds from the indispensableness of air, food, and, in certain climates, clothing, not in order to live, but in order not to stop living. In order to maintain himself, man constantly needs (according to Charles Comte) to appropriate things of various kinds. These things do not all exist in the same proportion.

"The light of the stars, air and water exist in such quantities that man can neither increase nor decrease them sensibly; each one can appropriate as much of them as his needs require *without prejudice to the enjoyment of others.*"

Hence Proudhon proceeds from Comte's own definitions. First of all he proves to him that the land is also an object of primary necessity, the usufruct of which must remain free to every one, within the limits of Comte's clause, that is *"without prejudice to the enjoyment of others."* Why then has land become private property? Charles Comte answers:

because it is *not unlimited*. He should have concluded, on the contrary, that because land is *limited* it may not be appropriated. The appropriation of air and water causes no prejudice to anybody because, as they are unlimited, there is always enough left. The arbitrary appropriation of land, on the other hand, prejudices the enjoyment of others precisely because the land is *limited*. The use of the land must therefore be regulated in the interests of *all*. Charles Comte's method of proving refutes his own thesis.

"Charles Comte," Proudhon (the Critical one, to be precise) reasons, "proceeds from the view that a nation can be the owner of a land; nevertheless, if property involves the right to use and misuse—*jus utendi et abutendi re sua**—even a nation cannot be adjudged the right to use and misuse land."

The real Proudhon does not speak of *jus utendi et abutendi* that the right of property "involves." He is too massy to speak of a right of property that the right of property involves. *Jus utendi et abutendi re sua* is, in fact, the right of property itself. Hence Proudhon directly refuses a people the right of property over its territory. To those who find that exaggerated he retorts that in all epochs that imaginary right of national property gave rise to suzerainty, tribute, royal prerogative, corvée, etc.

The real Proudhon reasons as follows against Charles Comte: Comte wishes to expound how property arises and he begins with the hypothesis of a nation as owner. He thus falls into a *petitio principii*. He makes the state sell lands, he lets industrialists buy those estates, that is to say, he presupposes the *property relation* that he wishes to prove.

The Critical Proudhon scraps the French *decimal system*. He keeps the *franc* but replaces the *centime* by the "*Dreier*."

"If I cede a piece of land," Proudhon (the Critical one) continues, "I not only rob myself of the harvest; I deprive

---

* The right to use and misuse one's own thing.—*Ed.*

my children and children's children of a lasting good. Land has value not only today, it has also the value of its capacity and its future."

The real Proudhon does not speak of the fact that land has value not only today but also in the future: he opposes the full present value to the value of its capacity and its future which depends on my skill in exploiting the land. He says: "Destroy the land, or what comes to the same for you, sell it: you not only alienate one, two or more harvests; you annihilate all the produce you could have obtained from it, you, your children and your children's children."

For Proudhon the question is not to bring out the contrast between one harvest and the lasting good—the money I get for the field can, as capital, also become a "lasting good" —but the contrast between the present value and the value the land can acquire through prolonged cultivation.

"The new value," Charles Comte says, "that I give to a thing by my work is my property, Proudhon" (the Critical) "thinks he can refute him in the following way: *Then* a man must cease to be an owner the moment he ceases to work. Ownership of the product can by no means "involve ownership of the material from which the product was made."

The real Proudhon says:

"Let the worker appropriate his product, but I do not understand how ownership of the product involves ownership of the matter. Does the fisherman who manages to catch more fish than the others on the same bank become by his skill the owner of the place where he fishes? Was the skill of a hunter ever considered as a title to ownership of game in a canton? The same applies to agriculture. In order to transform *possession* into *property another condition* is necessary besides work, or a man would cease to be an owner as soon as he ceased to be a worker."

Cessante causa, cessat effectus. When the owner is owner *only* as a worker, he ceases to be an owner as soon as he ceases to be a worker. "According to *law*, it is *prescription* which creates ownership; *work* is only the perceptible sign, the material act by which occupation is *manifested*."

"The system of appropriation through work," Proudhon goes on, "is therefore *contrary* to *law*; and when the supporters of that system claim it as an explanation of their laws they are *contradicting themselves*."

To say further, according to this opinion, that the cultivation of the land, for example, "creates fullest ownership of the same" is a *petitio principii*. It is a fact that a new productive capacity of matter has been created. But what was to be proved was that ownership of matter itself was thus created. Man has not created matter itself. And he cannot even create any productive capacity if the matter does not exist beforehand.

The Critical Proudhon makes *Gracchus Baboeuf* a partisan of *freedom*, but in the massy Proudhon he is a partisan of equality (*partisan de l'égalité*).

The *Critical Proudhon*, who wanted to estimate Homer's fee for the *Iliad*, says: "The fee which I pay Homer must be equal to what he *gives me*. But how is the value of what he gives to be determined?"

The Critical Proudhon is too elevated above the trifles of political economy to know that the *value* of an object and what that object *gives* somebody else are two different things. The real Proudhon says: "The fee of the poet must be equal to his *product*: what then is the value of that product?" The real Proudhon supposes that the *Iliad* has an infinite *price* (or exchange-value, *prix*), while the Critical Proudhon supposes that it has an infinite *value*. The real Proudhon opposes the value of the *Iliad*, *its value in the economic* sense (*valeur intrinsèque*), to its exchange-value (*valeur échangeable*); the Critical Proudhon opposes its "value for exchange" to its "intrinsic value," i.e., its value as a poem.

The real Proudhon says: "Between material retribution and talent there is no common measure. In *this* respect the situation of all producers is the same. Consequently any comparison between them, any classification according to fortune is impossible." (*Entre une récompense matérielle et le talent il n'existe pas de commune mesure; sous ce rapport la condition de tous les producteurs est égale; conséquemment toute comparaison entre eux et toute distinction de fortunes est impossible.*)

The Critical Proudhon says: "*Relatively*, the position of all producers is the same. Talent cannot be weighed materially.... Any comparison of the producers among themselves, any *exterior distinction* is impossible."

In the Critical Proudhon we read that "the man of science must *feel* himself *equal* in society, because his talent and his insight are *only* a product of the insight of society." The real Proudhon does not speak anywhere about the feelings of talent. He says that talent must lower itself to the level of society. No more does he assert that the man of talent is *only* a product of society. On the contrary, he says: "The man of talent has contributed to produce in himself a useful instrument.... There exist in him at once a free worker *and* an accumulated social capital."

The Critical Proudhon goes on to say: "Besides, he must be thankful to society for releasing him from other work so that he can apply himself to science."

The real Proudhon nowhere resorts to the gratitude of the man of talent. He says: "The artist, the scientist, the poet, receive their just reward by the mere fact that society allows them to apply themselves exclusively to science and art."

Finally, the Critical Proudhon works the wonder of making a society of 150 workers able to maintain a "*marshal*" and therefore, probably, an *army*. In the real Proudhon the marshal is a "*farrier*" (*maréchal*).

Critical Gloss No. 4

"If he" (Proudhon) "maintains the concept of salary, if he sees in society an institution that gives us work and pays us for it, he has all the less right to recognize time as the measure for payment as he but shortly before, agreeing with *Hugo Grotius*, professed that time is indifferent as to the *validity* of an object."

This is the only point on which Critical Criticism attempts to solve its problem and to prove to Proudhon that from the standpoint of political economy he is argumenting wrongly against political economy. Here Criticism *disgraces* itself in truly Critical fashion.

Proudhon agrees with Hugo Grotius and argues that *prescription* is no title to change *possession* into *property* or a "*legal principle*" into another principle, any more than time can change the truth that the three angles of a triangle are together equal to two right angles into the truth that they are equal to three right angles. "Never," cries Proudhon, "will you succeed in making length of time, which of itself creates nothing, changes nothing, modifies nothing, able to *change* the *user* into a *proprietor*."

Herr Edgar's conclusion is: Since Proudhon said that mere time cannot *change* one legal principle into another, that by itself it cannot change or modify anything, he is inconsistent when he makes *labour time* the measure of the political-economic value of the product of work. Herr Edgar manages this Critically Critical remark by translating "*valeur*"* by "*Geltung*,"** so that he can use the word for validity of a legal principle in the same sense as for the commercial value of a product of work. He manages it by identifying empty length of time with time filled with labour. Had Proudhon said that time cannot change a fly into an elephant, Critical Criticism

---

* Value.—*Ed.*
** Validity.—*Ed.*

could have said with the same justification: he has therefore
no right to make labour time the measure of wages.

Even Critical Criticism must be capable of grasping that
the *labour time* necessarily *expended* on the production of an
object is included in the *cost of production* of that object, that
the *cost of production* of an object is what it *costs* and what
it can be *sold* for, abstraction being made of the influence of
competition. Besides the labour time and the material of labour, economists include in the cost of production the rent
paid to the owner of the land, interest and the profit of the
capitalist. The latter are excluded by Proudhon because he
excludes private property. Hence there remain only the labour time and the expenses. By making labour time, the immediate existence of human activity as activity, the measure
of wages and the determination of the value of the product,
Proudhon makes the human side the decisive factor. In old
political economy, on the other hand, the decisive factor was
the ponderable power of capital and of landed property. In
other words, Proudhon reinstates man in his rights, but still
in a political-economic and therefore contradictory way. How
right he is from the standpoint of political economy can be
seen from the fact that *Adam Smith,* the founder of modern
political economy, develops in the very first pages of his book,
*An Inquiry into the Nature and Causes of the Wealth of
Nations* the idea that *before* the invention of private property,
that is to say, presupposing the *non-existence of private
property, labour time* was the measure of *wages* and of the
value of the product of labour, which was not yet distinguished from wages.

But even let Critical Criticism suppose for an instant that
Proudhon did not proceed from the premise of wages. Does
it believe that the *time* which the production of an object requires was *ever* not a substantial factor in the "*validity*" of
the object? Does it believe that time will lose its *costliness*?

As far as straightforward material production is concerned, the decision whether an object is to be produced or not, i.e., the decision on the *value* of the object, will depend substantially on the labour time required for its production. For it depends on that time whether society has time to develop humanly.

And even in the case of production *of the mind,* must I not, if I proceed reasonably in other respects, consider the time necessary for the production of an intellectual work when I determine its scope, its character and its plan? Otherwise I am risking at least that the object that is in my idea will never become an object in reality, and will therefore acquire no more than the value of an imaginary object, i.e., an *imaginary value.*

The criticism of political economy from the standpoint of political economy recognizes all the essential definitions of human activity, but only in an alienated, estranged form. Here, for example, it changes the importance of labour time for *human work* into its importance for *wages,* for wage-labour.

Herr Edgar continues: "In order to force talent to adopt that measure, Proudhon *misuses* the concept of *free contract* and asserts that society and its individual members have the right to reject the products of talent."

Talent in the *followers of Fourier* and *Saint Simon* bases itself on political-economic principles and puts forward exaggerated *fee claims,* giving its imagination of its infinite value as measure of the *exchange-value* of its products; Proudhon answers it in the same way as political economy answers the claim for a price much higher than the so-called natural price, that is, higher than the cost of production of the object offered. He answers by free contract. But Proudhon does not *misuse* this relation in the sense of political economy; actually, he supposes that to be real which the economists consider as nominal and illusory—the *freedom* of the contracting parties.

Characterizing Translation No. 4

The Critical Proudhon finally reforms *French society* by as deep a transformation of the French proletarians as of the French bourgeoisie.

He denies the French proletarians *"strength"* because the real Proudhon reproaches them with a lack of *virtue (vertu)*. He makes their *skill* in work problematic—"you are *perhaps* skilled in work"—because the real Proudhon unconditionally recognizes their skill in work (*"Prompts au travail vous êtes*, etc."). He makes out of the French bourgeois *dull* burghers where the real Proudhon opposes the ignoble bourgeois (*bourgeois ignobles*) to the blemished nobles (*nobles flétris*). He changes the happy-medium burghers (*bourgeois juste-milieu*) into "our *good* burghers," for which the French bourgeoisie must be grateful. Hence, where the real Proudhon says the *"ill"* will" (*la malveillance de nos bourgeois*) of the French bourgeois is growing, the Critical Proudhon consistently makes the *"carefreeness of our burghers"* grow. The real Proudhon's bourgeois is so far from being carefree that he shouts to himself: "Let us not be afraid! Let us not be afraid!" Those are the words of a man who wishes to reason himself out of fear and worry.

By creating the Critical Proudhon in its translation of the real Proudhon, Critical Criticism has shown the mass what a Critically perfect translation is. It has given directions for "translation as it ought to be." It is therefore rightly against bad, massy translations:

"The German public wants the booksellers' wares ridiculously cheap, so the publisher needs a cheap translation; the translator does not want to starve at his work, he cannot even perform it with mature reflexion" (with all the calm of knowledge) "because the publisher must anticipate rivals by quick delivery; even the translator has to fear competition, to fear someone else producing the ware quicker and cheaper; he therefore dictates his manuscript offhand to some poor scribe —as quickly as he can in order not to pay the scribe his hourly wage for nothing. He is more than happy when he can next day satisfy the harassing type-setter. By the way, the translations with which we are flooded are but an illustration of the *impotence* of German literature today," etc. (*Allgemeine Literatur-Zeitung*, No. VIII, p. 54).

Critical Gloss No. 5

"The proof of the impossibility of property that Proudhon draws from the fact that mankind is consumed particularly by the interest and profit system and by the disproportion between consumption and production lacks its counterpart, namely, the proof that private property is historically possible."

Critical Criticism has the fortunate instinct not to go into Proudhon's reasoning on the interest and profit system, etc., i.e., into the most important part of his argument. The reason is that on this point not even a pretence of criticism of Proudhon can be offered without absolutely positive knowledge of the movement of private property. Critical Criticism tries to make up for its impotence by observing that Proudhon has not proved the historical possibility of property. Why does Criticism, which has nothing but words to give, expect others to give it *everything*?

"Proudhon proves the impossibility of property by the fact that the worker cannot buy back the product of his work out of his wage. Proudhon does not give an exhaustive proof of this by expounding the essence of capital. The worker cannot buy back his product because it is always a common product, while he is never anything but an individual paid man."

Herr Edgar, in contrast to Proudhon's deduction, could have expressed himself still more exhaustively on the fact that the worker *cannot* buy back his product because he *must buy it back*. It is already contained in the definition of buying that his relation to his product is a relation to an object that he no longer has, an estranged object. Among other things, Herr Edgar's exhaustive argument does not exhaust the question why the capitalist, who himself is *nothing* but an *individual* man, and what is more, a man *paid* by interest and profit, can buy back not only the product of labour, but still more than that product. To explain this Herr Edgar would have to explain the relation of labour and capital, that is, to expound the essence of capital.

The above quotation from the criticism shows most palpably how Critical Criticism immediately makes use of what it has learnt from a writer to pass it off as wisdom it has itself discovered and use it with a Critical twist against the same writer. For it is from Proudhon himself that Critical Criticism drew the argument that it says Proudhon did not give and that Herr Edgar did. Proudhon says:

"*Divide et impera....* If the workers are separated one from another the wages paid to each one may exceed the value of each individual product; but that is not the point at issue.... Although you have paid all the individual powers you have not paid the collective power."

Proudhon was the *first* to draw attention to the fact that the sum of the wages of the individual workers, even if each individual labour be paid for completely, does not pay the collective power objectified in its product; that therefore the worker is not paid as a *part of the collective labour power.* Herr Edgar twists this into the assertion, that the worker is nothing but an individual paid man. Critical Criticism thus opposes a *general* thought of Proudhon's to the further *concrete* development that Proudhon himself gives to the same thought. It takes possession of that thought after the fashion of Criticism and gives voice to the secret of **Critical socialism** in the following sentence:

"The modern worker *thinks* only of himself, i.e., he demands pay only for his own person. It is he himself who fails to reckon with the enormous, the immeasurable power which arises from his co-operation with other powers."

According to Critical Criticism the whole evil lies in the workers' "*thinking.*" It is true that the English and French workers have formed associations in which they exchange opinions not only on their immediate needs as *workers,* but on their needs as *human beings.* Thus they show thorough and comprehensive consciousness of the "enormous" and "immeasurable" power which arises from their co-operation. But these *massy,* communist workers, employed, for instance, in the Manchester or Lyons workshops, do not believe that "*pure thinking*" will be able to argue away their industrial masters and their own practical debasement. They are most painfully aware of the *difference* between *being* and *thinking,* between *consciousness* and *life.* They know that property, capital, money, wage-labour and the like are no ideal figments of the brain but very practical, very objective sources of their self-estrangement and that they must be abolished in a practical, objective way for man to become man not only in *thinking,* in *consciousness,* but in massy *being,* in life. Critical Criticism, on the contrary, teaches them that they cease in reality to be wage-workers if in thinking they abolish the thought of wage-labour; if in thinking they cease to imagine themselves as wage-workers and no longer demand payment for their person in accordance with that extravagant imagination. As absolute idealists, as ethereal beings, they will then naturally be able to live on the ether of pure thought. Critical Criticism teaches them that they abolish real capital by overcoming in *thinking* the category Capital, that they *really* change and transform themselves into real human beings by changing their "*abstract ego*" in their consciousness and scorning as unCritical operations all *real* changes in their real existence, in the real conditions of their existence, that is, in their real ego. The "spirit," which sees in reality only categories, naturally reduces all human activity and practice to the dialectical thinking process of Critical Criticism. That is what distinguishes *its* socialism from *massy* socialism and communism.

After his great discourse Herr Edgar must naturally declare Proudhon's criticism "devoid of consciousness."

"*But* Proudhon wishes to be *practical too.*" "He thinks he has grasped." "And nevertheless," cries the calm of knowledge triumphantly, "we cannot even now credit him with the *calm of knowledge.*" "We quote a few passages to show how little he has considered his attitude to society."

Later we shall also quote a few passages from the works of Critical Criticism, (see the *Bank for the Poor* and the *Model Farm*) to show that it has not yet learnt the very first relations of political economy, let alone thought them over, and hence felt with its characteristic Critical tact that it is selected to pass judgement on Proudhon.

Now that Critical Criticism as the calm of knowledge has "*disposed of*" *all the massy* "*opposites*," has mastered all reality in the form of categories and dissolved all human activity into speculative dialectics, we shall see it reproduce the world out of speculative dialectics. It goes without saying that if the wonders of Critically speculative creation of the world are not to be "profaned," they may be presented to the profane mass only in the form of *mysteries*. Critical Criticism therefore appears in the person of *Wischnu-Szeliga* as a *mystery-monger*.[13]

CHAPTER V

CRITICAL CRITICISM AS A MYSTERY-MONGER,
OR
CRITICAL CRITICISM IN THE PERSON OF HERR SZELIGA

"Critical Criticism" personified in *Szeliga-Wischnu* provides an apotheosis of the *Mystères de Paris*. Eugène Sue is proclaimed a "Critical Critic." Hearing this, he may exclaim like Molière's *Bourgeois Gentilhomme*:

"Faith, I have been speaking prose for more than forty years without knowing it: I am infinitely grateful to you for telling me so."

Herr Szeliga prefaces his criticism with an *aesthetic* prologue.

"The aesthetic prologue" gives the following explanation of the general meaning of the "Critical" epos and in particular of the *Mystères de Paris*:

"The epos begets the thought that the present in itself is nothing, and not only" (*nothing* and not only!) "the eternal *boundary* between *past* and *future*, but" (nothing, and not only, but) "but the *gap* that *must continually be filled* and which separates *immortality* from *perishableness*. . . . *Such* is the *general meaning* of the *Mystères de Paris*."

The "aesthetic prologue" further asserts that "if the *critic* wished he could also be a *poet*."

The whole of Herr Szeliga's criticism will prove that assertion. It is "*a poem*" in every respect.

It is also a product of "*free* art" according to the definition of the latter in the "aesthetic prologue"—it "invents *some-*

thing quite new, something that absolutely never existed before."

Finally, it is even a *Critical epos*, for it is "a gap that must be continually filled," and which "separates immortality"—Herr Szeliga's Critical Criticism—from "perishableness"—Eugène Sue's novel.

1) "The Mystery of Degeneracy in Civilization" and "The Mystery of Rightlessness in the State"

Feuerbach, we know, conceived the Christian ideas of the Incarnation, the Trinity, Immortality etc., as the mystery of the Incarnation, the mystery of the Trinity, the mystery of Immortality. Herr Szeliga conceived all present world conditions as mysteries. But whereas *Feuerbach* disclosed *real mysteries*, Herr *Szeliga* makes *mysteries* out of real *trivialities*. His art is not that of disclosing what is hidden, but of hiding what is disclosed.

Thus he proclaims as *mysteries* degeneracy (criminals) within civilization and rightlessness and inequality in the state. So either socialist literature, which revealed these mysteries, is still a mystery to Herr Szeliga, or he wants to make a private mystery of "Critical Criticism" out of the best-known results of that literature.

We therefore need go no deeper into Herr Szeliga's discourse on these mysteries; we shall merely draw attention to a few of the most brilliant points.

"Before the law and the judge everything is *equal*, the high and the low, the rich and the poor. This sentence comes at the head of the credo of the *state*."

Of the state? On the contrary, the credo of most states starts by making the high and the low, the rich and the poor *unequal* before the *law*.

"The lapidary Morel in his naive probity most clearly expresses the mystery" (the Mystery of the contradiction between poor and rich) "when he says: If only the rich knew! If only the rich knew! The misfortune is that they do not know what poverty is."

Herr Szeliga does not know that Eugène Sue commits an *anachronism* out of courtesy to the French bourgeoisie when he puts the motto of the burghers of Louis XIV's time "*Ah! si le roi le savait!*" in a modified form: "*Ah! si le riche le savait!*" into the mouth of the working man Morel who lived in the time of *Charte vérité*.[14] In England and France, at least, that *naive* relation between rich and poor has ceased. There the scientific representatives of wealth, the economists, have spread a very detailed understanding of the physical and moral misery of poverty. They have made up for that by proving that misery must remain because the present condition must remain. In their solicitude they have even ✳ calculated the *proportions* in which poverty must be decimated for the good of the wealth and its own.

If Eugène Sue depicts the taverns, hide-outs and language — of *criminals*, Herr Szeliga discloses the "*mystery*" that what the "author" wanted was not to depict that language or those hide-outs, but "to teach us the mysteries of the mainsprings of evil, etc." "For criminals are *at home* precisely in the most crowded places."

What would a natural scientist say if one were to prove to him that the bee's cell does not interest him as the bee's cell, that it has no mystery for one who has not studied it, because the bee is "at home precisely" in the open air and on the flower? The hide-outs of the criminals and their language reflect the characters of the criminal, they are part of his existence, their description is part of his description as the description of the *petite maison* is part of the description of the *femme galante*.

For Parisians in general and even for the Paris police the hide-outs of criminals are such a "mystery" that at this very moment broad light streets are being laid out in the *Cité* to give the police access to them.

Finally, Eugène Sue himself states that in the descriptions mentioned above he was relying on the "timid curiosity" of his readers. Eugène Sue relied on the timid curiosity of his readers in all his novels. It is sufficient to recall *Atar Gull, Salamander, Plick and Plock,* etc.

2) "The Mystery of Speculative Construction"

The mystery of the Critical presentation of the *Mystères de Paris* is the mystery of *speculative Hegelian construction.* Once Herr Szeliga has proclaimed "degeneracy within civilization" and rightlessness in the state "Mysteries," i.e., has dissolved them in the category "*Mystery,*" he lets "Mystery" begin its *speculative career.* A few words will suffice to characterize speculative construction *in general*; Herr Szeliga's treatment of the *Mystères de Paris* will give the application *in detail.*

If from real apples, pears, strawberries and almonds I form the general idea "*Fruit,*" if I go further and *imagine* that my abstract idea "Fruit," derived from real fruit, is an entity existing outside me, is indeed the *true* essence of the pear, the apple, etc.; then, in the *language of speculative philosophy* I am declaring that "Fruit" is the *substance* of the pear, the apple, the almond, etc. I am saying, therefore, that to be a pear is not essential to the pear, that to be an apple is not essential to the apple; that what is essential to these things is not their real being, perceptible to the senses, but the essence that I have extracted from them and then foisted on them, the essence of my idea—"Fruit." I therefore declare apples, pears, almonds, etc. to be mere forms of existence, *modi,* of "Fruit." My finite understanding supported by my senses does, of course, *distinguish* an apple from a pear and a pear from an almond; but my speculative reason declares these sensuous differences unessential, indifferent. It sees in the apple *the same* as in the pear, and in the pear the same as in the almond, namely "Fruit." Particular real fruits are no more than semblances whose true essence is "the Substance"—"Fruit."

By this method one attains no particular *wealth of definition*. The mineralogist whose whole science consisted in the statement that all minerals are really "Mineral" would be a mineralogist only in *his imagination*. For every mineral the speculative mineralogist says "Mineral" and his science is reduced to repeating that word as many times as there are real minerals.

Having reduced the different real fruits to the *one* fruit of abstraction—"Fruit," speculation must, in order to attain some appearance of real content, try somehow to find its way back from "Fruit," from *Substance* to the *different* profane real fruits, the pear, the apple, the almond, etc. It is as hard to produce real fruits from the abstract idea "Fruit" as it is easy to produce this abstract idea from real fruits. Indeed it is impossible to arrive at the *opposite* of an abstraction without *relinquishing* the abstraction.

The speculative philosopher therefore relinquishes the abstraction "Fruit," but in a *speculative, mystical* fashion— with the appearance of *not* relinquishing it. Thus he rises above his abstraction only in appearance. He argues like this:

If apples, pears, almonds and strawberries are really nothing but "Substance," "Fruit," the question arises: Why does "Fruit" manifest itself to me sometimes as an apple, sometimes as a pear, sometimes as an almond? Why this *appearance of diversity* which so strikingly contradicts my speculative conception of "*Unity*"; "Substance"; "Fruit"?

This, answers the speculative philosopher, is because fruit is not dead, undifferentiated, motionless, but living, self-differentiating, moving. The diversity of profane fruits is

significant not only to *my* sensuous understanding, but also
to "Fruit" itself and to speculative reasoning. The different
profane fruits are different manifestations of the life of the
one "Fruit"; they are crystallizations of "Fruit" itself. In the
apple "Fruit" gives itself an apple-like existence, in the pear
a pear-like existence. We must therefore no longer say as
from the standpoint of Substance: a pear is "Fruit," an apple
is "Fruit," an almond is "Fruit," but "Fruit" presents itself
as a pear, "Fruit" presents itself as an apple, "Fruit" presents itself as an almond; and the differences which distinguish apples, pears and almonds from one another are the
self-differentiations of "Fruit" making the particular fruits
subordinate members of the life-process of "Fruit." Thus
"Fruit" is no longer a contentless, undifferentiated unity; it
is oneness as *allness*, as "*totalness*" of fruits, which constitute an "*organic ramified series*." In every member of that
series "Fruit" gives itself a more developed, more explicit
existence, until it is finally the "*summary*" of all fruits and
at the same time living *unity* which contains all those fruits
dissolved in itself just as much as it produces them from
within itself, as, for instance, all the limbs of the body are
constantly dissolved in blood and constantly produced out
of the blood.

We see that if the Christian religion knows only *one* Incarnation of God, speculative philosophy has as many incarnations as there are things, just as it has here in every fruit an
incarnation of the "Substance," of the Absolute "Fruit." The
main interest for the speculative philosopher is therefore to
produce the *existence* of the real profane fruits and to say in
some mysterious way that there are apples, pears, almonds
and raisins. But the apples, pears, almonds and raisins that
we get in the speculative world are nothing but *semblances*
of apples, *semblances* of pears, *semblances* of almonds and
semblances of raisins; they are moments in the life of "Fruit,"
that abstract *being of reason*, and therefore themselves ab-

stract *beings of reason*. Hence what you enjoy in speculation is to find all the real fruits there, but as fruits which have a higher mystic significance, which are grown out of the ether of your brain and not out of the material earth, which are incarnations of "Fruit," *the Absolute Subject*. When you return from the abstraction, the *preternatural* being of reason, "Fruit," to real *natural* fruits, you give, contrariwise, the natural fruits a preternatural significance and transform them into so many abstractions. Your main interest is then to point out the *unity* of "Fruit" in all the manifestations of its life —the apple, the pear, the almond—that is, the *mystical interconnection* between these fruits, how in each one of them "Fruit" develops *by degrees* and *necessarily* progresses, for instance, from its existence as a raisin to its existence as an almond. The value of profane fruits *no longer* consists in their *natural* qualities *but* in their *speculative* quality which gives each of them a definite place in the life-process of "Absolute Fruit."

The ordinary man does not think he is saying anything extraordinary when he states that there are apples and pears. But if the philosopher expresses those existences in the speculative way he says something *extraordinary*. He works a *wonder* by producing the real *natural being*, the apple, the pear, etc., out of the unreal *being of reason* "Fruit," i.e., by *creating* those fruits out of *his own abstract reason*, which he considers as an Absolute Subject outside himself, represented here as "Fruit." And in every existence which he expresses he accomplishes an act of creation.

It goes without saying that the speculative philosopher accomplishes this constant creation only by representing universally known qualities of the apple, the pear, etc., which exist in reality, as definitions *discovered* by him; by giving the *names* of the real things to what abstract reason alone can create, to abstract formulae of reason; finally, by declaring his *own* activity, by which *he passes* from the idea of an

apple to the idea of a pear, to be the *self-activity* of the Absolute Subject, "Fruit."

In the speculative way of speaking, this operation is called
comprehending the *substance* as the *subject*, as an *inner
process*, as an *Absolute Person* and that comprehension constitutes the essential character of *Hegel's* method.

These preliminary remarks were necessary to make Herr
Szeliga intelligible. After thus far dissolving real relations,
e.g., right and civilization, in the category of mysteries and
thereby making "Mystery" a substance, he now rises to the
real speculative *Hegelian* height and transforms "Mystery"
into self-existing subject *incarnating* itself in real situations
and persons so that the manifestations of its life are count-
esses, marquises, *grisettes*, porters, notaries and charlatans,
love intrigues, balls, wooden doors, etc. Having produced
the category "Mystery" out of the real world, he produces
the real world out of that category.

The mysteries of *speculative construction* in Herr Szeliga's
presentation will be all the *more visibly* disclosed as he has
an indisputable *double* advantage over *Hegel*. First, Hegel
has the sophistic mastery of being able to present as a process of the imagined being of reason itself, of the Absolute
Subject, the process by which the philosopher goes by sen-
sory perception and imagination from one object to another. Besides, Hegel very often gives a *real* presentation, embracing the *thing* itself, within the *speculative* presentation.
This real reasoning *within* the speculative reasoning mis-
leads the reader into considering the speculative reasoning
as real and the real as speculative.

With Herr Szeliga both these difficulties vanish. His dialectics have no hypocrisy or pretence. He performs his tricks
with the most laudable honesty and the most sincere
straightforwardness. But then he *nowhere* develops any *real
content*, so that his speculative construction is free from all
disturbing complications, from all ambiguous disguises, and

appeals to the eye in its naked beauty. In Herr Szeliga we also see a brilliant illustration of how speculation on the one hand apparently freely creates its object *a priori* out of itself, and on the other hand, for the very reason that it wishes to get rid by sophistry of its reasonable and natural dependence on the *object*, falls into the most unreasonable and unnatural *bondage* to the object whose most accidental and individual attributes it is obliged to construe as absolutely necessary and general.

3) "The Mystery of Educated Society"

After leading us through the lowest layers of society, for example through the criminals' taverns, Eugène Sue transports us to "high society," to a *ball* in Quartier Saint Germain.

This *transition* Herr Szeliga construes as follows: "*Mystery* tries to evade observation by a new twist: so far it appeared as the absolutely enigmatic, elusive, and negative, in contrast to the true, real and positive; now it withdraws into the latter as its *invisible content*. But by doing so it gives up the absolute impossibility of being known."

"Mystery" which has so far appeared in contrast to the "true," the "real," the "positive," that is, to law and education, "now withdraws into the latter," i.e., into the realm of education. It is certainly a mystery *for* Paris, if not *of* Paris, that "high society" is the exclusive realm of education. Here Szeliga does not pass from the mysteries of the criminal world to those of aristocratic society; "Mystery" becomes the "invisible content" of educated society, its *real essence*. It is "*not a new twist*" of Herr Szeliga's to lead on to new observations; "Mystery" *itself* takes this "new twist" in order to evade observation.

Before really following Eugène Sue where his heart leads him—to an aristocratic ball, Herr Szeliga makes use of

6*

the *hypocritical* twists of speculation which construes *a priori.*

"One can *naturally foresee* what a solid shell "Mystery" will *choose* to hide in; it *seems, in fact,* that it is of *compact solidity* ... that ... *hence* it may *be expected* that *in general* ... *nevertheless* a new attempt to break through to the core is *here indispensable.*"

Enough. Herr Szeliga has gone so far that the "*metaphysical* subject, Mystery, now steps forward, light, composed and coquet."

In order now to change aristocratic society into a "mystery," Herr Szeliga gives us a few considerations on "*education.*" He presumes aristocratic society to have all sorts of qualities that no man would look for in it, in order later to find the "mystery" that it has not got those qualities. Then he presents that discovery as the "mystery" of educated society. Herr Szeliga wonders, for example, whether "*general reason*" (does he mean speculative logic?) constitutes the content of its "*drawing-room talk,*" whether "the *rhythm* and *measure* of love *alone* makes" it a "harmonious whole," whether "what we call *general education* is the form of the *general,* the *eternal,* the *ideal,*" i.e., whether what we call education is metaphysical imagination. It is not difficult for Herr Szeliga to prophesy *a priori* in answer to his questions: "It *may be expected, however* ... that the answer will be a negative one."

In Eugène Sue's novel, the transition from the common world to the refined world is a normal transition for a novel. The *disguise of Rudolph,* Prince of Geroldstein, gives him entry into the lower sections of society as his title gives him access to the higher sections. On his way to the aristocratic ball he is by no means engrossed in the contrasts of contemporary life: it is the contrasts of his *own* disguise that he finds *piquant.* He informs his docile suite how extraordinarily interesting he finds himself in the various situations.

"I find these contracts *piquant* enough," he says, "one day a fan painter, settling down in a hole in *rue aux Fèves*; this morning a salesman offering a glass of black currant wine to Madame Pipelet, and this evening ... one of the privileged by the grace of God who reign over the world."

When Critical Criticism is ushered into the ball it sings:

Sense and reason forsake me near,
In the midst of the potentates here![15]

It pours forth in *dithyrambs* as follows:

"Here magic brings the glow of the sun at night, the verdure of spring and the splendour of summer in winter. We immediately feel in a mood to believe in the miracle of the divine presence in the breast of man, especially when beauty and grace uphold the conviction that we are in the immediate proximity of ideals." (!!!)

Inexperienced, credulous *Critical country parson!* Only your Critical ingenuity can be raised by an elegant Parisian ball-room "to a mood" in which you believe in "the miracle of the divine presence in the breast of man," and see in Parisian lionesses "immediate ideals" and angels corporeal!

In his *unctuous* simplicity the Critical parson listens to the two "most beautiful among the beautiful," Clémence d'Harville and Countess Sarah MacGregor. One can guess what he wishes to *hear* from them:

"In what way we can be the *blessing* of beloved children and the *fulness* of happiness of a husband!" ... "We hark ... we wonder ... we believe not our ears."

We secretly feel a spiteful pleasure when the listener is disappointed. The ladies speak neither of "blessing," "fulness" nor "general reason," but "of an infidelity of Madame d'Harville to her husband."

We get the following naive revelation about one of the ladies, Countess MacGregor:

She was "*enterprising enough* to become *mother to a child as the result* of a secret marriage."

Unpleasantly affected by the *enterprise* of Countess Mac-Gregor, Herr Szeliga has sharp words for her:

"We find that all the Countess's strivings are for selfish individual profit."

Indeed, he sees no good portent in the attainment of her purpose—her marriage to the Prince of Geroldstein:

"Of which we can *by no means* expect that she will avail herself of it for the *happiness* of the Prince of Geroldstein's *subjects.*"

The puritan ends his sermon with "profound earnestness": "Sarah" (the *enterprising* lady), "*incidentally, is hardly* an exception in this brilliant circle, *although* she is one of its *summits.*"

Incidentally, hardly! *Although!* And is not the "summit" of a circle an exception?

Here is what we learn about the character of two other ideals, the Marquise d'Harville and the Duchess of Lucenay:

They "lack satisfaction of the heart." They have not found in marriage the object of their love, so they seek it outside marriage. In marriage love has remained a *mystery* for them and the imperative urge of the heart drives them to pierce that mystery. *So* they give themselves up to *secret love.* These "victims" of "loveless marriage are driven against their will to debase love to something exterior, to a so-called relation and take the romantic, *mystery,* for the interior, the vivifying, the essential of love."

The merit of this dialectical reasoning is to be assessed all the higher as it is of more general application.

He, for example, who is not allowed to *drink* at home and yet feels the need to drink looks for the "object" of drink "*outside*" the house and "so" takes to *secret drinking.* He will even be driven to consider mystery as an essential ingredient of drinking, although he will not debase drink to a mere "exterior" indifferent thing, any more than our ladies did with love. For, according to Herr Szeliga, it is not love, but marriage without love, that they debase to what it really is, to something exterior, to a so-called relation.

Herr Szeliga goes on to ask: "What is the *mystery* of love?"

We have just had it construed in such a way that "mystery," is the "*essence*" of this kind of love. How is it that we now look for the mystery of the mystery, the essence of the essence?

"Not the shady paths in the thickets," declaims the parson, "not the *natural* semi-obscurity of moonlight night or the artificial semi-obscurity of costly curtains and draperies; not the soft enrapturing notes of the harp and the organ, not the attraction of what is forbidden. . . ."

Curtains *and* draperies! Soft *and* enrapturing notes! Even the *organ*! Let the reverend parson stop thinking of *church*! Who would bring an organ to a love tryst?

"All this" (curtains, draperies and the organ) "is only the *mysterious*."

And is not the *mysterious* the mystery of mysterious love? By no means:

"The mysterious in it is what excites, what inebriates, what enraptures, the *power of sensuality*."

In the "soft and *enrapturing*" notes the parson already had the enrapturing. Had he brought turtle soup and champagne to his rendezvous instead of curtains and organs, the "*exciting* and *inebriating*" would have been present too.

"We will not admit," the reverend gentleman argues, "the power of sensuality; it has such tremendous power over us only because we cast it out of us and will not recognize it as our own nature which we should be in a position to dominate if it tried to make itself felt at the expense of reason, of real love and of will-power."

The parson advises us after the fashion of speculative theology to *recognize* sensuality as our *own* nature, in order later to be able to *dominate* it, i.e., to retract recognition of it. True, he wishes to dominate it only when it tries to make itself felt at the expense *of reason*—will-power and love as *opposed* to sensuality are only the will-power and love *of* Reason. The unspeculative Christian also recognizes *sensuality* as long as it does not make itself felt at the expense of real reason, i.e., of faith, of real love, i.e., of love of God, of real will-power, i.e., will in Christ.

The parson immediately betrays his real meaning when he continues:

"If then love ceases to be the essential in marriage and in morality, *sensuality* becomes the mystery of love, of morality, of educated society—sensuality in its *narrow* meaning, in which it is *trembling in the nerves* and a *burning stream* in the veins, and also in the broader meaning, in which it is elevated to the *semblance* of spiritual power, to lust for power, ambition, craving for glory.... Countess MacGregor is a representative" of the latter meaning "of sensuality as the mystery of educated society."

The parson hits the nail on the head. To dominate *sensuality* he must first of all overcome the *nervous current* and the quick *circulation of the blood.*—Herr Szeliga believes in the "narrow" meaning that greater warmth in the body comes from the heat of the blood in the veins; he does not know that *warm-blooded animals* are so called because the temperature of their blood is subject to little modification, remains at a constant level.—As soon as there is no more nervous current and the blood in the veins is no longer hot, the *sinful body,* the seat of sensual lust, becomes *a corpse* and the souls can converse unhindered about "general reason," "true love," and "pure morals." The parson debases sensuality to such an extent that he abolishes the very elements which inspire sensual love—the rush of the blood, which proves that man does not love only by insensitive phlegm; the nervous current which connects the organ that is the main seat of sensuality with the brain. He reduces true sensual love to the *mechanical secretio seminis* and lisps with an ill-renowned German theologian:

"Not for the sake of sensual love, not for the lust of the flesh, but because the Lord said, increase and multiply."

Let us now compare the speculative construction with Eugène Sue's novel. It is not *sensuality* which is presented as the mystery of love, but mysteries, adventures, obstacles, fears, dangers, and especially the attraction of what is forbidden.

"Why," we read, "do many women take as lovers men who are not worth their husbands? Because the *greatest charm of love* is the enjoyable attraction of *the forbidden fruit....* Grant that if the fears, anxieties, difficulties, mysteries and dangers are taken away from that love there remains but little, to be precise, the lover ... in his original simplicity; in a word it would always be more or less the adventure of the man who was asked, 'Why do you not marry that widow, your mistress?' 'Alas, I thought of that,' he answered, 'but then I would not know where to spend my evenings.'"

Whereas Herr Szeliga says explicitly that the mystery of love is not in the attraction of what is forbidden, Eugène Sue says just as explicitly that it is the "greatest charm in love" and the reason for all love adventures *extra muros.*

"Prohibition and smuggling are as inseparable in love as in trade."[16]

Eugène Sue similarly maintains, contrary to his speculative commentator, that:

"the propensity to pretence and craft, the liking for mysteries and intrigues is an essential quality, a natural propensity and an imperative instinct of the nature of woman."

The only thing which embarrasses Eugène Sue is when that propensity and liking is directed against *marriage.* He would like to give the instinct of woman's nature a more harmless and useful application.

Herr Szeliga makes Countess MacGregor a representative of the kind of *sensuality* which "rises to a semblance of spiritual power," but in Eugène Sue she is a *person of abstract reason.* Her "ambition" and her "pride," far from being forms of sensuality, are born of an abstract reason which is completely independent of sensuality. That is why Eugène Sue explicitly notes that "the burning aspirations of love could never make her *icy* breast heave; *no* surprise of the *heart* or the *senses* could upset the pitiless calculations of that crafty, selfish, ambitious woman."

This woman's essential feature is the selfishness of abstract *reason* that never suffers from the sympathetic senses and on which the blood has no influence. Her soul is therefore described as "dry and hard," her mind as "artfully wicked," her character as "treacherous" and—what is typical of a person of abstract reason—as "absolute," her dissimulation as "profound." Let it be noted incidentally that Eugène Sue motivates the career of the Countess just as stupidly as that of most of the characters of his novel. An old nurse gives her the idea that she must become a "crowned head." Convinced of this, she undertakes journeys to capture a crown through marriage. Finally she commits the inconsistency of considering a petty German "*Serenissimus*" as a "crowned head."

After his expectorations against *sensuality* our Critical saint deems it necessary to show why Eugène Sue takes us to a ball in high society, a method which is popular in nearly all French novelists, whereas the *English* more often show us the upper world at the chase or in a country mansion.

"For his" (i.e., Herr Szeliga's) "conception it cannot be indifferent, and therefore merely accidental" (in Herr Szeliga's construction) "that Eugène Sue introduces us into high society at a ball."

Now the horse has been given the rein and it trots briskly towards his necessary end through a series of conclusions reminding one of the late Wolf.

"*Dancing* is the most common manifestation of *sensuality as a mystery*. The immediate *contact*, the embracing of the two sexes" (?) "necessary to form a couple are allowed in dancing because, in spite of appearances, and the really" (really, Reverend Sir?) "perceptible pleasant sensation" is not considered as "*sensual* contact and embracing" (but probably as contact and embracing of universal reason?).

And then comes a closing sentence which staggers more than it dances:

"*For if it were* in actual fact considered as sensual it *would— be impossible to understand why* society is so lenient only as regards dancing *whereas it on the contrary* so severely censures similar freedom exhibited *in other circumstances* as an unpardonable violation of morals and decency deserving to be branded and mercilessly cast out."

The reverend parson speaks here neither of *cancan* nor of the *polka*, but of dancing in general, of the *category* Dancing, which is not performed anywhere except in his Critical cranium. If he saw a single dance at the Chaumière in Paris his Christian-German soul would be outraged by the boldness, the frankness, the graceful petulance and the music of that most sensual movement. His own really perceptible "pleasant sensation" would make it perceptible to him that "in actual fact it would be impossible to understand why the dancers themselves, while on the other hand they" give the spectator the inspiring impression of frank human sensuality—"which, exhibited in the same way in other circumstances"—to be exact in Germany—"would be severely censured as an unpardonable violation." etc., etc.—why those dancers, at least, so to speak, in their own eyes, not only should and may, but can and must necessarily be frankly sensual human beings!!

The Critic introduces us to the *ball* for the sake of *the essence of dancing*. He encounters a great difficulty. There *is* dancing at that ball, but only in imagination. The fact is that Eugène Sue does not say a word describing the dancing. He does not mix among the throng of dancers. He makes use of the ball only to bring his main aristocratic characters together. In despair, Criticism comes to help out and *supplement* the author, and its own "fancy" easily provides a description of ball incidents, etc. If according to Criticism's rules Eugène Sue was not directly interested in the criminals' hide-outs and language when he described them, the dance, on the other hand, which *not he* but his "fanciful" critic describes, necessarily interests him infinitely.

Let us continue.

"*Actually,* the secret of sociable tone and tact—the secret of that extremely unnatural thing—is the longing to return to nature. That is why the appearance of a person like Cecily in educated society has such an electrifying effect and is crowned with such extraordinary success. She grew up a slave among slaves, without any education, and the only source of life she has to rely upon is her nature. Suddenly transported into a palace with all its constraint and customs, she soon learns to see through the secret of the latter. . . . In this sphere, which she can undoubtedly hold in sway because her power, the power of her nature, has an enigmatic magic, Cecily must necessarily stray into losing all sense of measure, whereas formerly, when she was still a slave, the same nature taught her to resist all nonsense on the part of the powerful lord and to remain true to her love. *Cecily* is the *mystery of educated society disclosed.* The scorned senses finally overflow all resistance and break forth completely uncurbed," etc.

Those of Herr Szeliga's readers who have not read Sue's novel will certainly think that Cecily is the lioness of the ball in question. In the novel she is in a German jail while the dancing goes on in Paris.

Cecily, as a slave, remains true to the Negro doctor David because she loves him "passionately" and because her owner, Mr. Willis, is *"brutal"* in courting her. The reason for her change to a dissolute life is a very simple one. Transported into the "European world," she "blushes" at being "married to a Negro." On arriving in Germany she is *"at once"* depraved by a wicked man and her "Indian blood" comes into its own. This the hypocritical Sue, for the sake of "sweet morals and tender commerce," feels it his duty to describe as "natural perversity."

The mystery of Cecily is that she is a *half-breed*. The mystery of her sensuality is *the heat of the tropics*. Parny sang the half-breed in his beautiful lines to Eléonore. Over a hundred seafaring tales tell us how dangerous she is to sailors.

"Cecily," Eugène Sue tells us, "was the incarnation of burning sensuality which only the heat of the tropics can kindle. . . . Everybody has heard of those coloured girls who are fatal, so to speak, to Europeans; of those charming vampires who inebriate their victim with terrible seductions . . . and leave him nothing, as the forcible expression of the country says, but his tears to drink and his heart to gnaw."

Cecily by no means produced such a magic effect precisely on people of the aristocratically educated *blasé* society. . . .

"Women of the type of Cecily have a sudden effect, a magic omnipotence over men of *brutal sensuality* like *Jacques Ferrand*," Sue tells us.

Since when have men like Jacques Ferrand been representative of fine society? But Critical Criticism must construe **Cecily** as a moment in the life-process of Absolute Mystery.

4) "The Mystery of Probity and Piety"

Granted, "*Mystery*, as *that* of educated society, withdraws from its *opposite* into the *interior. Nevertheless*, high society *still* has *its own* exclusive circles in which it preserves *the* holy. It is, *as it were*, the chapel for this holy of holies. *But* for people in the yard the chapel itself is the *mystery*. Education, *therefore*, in its exclusive position is the same for the people ... as vulgarity is for the educated."

Granted, nevertheless, still, as it were, but, therefore—those are the magic hooks which hold together the links of the *chain of speculative reasoning*. Herr Szeliga has made *Mystery* withdraw from the world of criminals into high society. Now he has to construe the mystery that high society has its *exclusive* circles and that the mysteries of those circles are mysteries for the people. Besides the magic hooks already mentioned this construction requires the transformation of a *circle* into a *chapel* and the transformation of non-aristocratic society into a *yard* in front of that chapel. Again it is a mystery *for* Paris that all the spheres of bourgeois society are only *a yard* in front of the chapel of high society.

Herr Szeliga has a double aim. First of all, Mystery which has become incarnate in the exclusive circle of *high society* must be declared "*common property of the world*." Secondly, the *notary Jacques Ferrand* must be construed as a link in the life of Mystery. Here is the way Herr Szeliga reasons:

"Education cannot and will not bring all sections and varieties into its circle yet. Only *christianity* and *moral* are able to found a universal kingdom on earth."

Herr Szeliga, identifies education, civilization, with *aristocratic* education. That is why he cannot understand that *industry* and *trade* found quite different universal kingdoms than Christianity and moral, domestic happiness and civic prosperity. But how do we come to the *notary Jacques Ferrand*? Quite simply!

Herr Szeliga transforms *Christianity* into an *individual* quality, *"piety,"* and *moral* into *another individual* quality, *"probity."* He combines these two qualities in *one* individual whom he christens *Jacques Ferrand*, because Jacques Ferrand does not possess these two qualities but only pretends to. And thus Jacques Ferrand becomes the "mystery of probity and piety." His "testament," on the other hand, is "the mystery of *seeming* probity and piety," and no longer of probity and piety themselves. If Critical Criticism wished to construe this testament as a mystery, it would have to declare seeming probity and piety to be the mystery of this testament, not the other way round, the testament to be the mystery of seeming probity and piety.

The Paris college of notaries considered Jacques Ferrand as a lampoon against itself and managed to get him removed from the performances of the *Mystères de Paris*; but Critical Criticism, though *"polemizing against the aerial kingdom of conceptions,"* sees in a Paris notary not a Paris notary but religion and moral, probity and piety. The trial of the notary *Léhon* ought to have taught it better. The position held by the *notary* in Eugène Sue's novel is closely connected with his official position.

"Notaries are in the temporal realm what priests are in the spiritual: they are the *depositories of our secrets"* (Monteil, *Histoire des Français des divers états, etc.* Vol. IX, p. 37).

The notary is the temporal confessor. He is a *puritan* by profession, and "honesty," Shakespeare says, is "no Puritan." He is at the same time the go-between for all possible purposes, the manager of all civil intrigues and schemes.

With the notary Ferrand, whose whole mystery consists in his hypocrisy and his profession we do not seem to have made a step forward yet. But listen:

"If for the notary hypocrisy has become a matter of complete consciousness and for Madame Roland instinct, *as it were*, between them there is the great mass of those who cannot get to the bottom of the mystery and yet feel an involuntary desire to do so. It is therefore not superstition that takes great and small to the sombre dwelling of the charlatan Bradamanti (Abbé Polidori); no, it is the search for Mystery, to justify themselves to the world."

"Great und small" flock to Polidori not to find out a definite secret which will justify them to the whole world, but to look for "Mystery" in general, Mystery as the Absolute Subject, *in order to* justify themselves to the world; as if to chop wood one looked, not for a chopper, but for Instrument *in abstracto.*

All the secrets that Polidori possesses are limited to a means for abortion and a poison for murder.—In a speculative frenzy Herr Szeliga makes the *"murderer"* resort to Polidori's poison "because he wants to be not a murderer, but respected, loved and honoured." As if in a case of murder it were a matter of respect, love or honour and not of one's *neck*! But the *Critical* murderer is not bothered about his neck, but only about "Mystery." As not everybody commits murder or becomes pregnant illegitimately how is Polidori to put *everybody* in the desired possession of Mystery? Herr Szeliga probably confuses the charlatan Polidori with the scholar *Polydorus Virgilius* who lived in the sixteenth century and, who, although he did not discover any mystery, tried to make the history of those who did, the *inventors*, the "common property of the world" (see *Polidori Virgilii, liber de rerum inventoribus*, Lugduni MDCCVI).

Mystery, Absolute Mystery, as it has finally made itself the "common property of the world," is therefore the secret of abortion and poisoning. Mystery could not make itself "the common property of the world" more skilfully than by turning itself into mysteries which are mysteries for nobody.

5) "Mystery, a Mockery"

"Mystery has *now* become common property, the mystery of the whole world and of every individual. Either it is my art or my instinct, or I can buy it as a purchasable ware."

What mystery has now become the common property of the world? The mystery of rightlessness in the state, the mystery of educated society, the mystery of adulterating wares, the mystery of making eau-de-cologne or the mystery of "Critical Criticism"? None of all those, but Mystery *in abstracto*, the category Mystery!

Herr Szeliga intends to present the *servants* and *the porter Pipelet and his wife* as the incarnation of Absolute Mystery. He wants to construe the *servant* and the *porter* of "Mystery." How does he manage to come out of *pure category* to the "*servant*" who "*spies at a locked door*," to come out of *Mystery as the Absolute Subject* that thrones above the *roof* in the heavens of abstraction, and plunge down to the ground floor where the porter's lodge is?

First he subjects the category "Mystery" to a speculative process. When by the intermediary of means for abortion and poisoning Mystery has become the common property of the world, it is

"*therefore no longer concealment* and *inaccessibility itself at all*, but *it conceals itself*, or better still" (always better!) "I conceal it, *I make it inaccessible*."

With this transformation of Absolute Mystery from *substance* to *concept*, from the *objective* stage in which it is concealment itself into the *subjective* stage in which it conceals itself, or better still, in which *I conceal it*, we have not made a single step forward. On the contrary, the difficulty seems to grow, for a mystery in the head or the breast of man is more inaccessible and concealed than at the bottom of the sea. That is why Herr Szeliga at once helps his *speculative* progress along with the *immediate* help of *empirical* progress.

"*It is behind locked doors*"—hark! hark! "that *henceforth*"
—henceforth!—"Mystery is hatched, brewed and accomplished."

Herr Szeliga has "henceforth" changed the speculative *ego*
of Mystery into a very empirical, very *wooden* reality—a
door.

"*With that*"—i.e., with the closed door, not with the transition from the closed substance to the concept—"there exists
also the possibility of overhearing, eavesdropping, and spying on it."

It is not *Herr Szeliga* who discovered the "mystery" that
one can eavesdrop by locked doors. The massy proverb even
says that walls have ears. On the other hand it is a quite
Critical speculative mystery that only "*henceforth*," after the
descent into the hell of the criminals' hide-outs and the as-
cension into educated society, and after Polidori's miracles,
mysteries can be brewed *behind* locked doors and overheard
through closed doors. It is just as great a Critical mystery
that locked doors are a *categorical necessity* for the hatching,
brewing and accomplishing of mysteries—how many mysteries are hatched, brewed and accomplished behind bushes!
—as well as for spying them out.

After this brilliant dialectic feat of arms Herr Szeliga naturally goes on from *spying* itself to the *grounds for spying*.
Here he reveals the mystery that *malicious exultation* is the
grounds for it. From malicious exultation he goes on to *the
grounds for malicious exultation*.

"Everybody wishes to be better than the others," he says,
"because he keeps secret the mainsprings not only of his
good actions, but of his bad ones too, which he tries to hide
in impenetrable darkness."

The sentence should be the other way round: Everybody
not only keeps the mainsprings of his good actions secret,
but tries to conceal his bad ones in quite impenetrable darkness because he wishes to be better than the others.

Thus it seems we have gone from *Mystery that conceals itself* to the *ego* that conceals: from the *ego* to the *locked door*, from the *locked door* to *spying*, from *spying* to the *grounds for spying*, malicious exultation; from *malicious exultation* to the *grounds for malicious exultation*, the *desire to be better than the others.* We shall soon have the pleasure of seeing the *servant* standing at the locked door. For the general desire to be better than the others leads us directly to this: that "everybody is inclined to find out the mysteries of the other." There is no difficulty in following this up with the witty remark:

"In this respect *servants* have the *best opportunity.*"

Had Herr Szeliga read the memoires from the Paris Police archives, Vidocq's memoires, the *livre noir* and the like, he would know that in this respect the *police* has still greater opportunity than the "best opportunity" that servants have; that it uses servants only for vulgar service, that it does not stand by doors or when the masters are in *négligé* but creeps under their sheets next to their naked body in the form of a *femme galante* or even of a legitimate wife. In Sue's novel the police spy *"Bras Rouge"* is one of the main agents in the plot.

What "henceforth" annoys Herr Szeliga most in servants — is that they are not *"disinterested"* enough. This *Critical misgiving* leads him to the *porter Pipelet and his wife.*

"The porter's position, on the other hand, gives him relative independence so that he can pour out free, disinterested, if vulgar and injurious mockery on the mysteries of the house."

At first this speculative construction of the porter is greatly embarrassed because in many Paris houses the servant and the porter are one and the same for some of the tenants.

The following facts will enable the reader to form an opinion of the Critical fantasy concerning the relatively independent disinterested position of the porter. The porter in

7*

Paris is the representative and spy of the owner of the house.
He is generally paid not by the owner of the house but by
the tenants. Because of that precarious position he often
combines the functions of spy with his official duties. During
the Terror, the Empire and the Restoration the porter was
one of the secret police's main agents. General Foy, for instance, was watched by his porter, who took all the letters
addressed to the general to be read by a police agent not far
away (see Froment, *La Police Dévoilée*). As a result "*portier*" and "*épicier*"* are considered insulting names and the
porter insists on being called "*concierge.***"

Far from being "disinterested" and harmless Eugène Sue's
Madame Pipelet immediately cheats Rudolph when giving
him his change; she recommends him the dishonest money-
lender living in the house and describes Rigolette to him as
an acquaintance who may be "agreeable": she teases the
major because he pays her badly and haggles with her—in
her vexation she calls him "a twopenny major,"—"that'll
teach you to give only twelve francs a month for your house-
keeping"— and because he is so "petty" as to keep a check
on his firewood, etc. She herself gives the grounds for "independent" behaviour: the major only pays her twelve francs
a month.

Herr Szeliga's "Anastasia Pipelet has, *in a way*, to declare
a running war on Mystery."

Eugène Sue makes Anastasia Pipelet a typical *Paris portière*. He wants "to dramatize the *portière* whom Henry
Monier portrayed with such mastery." But Herr Szeliga feels
bound to transform one of her qualities—"*backbiting*"—into
a separate being and then to make Madame Pipelet a representative of that being.

"The husband," Herr Szeliga continues, "the *portier* Alfred
Pipelet, helps her but with less luck."

---

* Grocer.—*Ed.*
** Caretaker.—*Ed.*

To console him for his bad luck Herr Szeliga makes him an *allegory*. He represents the *"objective"* side of Mystery, *"Mystery as Mockery."*

"The mystery which defeats him is a mockery, a joke, that is played on him."

Indeed, in its infinite pity divine dialectics makes "the unhappy, old, childish man" a *"strong man"* in the *metaphysical sense*, by representing him as a very worthy, very happy and very decisive moment in the life-process of Absolute Mystery. The victory over Pipelet is *"Mystery's most decisive defeat."* "A cleverer, more courageous man would not let himself be duped by a joke."

6) Turtle-Dove (Rigolette)

"There is still one step left. *Through its own consequence* — Mystery, as we saw in Pipelet and Cabrion, is driven to debase itself to mere joking. The *one* thing necessary *now* is that the individual should no longer agree to play that silly comedy. *Turtle-dove* takes that step in the most unprejudiced way in the world."

Anybody can see in two minutes through the mystery of this speculative joking and learn to practise it himself. We would give brief directions in this respect.

Problem. You must construe for me how man becomes master over beasts.

Speculative solution. Given half a dozen animals, such as the lion, the shark, the snake, the bull, the horse and the pug. From these six animals abstract the category "Animal." Imagine "Animal" to be an independent being. Consider the lion, the shark, the snake, etc., as disguises, incarnations, of *"Animal."* Just as you made your imagination, the *"Animal"* of your abstraction, a real being, now make real animals beings of abstraction of your imagination. You see that "Animal" which in the *lion* tears man to pieces, in the *shark* swal-

lows him up, in the *snake* stings him with venom, in the
bull tosses him with its horns and in the *horse* kicks him,
only barks at him when it presents itself as a *pug*, and
changes the fight against man into the mere *semblance of a
fight*. Through its *own consequence* Animal is driven, as we
have seen in the pug, to debase itself to a *mere joker*. When
a child or a childish man runs away from a pug, the only
thing is for the individual no longer to agree to play the silly
— comedy. The individual X takes this step in the most unprejudiced way in the world by using a bamboo cane on a pug.
You see how "Man," through the agency of the individual X
and the pug, has become master over "Animal," and consequently over animals, and in "*Animal*" *as a pug* has defeated *the lion as "Animal."*

Similarly Herr Szeliga's "Turtle-Dove" defeats the mystery of the present world system through the intermediary of
Pipelet and Cabrion. More than that! She is herself a manifestation of the category "Mystery."

— "She herself is not yet conscious of her high moral value,
therefore she is still a mystery to herself."

Eugène Sue makes Murph reveal the mystery of *non*-spec-
ulative Rigolette: She is "a very pretty *Grisette*." Eugène
Sue described in her the lovely human character of the Paris
girl of the people. Only his devotedness to the bourgeoisie
and his own personal love of exaggeration made him idealize
Grisette *morally*. He could not refrain from smoothing
down the asperities of her situation in life and her character, to be precise, her disdain for the form of marriage, her
naive attachment to the young *student* or the worker. It is
precisely in that attachment that she constitutes a really
human contrast to the hypocritical, narrow-hearted, self-
seeking wife of the bourgeois, to the whole circle of the bourgeoisie, that is, to the official circle.

7) The World System of the Mysteries
of Paris

"This world of mystery is *now* the general world system into which the individual action of the Paris Mysteries is transported."

Before, "however ..." Herr Szeliga "goes on to the *philosophical reproduction* of the epic event" he must "assemble in a general picture the sketches previously jotted down separately."

It must be considered as a real confession, a revelation — of Herr Szeliga's Critical Mystery when he says that he wishes to go on to the "philosophical reproduction" of the epic event. He has so far been "philosophically reproducing" the world system.

Herr Szeliga continues his confession:

"From our presentation it would appear that the individual mysteries dealt with have not their worth in themselves, each separate from the others, and are in no way magnificent novelties for gossip; their value consists in their constituting an *organically ramified series*, the *totality* of which is "Mystery."

In his fit of sincerity Herr Szeliga goes still further. He — admits that *"the speculative sequence"* is not the *real* sequence of the *Mystéries de Paris*.

"Granted, the mysteries do not appear in our epic in the relation of this *self-knowing sequence* (at the cost price?). *But* we are *not* dealing with the *logical*, obvious, *free organism of criticism* but with a *mysterious vegetable existence*."

We shall pass over Herr Szeliga's summary and go on immediately to the point that constitutes the "transition." In Pipelet we saw the "self-jesting of Mystery."

"In self-jesting Mystery judges itself. *Thereby* the mysteries, annihilating themselves in their last consequence, challenge every strong character to independent examination."

Rudolph, Prince of Geroldstein, *the man of "pure Criticism"* is destined to carry out that examination and the *"disclosure of the mysteries."*

If we deal with Rudolph and his feats only later, after having lost sight of Herr Szeliga for some time, it can already be foreseen, and to a certain degree the reader can have an idea and can even guess at his discretion, that instead of making him a *"mysterious vegetable being"* as he is in the Critical *Literatur-Zeitung*, we shall make him a *"logical, obvious, free* link" in the *"organism of Critical Criticism."*

CHAPTER VI

ABSOLUTE CRITICAL CRITICISM
OR
CRITICAL CRITICISM IN THE PERSON OF HERR BRUNO

1) Absolute Criticism's First Campaign

a) "Spirit" and "Mass"

So far Critical Criticism has seemed to deal more or less with the critical elaboration of various *massy* objects. We now find it dealing with the absolutely Critical object. *itself*. So far it has drawn its relative fame from critical debasement, rejection and transformation of *definite* massy objects and persons. It now draws its *absolute* fame from the critical debasement, rejection and transformation of the mass in general. Relative criticism was faced with relative limits. Absolute Criticism is faced with the absolute limit, the limit of the mass, the mass as limit. Relative criticism — in its opposition to definite limits was necessarily itself a *limited* individual. Absolute Criticism, in its opposition to the *general* limit, to limit in general, is necessarily an *absolute* individual. As the various massy objects and persons have merged in the *impure* pulp of the "*mass*," so has still seemingly objective and personal criticism changed into "*pure criticism*." So far criticism has appeared to be more or less a *quality* of the critical individuals, Reichardt, Edgar, Faucher, etc. Now it is a *subject* and Herr Bruno is its incarnation.

So far *massiness* has seemed to be more or less the quality of the objects and persons criticized; now objects and persons have become "*Mass*" and the "*Mass*" has become persons and objects. All previous critical attitudes were dissolved in the attitude of Absolute Critical wisdom to absolute massy stupidity. This *basic attitude* appears as the *meaning*, the *tendency* and the *keyword* of Criticism's previous deeds and struggles.

In accordance with its absolute character "pure" Criticism, as soon as it appears, will pronounce the differentiating "*catchword*," nevertheless, as the Absolute Spirit it must go through a dialectic process. Only at the end of its heavenly motion will its original concept truly be realized (see Hegel, *Encyclopaedia*).

"But a few months ago," Absolute Criticism announces, "the mass believed itself to be of gigantic strength and destined to world mastery within a time that it could count on its fingers."[17]

It was Herr *Bruno Bauer*, in *Die gute Sache der Freiheit* (his "*own*" cause, of course), in *Die Judenfrage*[18] and so forth, who counted on his fingers the time before the approaching world mastery, although he admitted he could not give the exact date. To the record of the sins of the mass he adds his own.

— "The mass thought itself in possession of so many truths which seemed obvious to it." "But one *possesses* a *truth* completely only ... when one follows it through *its* proofs."

For Herr Bauer as for Hegel, truth is an *automaton* that proves itself. Man must *follow* it. As in Hegel, the result of real development is nothing but the *truth proven*, i.e., brought to *consciousness*. Absolute Criticism may therefore ask with the most limited of theologians:

"*What* would be *the purpose of history* if its task were not precisely to *prove* these, the simplest of all truths (such as the movement of the earth round the sun)?"

Just as according to old teleologists plants exist to be eaten by animals and animals by men, history exists in order to serve as the act of consumption of theoretical eating—*proving*. Man exists so that history may exist and history exists so that the *proof of truths* may exist. In that **Critically** trivialized form we have the repetition of the speculative wisdom that man exists and that history exists so that *truth* may be brought to *self-consciousness*.

That is why *history*, like *truth*, becomes a person apart, a metaphysical subject of which real human individuals are but the bearers. That is why Absolute Criticism uses expressions like these:

"*History* will not be joked at ... *history* has exerted *its* greatest efforts to ... *history* has been engaged ... what would be the purpose of *history*? ... *history* provides the explicit proof; *history* proposes truths," etc.

If, as Absolute Criticism affirms, history has so far been — occupied with only *a few* such truths—the simplest of all— which in the end are self-evident, "this indigence to which previous human experiences were reduced proves first of all only Absolute Criticism's *own* indigence. From the un-Critical standpoint the result of history is, on the contrary, that the most complicated truth, the quintessence of all truth, *man*, understands himself in the end by himself."

"But truths," Absolute Criticism continues to argue, "which *seem* to the mass to be so crystal clear that they are understood of themselves *from the start* ... and that the mass deems proof superfluous, are not worth history supplying explicit proof of them; they constitute no part whatever of the problem which history is engaged in solving."

In its holy zeal against the mass Absolute Criticism flatters it in the most refined way. If a truth is *crystal clear* because it *seems* crystal clear to the mass; if history's *attitude* to truths *depends* on the *opinion* of the mass, the opinion of the mass is absolute, infallible, it is *law* for

history, and history proves only what the mass does *not*
consider as crystal-clear, what therefore needs proof. It is
the mass, therefore, that prescribes history's "task" and
"occupation."

Absolute Criticism speaks of "truths which are understood of themselves *from the start.*" In its Critical naiveness
it invents an absolute "*from the start*" and an abstract,
immutable "*Mass.*" There is just as little difference, in the
eyes of Criticism, between the "from the start" of the sixteenth century mass and the "from the start" of the
nineteenth century mass as between those masses themselves. It is precisely a feature of a truth which has become
true and *obvious* and is understood of itself that it "is
understood of itself *from the start.*" Absolute Criticism's
polemic against truths which are understood of themselves
from the start is a polemic against truths which, in general,
"are understood of themselves."

A truth which is understood of itself has lost its salt, its
meaning, its *value* for Absolute Criticism as for divine
dialectics. It has become flat, like stale water. On the one
hand, therefore, Absolute Criticism *proves* everything which
is understood of itself and, besides, many things which
have the luck of being incomprehensible and will therefore
never be understood of themselves. On the other hand it
considers as understood of itself everything which needs
some proof. Why? Because it is *understood of itself* that
real problems are *not* understood of themselves.

As "Truth," like history, is an ethereal subject separate
from the material mass, it addresses itself not to the
empirical man but to the "*innermost of the soul*"; in order
to be "*truly apprehended*" it does not act on his *vulgar
body,* which may live in the bowels of an English basement
or at the top of a French block of poky flats; it "drags" on
and on "through" his idealistic intestines. Absolute Criticism does certify that "the mass" has so far in its own way,

i.e., superficially, been touched by the truths that history has been so gracious as to "propose"; "but at the same time it prophesies that *the attitude of the mass* to *historical progress* will *completely change.*"

It will not be long before the mysterious meaning of this Critical prophecy is "crystal-clear" to us.

"All great actions of previous history," we are told, "were failures *from the start* and had no effective success because the mass became *interested* in and *enthusiastic* over them; in other words they were bound to come to a pitiful end because the idea in them was such that it had to be satisfied with a superficial comprehension and therefore to rely on the approbation of the mass."

It seems that comprehension ceases to be superficial when it suffices for, corresponds to an idea. It is only for *appearance' sake* that Herr Bruno brings out a *relation* between an *idea* and its *comprehension*, as it is also only for *appearance' sake* that he brings out a *relation* between unsuccessful historical *action* and the *mass*. If, therefore, Absolute Criticism condemns something as being "superficial," it is simply previous history whose actions and ideas were those of the "masses." It rejects *massy* history to replace it by *Critical* history (see Herr Jules Faucher on English problems of the day). According to previous *un-Critical* history, i.e., history not conceived in the sense of Absolute Criticism, it must further be precisely distinguished to what extent the *mass* was "*interested*" in aims and to what extent it was "*enthusiastic*" over them. The "*idea*" always disgraced itself insofar as it differed from the "*interest.*" On the other hand it is easy to understand that every massy "*interest*" asserting itself historically goes far beyond its real limits in the "*idea*" or "*imagination*" when it first came on the scene and is confused with *human* interest in general. This *illusion* constitutes what *Fourier* calls the *tone* of each historical epoch. The *interest* of the bourgeoisie in the 1789

Revolution, far from having been a *"failure,"* *"won"* every-thing and had *"effective success"* however much the *"pathos"* of it evaporated and the *"enthusiastic"* flowers with which that interest adorned its cradle faded. That *interest* was so powerful that it vanquished the pen of Marat, the guillotine of the Terror and the sword of Napoleon as well as the crucifix and the blue blood of the Bourbons. The Revolution was a "failure" only for the mass which did not find in the *political* "idea" the idea of its real *"interest,"* whose real life-principle did not therefore coin-cide with the life-principle of the Revolution; the mass whose real conditions for emancipation were substantially different from the conditions within which the bourgeoisie could emancipate itself and society. If the revolution, which can exemplify all great historical "actions" was a failure, it was so because the mass whose living conditions it did not substantially go beyond was an *exclusive, limited* mass, not an all-embracing one. If it was a failure it was not because it aroused the *"enthusiasm"* and *"interest"* of the mass, but because the most numerous part of the mass, the part most greatly differing from the bourgeoisie, did not find its *real* interest in the principle of the revolution, had no revolutionary principle of *its own*, but *only* an *"idea,"* and hence only an object of momentary *enthusiasm* and only apparent *exaltation*.

With the thoroughness of the historical action the size of the mass whose action it is will therefore increase. In Criti-cal history, according to which in historical actions it is not a matter of the active mass, of empirical action, or of the empiric *interest* of that action but rather only of "an idea" *"in them,"* affairs must naturally take a different course.

"In the mass," Criticism teaches us, *"not somewhere else,* as its former liberal spokesmen believed, *is the true enemy of the spirit to be found."*

The enemies of progress *outside* the mass are precisely those *products* of *self-debasement, self-rejection* and *self-estrangement* of the *mass* which have been endowed with independent being and a life of their *own*. The mass therefore rises against its *own* deficiency when it rises against the independently existing *products* of its *self-debasement* just as man, turning against the existence of God, turns against his *own religiosity*. But as those *practical* self-estrangements of the mass exist in the real world in an outward way, the mass must fight them in an *outward* way. It must by no means consider these products of its self-estrangement as mere *ideal* fancies, mere *estrangements of self-consciousness*, and must not wish to abolish *material* estrangement by a purely *inward spiritual* action. As early as 1789 Loustalot's journal[19] gave the motto:

> *The great appear great in our eyes*
> *Only because we kneel.*
> *Let us rise!*

But to rise it is not enough to do so *in thought* and to leave hanging over our *real sensual* head the *real palpable* yoke that cannot be subtilized away with ideas. Yet *Absolute Criticism* has learnt from Hegel's *Phenomenology* at least the art of changing *real objective* chains that exist *outside me* into *mere ideal*, mere *subjective* chains existing *in me*, and thus to change all *exterior* palpable struggles into pure struggles of thought.

It is on this Critical transformation that *the pre-established harmony between Critical Criticism and the censorship* is based. From the Critical point of view the writer's fight against the censor is not a fight of "man against man." The censor is nothing but *my own tact personified* for me by the solicitous police, my own tact struggling against my tactlessness and un-Criticalness. The struggle of the writer with the censor is only apparently, only in the eyes of wicked

sensuality, anything else than the *interior* struggle of the
writer *with himself. Insofar* as the censor is a *real individual different* from myself, a *police official* who mishandles
the product of my mind by applying an external standard
which has nothing to do with the matter in question; he is
but a *massy* imagination, an *un-Critical figment* of the
brain. When Feuerbach's *Theses on the Reform of Philosophy* were prohibited by the censor, it was not the official
barbarity of the censor that was to blame but the lack of
refinement of Feuerbach's *Theses.* "*Pure*" Criticism, un-
sullied by mass or matter, also has in the censor a purely
"ethereal" form, free from any massy reality.

Absolute Criticism has declared the "*mass*" to be the *true
enemy of the spirit.* This it develops as follows:

"The spirit now knows where to *look for its* only *adversary*—in the self-deception and the pithlessness of the
mass."

Absolute Criticism proceeds from *the dogma* of the
absolute competency of *the "spirit."* Furthermore, it proceeds from *the dogma of the extramundane* existence of the
spirit, i.e., of its existence outside the mass of humanity.
Finally it transforms "*the* spirit," "*progress,*" on the one
hand, and the "mass," on the other, into *fixed* beings, into
concepts, and relates them one to the other in that form
as given invariable extremes. It does not occur to Absolute
Criticism to investigate *the "spirit"* itself, to find out
whether it is not its own spiritualistic nature, its airy pretensions that justify "the phrase," "self-deception" and
"pithlessness." The spirit, on the contrary, is *absolute,* but
unfortunately at the same time it continually falls into
spiritlessness: it continually calculates without the master,
hence it must necessarily have *an adversary* that intrigues
against it. That *adversary* is the mass.

The position is the same with "*progress.*" In spite of
"*progress's*" pretensions, continual *retrogressions* and *cir-*

cular movements are to be observed. Not suspecting that the category "*Progress*" is completely empty and abstract, Absolute Criticism is so profound as to recognize "*progress*" as being absolute and to explain retrogression by supposing a "*personal adversary*" of progress, the *mass*. As "*the mass*" is nothing but the "*opposite of the spirit*," of progress, of "*Criticism*," it can also be defined only by that imaginary opposition; outside that opposition all that Criticism can say about the *meaning* and the existence of the mass is the *senseless*, because completely undefined:

"The mass, in *the sense* in which the "*word*" also embraces the *so-called* educated world."

"Also" and "so-called" are enough for its Critical definition. The "Mass" is therefore distinct from the *real* masses and exists as *the* "*Mass*" only for "*Criticism*."

All communist and socialist writers proceeded from the observation that, on the one hand, even the most favourable brilliant deeds seemed to remain without brilliant results, to end in trivialities, and, on the other, *all progress of the spirit* had so far been *progress against the mass of mankind*, driving it to an ever more dehumanized predicament. They therefore declare "*progress*" (see *Fourier*) to be an inadequate abstract *phrase*; they assumed (see *Owen* among others) a fundamental flaw in the civilized world; that is why they submitted the *real* bases of contemporary society to incisive *criticism*. To this communist criticism corresponded immediately in practice the movement of the *great mass* against which history had so far developed. One must be acquainted with the studiousness, the craving for knowledge, the moral energy and the unceasing urge for development of the French and English workers to be able to form an idea of the *human* nobleness of that movement.

How infinitely *profound* "Absolute Criticism" must be to have in face of these intellectual and practical facts, but a

one-sided conception of only *one aspect* of the relationship
—the continual foundering of the spirit—and, vexed at
this, to seek besides an *adversary* of the "Spirit" and find
it in the "*Mass*." In the end all this great Critical *discovery*
comes to *tautology*. According to Criticism, *the spirit* has so
far had a limit, an obstacle, in other words, an *adversary*,
because it has had *an adversary*. Who, then, is the adversary
of the Spirit? *Spiritlessness*. For the mass is defined only
as the "opposite" of the spirit, as *spiritlessness* or to take
more precise definitions of spiritlessness, "indolence,"
"superficiality," "self-complacency." What a fundamental
advantage over the communist writers it is not to have
traced spiritlessness, indolence, superficiality and self-complacency to their origin but to have branded them *morally*
and *exposed* them as the opposite of the spirit, of progress!
If these qualities are proclaimed qualities of *the Mass*, as
of a *subject* still distinct from them, that distinction is
nothing but a Critical *semblance* of distinction. Only in
appearance has Absolute Criticism a *definite* concrete
subject besides abstract qualities of spiritlessness, indolence, etc., for the "*Mass*" in the Critical conception is
nothing but those abstract qualities, another **word** for them,
a *fantastic personification* of them.

Meanwhile, the relation between "spirit and mass" has
still a *hidden* sense which will be completely revealed in
the course of the reasoning. We only indicate it here.
That relation *discovered* by Herr Bruno is, in fact, nothing
but a *Critically caricatural realization of Hegel's conception of history*; this, in turn, is nothing but the *speculative*
expression of the *Christian-Germanic* dogma of the opposition between *spirit* and *matter*, between *God* and the *world*.
This opposition is expressed in history, in the very world of
man, in only a few chosen *individuals* opposed as the *active*
spirit to the rest of mankind, as the *spiritless mass*, as
matter.

Hegel's conception of history assumes an *Abstract* or *Absolute Spirit* which develops in such a way that mankind is a mere *mass* bearing it with a varying degree of consciousness or unconsciousness. Within *empiric*, exoteric history he therefore has a *speculative*, esoteric history develop. The history of mankind becomes the history of the *abstract* spirit of mankind, a *spirit beyond all man!*

Parallel with this doctrine of Hegel's there developed in France that of the *Doctrinarians*[20] proclaiming the *sovereignty of reason* in opposition to the *sovereignty of the people* in order to exclude the masses and rule *alone*. This was quite consistent. If the activity of *real* mankind is nothing but the activity of a *mass* of human individuals then *abstract generality, Reason*, the Spirit must contrariwise have an abstract expression restricted to a few individuals. It then depends on the situation and imaginative power of each individual whether he will pass for a representative of that "spirit."

In *Hegel* the *Absolute Spirit* of history already treats the *mass* as material and finds its true expression only in *philosophy*. But with Hegel, *the* philosopher is only the organ through which the creator of history, the Absolute Spirit, arrives at self-consciousness *by retrospection* after the movement has ended. The participation of the philosopher in history is reduced to this retrospective consciousness, for real movement is accomplished by the Absolute Spirit *unconsciously*, so that the philosopher appears *post festum.**

Hegel is doubly inconsistent: first because, while declaring that philosophy constitutes the Absolute Spirit's existence he refuses to recognize the *real philosophical individual* as the *Absolute* Spirit; secondly, because according to him the Absolute Spirit makes history only *in appearance*.

---

* After the event.—*Ed.*

For as the Absolute Spirit becomes *conscious* of itself as the creative World Spirit only in the philosopher and *post festum*, its making of history exists only in the consciousness, in the opinion and conception of the philosopher, i.e., only in the speculative imagination. Herr Bruno Bauer eliminates Hegel's inconsistency.

First, he proclaims *Criticism* to be the Absolute Spirit and *himself* to be *Criticism*. Just as the element of criticism is banished from the mass, so the element of mass is banished from criticism. Therefore *Criticism* sees itself incarnate not in a *mass*, but in a small *handful* of chosen men, exclusively in Herr *Bauer* and his followers.

Herr Bauer further does away with Hegel's other inconsistency. No longer, like the Hegelian spirit, does he make history *post festum* and in imagination. He *consciously* plays the part of the *World Spirit* in opposition to the mass of the rest of mankind; he enters in the present into a *dramatic* relation with that mass; he invents and carries out history with a purpose and after mature meditation.

On the one side stands the Mass, that *material,* passive, dull and unhistorical element of history. On the other stand the *Spirit, Criticism,* Herr Bruno and Co. as the active element from which arises all *historical* action. The act of social transformation is reduced to the *brain work* of Critical Criticism.

Indeed, the relation of Criticism, and hence of Criticism incarnate, Herr Bruno and Co., to the mass is in truth the *only* historical relation of the present. The whole of present-day history is reduced to the movement of these two sides one against the other. All oppositions have been dissolved in this *Critical* opposition.

Critical Criticism, becoming *objective* only in its opposition to the Mass, *stupidity,* is consequently obliged continually *to produce* that opposition for itself, and Herrn

Faucher, Edgar and Szeliga have supplied sufficient proof of their virtuosity in their speciality, the *mass stupefaction* of persons and things.

Let us now accompany Absolute Criticism in its *campaign* against the *Mass*.

b) The Jewish Question, No. 1.
Setting of the Question

The "spirit," contrary to the mass, immediately behaves in a *critical way* by considering its own limited work, Bruno Bauer's *Die Judenfrage*, as absolute, and only the opponents of that work as sinners. In Reply No. 1[21] to attacks on that treatise, he does not show any inkling of its defects; on the contrary, he declares he has developed the "true," "*general*" (!) significance of the Jewish question. In later replies we shall see him obliged to admit his "*oversights*."

"The reception my book has had is the *beginning* of the proof that the very ones who so far have advocated freedom and still do advocate it must rise against the spirit more than any others; the defence I am now going to provide it with will supply further proof how thoughtless the *spokesmen of the mass* are; they have God knows what a great opinion of themselves for supporting emancipation and the dogma of the "*rights of man*."

On the occasion of a treatise by Absolute Criticism the "Mass" must necessarily have *begun* to prove its opposition to the Spirit; for it is its opposition to Absolute Criticism that *determines and proves* its *existence*.

The polemic of a few liberal and rationalist Jews against Herr Bruno's *Die Judenfrage* has naturally quite a different critical meaning than the massy polemic of the liberals against philosophy and of the rationalists against Strauss. Incidentally, the originality of the above quoted remark can be judged by the following passage from *Hegel*:

"We can here note the particular form of evil conscience manifest in the kind of eloquence with which that shallowness" (of the liberals) "plumes itself, and first of all in the fact that it speaks most of *spirit* where it has the *least*, and uses the word *life* where it is most dead and withered, etc."

As for the *"rights of man,"* it has been proved to Herr Bruno (*"Die Judenfrage," Deutsch-Französische Jahrbücher*[22]) that it is "*he himself,*" not the *spokesmen of the mass,* who has misunderstood and dogmatically mishandled the essence of those rights. Compared to his discovery that the rights of man are not *"innate"*—a discovery which has been made innumerable times in England during the last 40 years—Fourier's assertion that the right to fish, to hunt, etc., are innate rights of men is one of genius.

We give but a few examples of Herr Bruno's fight against *Philippson, Hirsch* and others. Even such poor opponents as these are not disposed of by Absolute Criticism. It is by no means preposterous of *Mr. Philippson,* as Absolute Criticism maintains, to say:

"Bauer imagines a peculiar kind of state ... a *philosophical ideal* of a *state.*"

Herr Bruno, who confuses the state with humanity, the rights of man with man and political emancipation with human emancipation, was bound, if not to conceive, at least to imagine a peculiar kind of state, a philosophical ideal of a state.

"Instead of writing his boring statement the rhetorician" (Herr Hirsch) "would have done better to refute my proof that the *Christian state,* having as its vital principle a definite religion, cannot allow adherents of another religion ... complete equality with its own estates."

Had the rhetorician *Hirsch* really refuted Herr Bruno's proof and shown, as is done in the *Deutsch-Französische Jahrbücher* that the state of estates and exclusive Christianity are not only an incomplete state but an incomplete

Christian state, Herr Bruno would have answered as he does to that refutation:

"Objections in this instance are meaningless."

Herr Hirsch is quite correct when in answer to Herr Bruno's statement:

"By pressure on the mainsprings of history the Jews provoked counter-pressure"

he recalls:

"Then they must have been something in the making of history, and if Bauer himself asserts this, he has no right to assert, on the other hand, that they did not contribute to the making of modern times."

Herr Bruno answers:

"An eyesore is something too—does that mean it contributes to develop my eyesight?"

Something which has been an eyesore to me since my birth, as the Jews have been to the Christian world, which grows and develops with me is not an ordinary sore, but a wonderful one, one that really belongs to my eye and must even contribute to a highly original development of my eyesight. The critical *"eyesore"* does not therefore hurt the rhetorician *"Hirsch."* However, the criticism quoted above revealed to Herr Bruno the significance of Jewry in "the *making* of modern times."

The theological mind of Absolute Criticism feels so offended by a *Rhine Landstag deputy's* statement that "the Jews are *queer* in their own Jewish way, not in our so-called Christian way," that it is still "calling him *to order* for using such an argument."

When another deputy maintained "*civil* equality can be given to Jews only where Jewry no longer exists" Herr Bruno observed:

"Correct! Correct, to be precise, when the critical point made by me in my treatise" (that point being that Christianity must also have ceased to exist), "is taken into account."

We see that in its Reply No. 1 to the attacks upon *Die Judenfrage* Absolute Criticism still considers the abolition of religion, atheism, to be the condition for *civil* equality. In its first stage it has therefore not *yet* acquired any deeper insight into the essence of the state than into the "*oversight*" of its "*work*."

Absolute Criticism feels offended when one of its *intended* "latest" scientific discoveries is betrayed as an already generally accepted view. A Rhineland deputy remarked:

"Nobody has yet maintained that France and Belgium were remarkable for particular clarity in recognizing principles in the organization of political relations."

Absolute Criticism could have objected that that assertion transported the present back into the past by representing as traditional the now trivial view that the principles of French policy are inadequate. Such a relevant objection would not have suited Absolute Criticism. On the contrary, it must give the old-fashioned view as that of the present and proclaim the now prevailing view a Critical mystery which *its* investigation still has to reveal to the mass. Hence it must say:

"It" (the antiquated prejudice) "has been asserted by *very many*" (the Mass); "but a *thorough investigation* of history will provide the proof that *even* after the great work done by France to comprehend the principles, *much still remains to be achieved*."

A thorough investigation of history itself will therefore not *achieve* the comprehension of the principles. It will only *prove* in its thoroughness that "*much still remains to be achieved*." A great achievement, especially after the works of the Socialists! Nevertheless Herr Bruno *already* achieves *much* for the comprehension of the present social situation by his remark:

"The *certainty* prevailing at present *is uncertainty*."

If Hegel says that the prevailing *Chinese* certainty is "Being," the prevailing *Indian* certainty is "Nothingness," etc., Absolute Criticism joins him in the "pure" way when it resolves the character of the present time in the logical category "*Uncertainty*" and all the purer as "Uncertainty," like "Being" and "Nothingness" belongs to the first chapter of speculative logic, to the chapter on "*Quality.*"

We cannot leave No. 1 of *Die Judenfrage* without a general remark.

One of the chief pursuits of Absolute Criticism consists in first bringing all questions of the day into *the right setting*. For it does not answer the *real* questions—it substitutes *quite different* ones. As it makes everything, it must also first *make* the "questions of the day," make them *its own* questions, the questions of Critical Criticism. If it were a question of the *Napoleonic Code*, it would prove that it is *properly* a question of the *Pentateuch*. Its *setting* of "questions of the day" is Critical *distortion* and *misplacement* of them. It thus distorted the Jewish question in such a way that it did not need to investigate *political emancipation*, which that question deals with, but could be satisfied with a criticism of the Jewish religion and a description of the Christian-German state.

This method, like all Absolute Criticism's originalities, is the repetition of a *speculative* witticism. *Speculative* philosophy, to be exact, *Hegel's* philosophy, must transpose all questions from the form of human common sense to the form of speculative reason and change the real question into a *speculative* one to be able to answer it. Having distorted *my* question on my lips and put *its own* question on my lips like the catechism, it could naturally have a ready answer to all my questions, also like the catechism.

c) Hinrichs No. 1. Mysterious Hints on Politics, Socialism and Philosophy

"*Political!*" Absolute Criticism is literally horrified at the presence of this word in Professor *Hinrichs'* lectures.[23]

"Whoever has followed the development of modern times and knows history will *also* know that the political movements at present taking place have *quite a different* (!) significance than a *political* one: at their base" (at their base! .. now for basic wisdom) "they have a *social*" (!) "significance, which, as we know" (!) "is such that *all* political interests appear *insignificant*" (!) "in comparison with it."

A few months before the Critical *Literatur-Zeitung* was published, there appeared, *as we know* (!), Herr Bruno's fantastic political treatise *Staat, Religion und Parthei*.

If *political* movements *have social significance*, how can political interests appear "*insignificant*" in comparison with their own social significance?

"Herr Hinrichs does not know his way about either in his own house or anywhere else in the world. ... He could not be at home anywhere *because* ..., *because* he still knows *nothing* about Criticism, which in the last four years has begun and carried on its *by no means* "*political*" (!) "but *social*" (!) "work."

Criticism, which according to the opinion of the mass carried on "by no means *political*" but "in *all* respects *theological*" work, is content with the word "*social*," even now that it has pronounced that *word* for the first time, not just for four years, but since its political birth.

Since socialist writings spread in Germany the view that *all* human aspirations and actions without exception have *social* significance, Herr Bruno can call his theological works *social* too. But what a *Critical* demand it is that Professor Hinrichs should derive socialism from an *acquaintance* with *Bauer's* works when the practical conclusions—wherever

there were any—of all of Bruno Bauer's works up to the publication of Professor Hinrichs' lectures were *political* ones! It
was impossible, un-Critically speaking, for Professor Hinrichs to supplement Herr Bruno's published works with his
unpublished ones. From the Critical point of view, the mass,
of course, is obliged to interpret all Absolute Criticism's
massy as well as "political" "movements" in the spirit of the
future and of Absolute Progress! But so that once Herr Hinrichs has been acquainted with *Literatur-Zeitung* he may
never again forget the word "*social*" or fail to recognize the
"*social*" character of *Criticism*, *Criticism* prohibits the word
"*political*" for the third time before the whole world and
solemnly repeats the word "*social*" for the third time.

"If the *true* tendency of modern history is taken into account it is no longer a *question* of *political but* ... but *of
social* significance," etc.

As Professor Hinrichs is the scapegoat for the former
"political" movements, so he is too for the "*Hegelian*"
movements and expressions that Absolute Criticism used
intentionally up to the publication of *Literatur-Zeitung* and
continually uses unintentionally in it.

Once "*real Hegelian*" and twice "*Hegelian philosopher*"
are thrown in Hinrichs' face as catchwords. Herr Bruno
even "*hopes*" that the "banal expressions which had such
tiring circulation in all books of the *Hegelian* school" (in
particular in his own books), being *so* "*exhausted*" in Professor Hinrichs' lectures, will soon reach the end of their
journey. From the "*exhaustion*" of *Professor Hinrichs* Herr
Bruno expects the abolition of *Hegel's philosophy* and
thereby *his own redemption* from it.

Thus in its *first campaign* Absolute Criticism overthrows
the gods "*Politics*" and "*Philosophy*" it has itself so long
been worshipping, declaring them to be idols of Professor
Hinrichs.

Glorious first campaign!

2) Absolute Criticism's Second Campaign

a) Hinrichs No. 2. "Criticism" and "Feuerbach." Damnation of Philosophy

As the result of its first campaign *Absolute Criticism* can consider *"philosophy"* as dealt with and term it outright an ally of the *"Mass."*

"Philosophers were predestined to fulfil the heart's desires of the '*Mass.*'" And "the Mass *wants* simple concepts in order to have nothing to do with the thing itself—shibboleths, so as to have finished with everything from the start, phrases by which Criticism can be done away with."

And "philosophy" fulfils this longing of the "Mass!"

Staggering after its victories, Absolute Criticism breaks out in *Pythian* violence against philosophy. *Feuerbach's Philosophy of the Future* is the concealed cauldron whose fumes inspire Absolute Criticism's victory-inebriated head.*
It read Feuerbach's work in March. The fruit of that reading and at the same time the criterion of the earnestness with which it was undertaken is Article No. 2 against Professor Hinrichs.

In this article Absolute Criticism, which has never freed itself from the Hegelian way of viewing things, storms at the iron bars and walls of its prison. The *"simple concept,"* the terminology, the whole mode of thinking of philosophy, indeed, the whole of philosophy, is rejected with disgust. In its place we suddenly find the *"real wealth of human relations,"* the *"immense content of history,"* the *"significance of man,"* etc. *"The mystery of the system"* is declared *"revealed."*

But who, then, revealed the mystery of the "system"? *Feuerbach.* Who annihilated the dialectics of concepts, the

---

* Engels here makes a pun on "Feuerbach" (literally stream of fire) and "Feuerkessel" (boiler).—*Ed.*

war of the gods known to the philosophers alone? *Feuer-bach.* Who substituted for the old rubbish and for "infinite self-consciousness" not, it is true, "the significance of man" —as though man had another significance than that of being man—but *Man*? *Feuerbach*, and *Feuerbach alone*. And he did more. Long ago he did away with the very categories that "Criticism" now wields—the "real wealth of human relations, the immense content of history, the struggle of history, the fight of the mass against the spirit," etc.

Once man is apprehended as the essence, the basis of all human activity and situations, only "Criticism" can invent *new categories* and transform *man* himself into a category and into the principle of a whole series of categories as it is doing now. It is true that in so doing it steps on to the only road to salvation that remained for terrorized and persecuted *theological* inhumanity. *History* does *nothing*, it "possesses *no* immense wealth," it "wages *no* battles." It is *man*, real living man, that does all that, that possesses and fights; "history" is not a person apart, using man as a means for *its own* particular aims; history is *nothing but* the activity of man pursuing his aims. If *Absolute* Criticism, after *Feuerbach's* inspired arguments, still takes the liberty of dishing up the old trash in a new form at the same time abusing it as "*Massy*" trash—which it has all the less right to do as it never stirred a finger to abolish philosophy—that fact alone is sufficient to bring the "*mystery*" of Criticism to light and to assess the Critical naiveness with which it says to Professor Hinrichs whose "*exhaustion*" once did it such a great service:

"The *damage* is to those who have not gone through any development and therefore *could not alter themselves even if they wished to*; and if it gets so far, the *new* principle—but no! The new *cannot* be made *into a phrase, separate turns of speech cannot be borrowed from it.*"

Absolute Criticism boasts over Professor Hinrichs that it solved "*the mystery of faculty sciences.*" Has it then solved the "mystery" of philosophy, jurisprudence, politics, medicine, political economy and so forth? Not at all! It has, be it noted, it has shown in the *Die Gute Sache der Freiheit* that science as a source of livelihood, and free science, freedom of teaching and faculty statutes contradict each other.

If "Absolute Criticism" were honest it would have admitted where it got its pretended illumination on the "Mystery of Philosophy" from. It is a good thing all the same that it did not put into *Feuerbach's* mouth such nonsense as the misunderstood and distorted sentences that it had borrowed from him, as it has done with other people. By the way, it is typical of "Absolute Criticism's" *theological* viewpoint that while the German philistines are now beginning to understand Feuerbach and to adopt his conclusions, it is unable to grasp a single sentence of his correctly or to use it properly.

Criticism makes real progress in comparison with its feats of the first campaign when it "defines" the struggle of "*the Mass*" against the "*Spirit*" as "*the aim*" of all history up to date; when it declares the "*Mass*" to be "*pure nothingness*" of "misery;" when it calls *the* "Mass" purely and simply "*Matter*" and contrasts "*the Spirit*" as truth to "Matter." Is "Absolute Criticism" then not *genuinely Christian-German*? After the old contradiction between spiritualism and materialism has been fought out on all sides and overcome once for all by *Feuerbach*, "Criticism" again makes a basic dogma of it in its ugliest form and gives the victory to the "*Christian-German spirit.*"

Finally, it must be considered as a development of the mystery contained in Criticism's first campaign that it now identifies the contradiction between *spirit* and *mass* with the contradiction between " *Criticism*" and the Mass. Later it will proceed to identify *itself* with *"Criticism in general"* and therefore to represent itself as *"The Spirit,"* the Absolute and the Infinite, and the Mass, on the other hand, as finite, coarse, brutal, dead, and inorganic—for that is what "Criticism" understands by matter.

How immense is the wealth of history since it is exhausted by the attitude of humanity to *Herr Bauer*!

b) The Jewish Question No. 2.
Critical Discoveries on Socialism, Jurisprudence and Politics (Nationality)

The massy material Jews are preached the *Christian* doctrine of *freedom of the spirit, freedom in theory,* that *spiritualistic* freedom which *imagines* itself to be free even in chains, whose soul is satisfied with *"the idea"* and embarrassed by any kind of massy existence.

"The Jews are *emancipated* to the extent of their progress in *theory*, they are *free* to the extent that they *wish to be free*."[24]

From that proposition one can immediately measure the critical gap which separates *massy*, profane communism and socialism from *Absolute* socialism. The first proposition of profane socialism rejects emancipation *in mere theory* as an illusion and for *real* freedom it demands besides the idealistic *"will"* quite palpable material conditions. How low *"the* Mass" is in comparison with holy Criticism, the Mass which considers material, practical upheavals necessary to win the time and means required even to deal with *"theory"*!

Let us leave purely spiritual socialism an instant for *politics*!

Herr *Riesser* argues against Bruno Bauer that *his* state (i.e., the *Critical* state) must exclude "Jews" and "Christians." Herr Riesser is right. Since Herr Bauer confuses *human* emancipation with *political* emancipation, since the state can react to adverse elements—and Christianity and Judaism are considered as treasonable elements in the *Judenfrage*—only by forcible expulsion of the *persons* representing them (the Terror, for instance, wished to do away with corn hoarding by guillotining the hoarders), Herr Bauer must have both Jews and Christians hanged in his "Critical state." Having confused political emancipation with human emancipation, he had to be consistent and confuse the *political means* of emancipation with the *human means*. But as soon as Absolute Criticism hears the *definite* meaning of its deductions formulated, it gives the answer *Schelling* once gave to his opponents who substituted *real* thoughts for his phrases:

"*Criticism's* opponents are its opponents because they not only measure it with their *dogmatic* yardstick but consider it as *dogmatic* itself: they oppose criticism because it will not recognize their dogmatic distinctions, definitions and evasions."

It is, indeed, adopting a dogmatic attitude to Absolute Criticism, as to Herr *Schelling*, to attribute to it *definite*, real significance, thought and views. In order to be accommodating and to prove to Herr Riesser its humanity "Criticism," however, decides to resort to dogmatic distinctions, definitions, and, to be precise, to *evasions*."

Thus we read:

"Had I in that work" (*Die Judenfrage*) "had the *will* or the *right* to go *beyond* criticism, I *ought*" (!) "to *have spoken*" (!) "not of the *state*, but of *society*, which excludes nobody but from which only those exclude themselves who do not wish to take part in its development."

Here Absolute Criticism makes a *dogmatic distinction* between what it ought to have done if it had not done the contrary and what it actually did. It explains the narrowness of its *Die Judenfrage* by the "*dogmatic evasions*" of having the *will* and having the *right* which prohibited it from "going *beyond criticism.*" What? "Criticism" should go *beyond* "*criticism.*" This quite *massy* notion occurs to Absolute Criticism because of the dogmatic necessity for, on the one hand, asserting its conception of the Jewish question as absolute, as Criticism, and, on the other hand, admitting a more comprehensive conception.

The *mystery* of its "*not having the will*" and "*not having the right*" will later be revealed as the Critical *dogma* according to which all apparent limitations of "Criticism" are nothing but necessary *adaptations* to the powers of comprehension of the Mass. —

It had not the *will!* It had not the *right* to go beyond its narrow conception of the Jewish question! But what would it have done had it had the *will* or the *right*? It would have given a *dogmatic definition*. It would have spoken of "*society*" instead of "state" in other words it would not have studied the *real* relation of Jewry to *civil* society *today*! It would have given a *dogmatic definition* of *the* "society" as distinct from the "state" in the sense that whereas *the state* expels those who do not wish to take part in its development, *such people exclude themselves* from society!

Society behaves just as exclusively as the state, only in a more polite form: it does not throw you out, but it makes it so uncomfortable for you that you go out of your own will.

In substance the state does not behave otherwise, for it does not expel anybody who is satisfied with *its* demands and orders and *its* development. In its *perfection* it even closes its eyes and declares *real* contradictions to be *nonpolitical* contradictions which do not disturb it. Besides, Absolute Criticism itself has argued that the state excludes Jews only because and insofar as the Jews exclude the state and hence exclude *themselves* from the state. If these relations have a more courteous, a more hypocritical and more crafty form in *Critical* "society" that only proves that "*Critical*" "*society*" is more hypocritical and less developed in its structure.

Let us follow Absolute Criticism deeper in its "dogmatic distinctions" and "definitions," to be precise, in its "*evasions.*"

Herr Riesser, for example, demands of the critic "that he *distinguish* what belongs to the domain of law" from "what is beyond it."

The Critic is indignant at the impertinence of this *juridical* demand.

"So far," he retorts, "both feeling and conscience have, *however*, interfered in law, supplemented it, and, because of the quality based on its *dogmatic form*" (not, therefore, on its dogmatic *essence?*) "have always had to supplement it."

The Critic forgets that *law*, on the other hand, *distinguishes* itself quite explicitly from "feeling and conscience," that this distinction is based on the one-sided *essence* of *law* as well as on its dogmatic *form*, that it is even one of the *main dogmas* of law; that, finally, the practical implementation of that distinction is just as much the peak of the *development of law* as the separation of religion from all profane content makes it *abstract, absolute* religion. The fact that "feeling and conscience" interfere in law is sufficient reason for *the Critic* to speak of feeling and conscience when it is a matter of *law* and of *theological* dogmatics when it is a matter of *juridical* dogmatics.

The "definitions and distinctions" of Absolute Criticism have prepared us sufficiently to hear its latest "*discoveries*" about "*society*" and "*law.*"

"The world form that *Criticism* is preparing and the *thought* of which it is *even first* preparing is *no merely legal* form but" (collect yourself, Reader) "a form *of society* about which *at least* this much" (this little?) "*can* be said: whoever has not made his contribution to its formation and does not live with his feeling and conscience in it, does not feel at home in it and cannot take part in its history."

The world form that "Criticism" is preparing is defined as *not merely* legal, *but* social. This definition can be interpreted in two ways. The sentence quoted may be taken as "*not* legal *but* social" or "not merely legal, but *also* social." Let us consider its content according to both readings, beginning with the first. Earlier, Absolute Criticism defined the new "world form" distinct from the "*state*" as "society." Now it defines the noun "*society*" by the adjective "*social*." If Herr Hinrichs was three times given the *word* "*social*" in contrast to his "*political*," Herr Riesser is now given "*social society*" in contrast to his "*legal*." If the *Critical* explanations for Herr Hinrichs came to the formula "social" + "social" + "social" $= 3\ a$, Absolute Criticism passes in its second campaign from *addition* to *multiplication* and Herr Riesser is referred to society multiplied by itself, society to the *second* power, social society $= a^2$. In order to complete its deductions on society all Absolute Criticism now has to do is to go on to fractions, to extract the *square root* of society, and so forth.

If on the other hand we take the second reading: the "*not merely* legal *but also* social" world form, this hybrid world form is nothing but the *world form* existing *today*, the world form of *society today*. It is a great, a venerable *Critical miracle* that "Criticism" in its pre-world thinking is only just *preparing* the *future* existence of the world form which *already exists today*. But however it be with "not merely legal but also social society" Criticism can for the time being say no more about it than "*fabula docet*"* the *moral* application. Those who do not believe in that society with their feeling and their conscience will "not

* The fable teaches.—*Ed.*

9*

feel at home" in it. In the end, nobody will live in that society except "pure feeling" and "pure conscience," that is, "the Spirit," "Criticism" and its supporters. The *Mass* will be excluded from it one way or another so that "massy society" will dwell outside "social society."

In a word, this society is nothing but the *Critical heaven* from which the real world is excluded as being the *un-Critical hell*. In its pure thinking Absolute Criticism is preparing this transfigured *world form* of the antithesis between *"Mass"* and *"Spirit."*

From the same *Critical* depths as these explanations on *"society"* come the explanations Herr Riesser is given on the destiny of *nations.*

The Jews' desire for emancipation and the desire of Christian states to "classify" the Jews in "their government scheme"—as though the Jews had not long ago been classified in the Christian government schemes!—leads Absolute Criticism to prophecies on the *"decay of nationalities."* See by what a complicated detour Absolute Criticism arrives at the present historical movement—by the *detour of theology.* The following illuminating words of the oracle show us what great results Criticism achieves in this way:

"*The future* of all nationalities—is—*very—gloomy*!"

But let the future of nationalities be as gloomy as it may, for Criticism's sake. The one essential thing is *clear*: the *future* is the *work of Criticism.*

"*Destiny*," it exclaims, "may decide as it will: we now know that it is *our work.*"

As God leaves *his* creation, man, his own will, so *Criticism* gives destiny, which is *its creation*, its *own will. Criticism*, which makes destiny, is, like God, *almighty.* Even the "resistance" which it "*finds* outside itself," is its work. "Criticism *makes* its adversary." "Massy indignation" against it is therefore "dangerous" only for "the Mass" itself.

But if Criticism, like God, is *almighty*, it is also *all-wise* like him and is capable of combining its almightiness with the *freedom*, the *will* and the *natural attributes* of human individuals.

"It would not be the *epoch-making* force if it did not have the effect of *making each one* what he *wills* to be and showing each one irrevocably the standpoint *corresponding to his nature and his will*."

Leibnitz could not have given a happier presentation of the pre-established harmony between the almightiness of God and human freedom and the natural attributes of man.

If "Criticism" seems to clash with psychology by *not distinguishing* between the *will* to be something and the *ability* to be something, it must be borne in mind that it has decisive grounds to declare such a *"distinction"* *"dogmatic."*

Let us steel ourselves for the third campaign! Let us recall once more that "Criticism *makes its* adversary!" But how could it make its adversary *the "Phrase"* if it were not a phrase-monger?

3) Absolute Criticism's Third Campaign

a) Absolute Criticism's Self-Apology.
Its "Political" Past

Absolute Criticism begins its third campaign against the *"Mass"* with the question:

"*What is now the object of criticism?*"[25]

In the same number of *Literatur-Zeitung* we find the information:

"*Criticism* wishes *nothing* but to know *things*."

According to that the *object* of Criticism is all things. It would be senseless to inquire about some particular, definite object peculiar to Criticism. The contradiction easily resolves itself when one remembers that all things "merge" into Critical things and all Critical things into *the Mass*, as *the "Object"* of *"Absolute Criticism."*

First of all Herr Bruno describes his *infinite pity* for the "Mass." He makes *"the gap* that separates him from the *crowd"* an object of *"persevering study."* He wants *"to find out the significance of that gap for the future"* (this is what above was called knowing *"all"* things) and at the same time *"to abolish it."* In truth he therefore already knows the *significance* of that gap. It consists in being *abolished* by him.

As each man's self is nearest to him *"Criticism"* first sets about abolishing its *own massiness*, like the Christian ascetics who began the campaign of the spirit against the flesh with the mortification of their *own* flesh. The *"flesh"* of "Absolute Criticism" is its *really massy* literary *past* (filling 20-30 volumes). Herr Bauer must therefore free the literary biography of "Criticism"—which coincides exactly with his own literary biography—from its *massy appearance*; he must retroactively *improve* and *explain* it and by that *apologetic* commentary *"place its earlier works in safety."*

He begins by explaining by a double cause the error of the *mass* who, until the downfall of *Deutsche Jahrbücher*[26] and *Rheinische Zeitung*,[27] consider Herr Bauer as one of *their own*. The first mistake that was made was to consider the literary movement *not "purely as literary."* At the same time the opposite mistake was made, that of considering the literary movement as "a merely" or "a purely" *literary* movement. There is no doubt that the *"Mass"* was mistaken in any case, because it made two mutually incompatible errors *at the same time*.

Absolute Criticism takes this opportunity of crying to those who railed the "German nation" as a *"blue stocking"*:

"Name one single historical epoch which was not author-
itatively *outlined beforehand by the "pen"* and had not to
accept to be shattered by a stroke of the pen!"

In his Critical naiveness Herr Bruno separates *"the pen"*
from *the subject who writes* and the subject who writes as
"abstract *writer*" from the living *historical man* who wrote.
This allows him to go into ecstasy over the *wonder-working*
power of the *"pen."* He might just as well have asked
which historical movement was not outlined beforehand by
"poultry" or "the goose girl."

Later we shall be told by the same Herr Bruno that so far
not one historical epoch, not a single one, has been recognized. How could the *"pen,"* which was unable to *outline*
"any single" epoch *after* the event, have *outlined them all*
beforehand?

Nevertheless, Herr Bruno proves the correctness of his
view by *deeds*, by himself *"outlining beforehand"* his own
"past" with *apologetic "strokes of the pen."*

Criticism, which was involved on all sides not only in the
general limitation of the world and of the epoch but in
quite a particular and personal limitation, and yet assures
us that it has nevertheless been *"absolute, perfect and pure"*
in all its works for as long as man can think, has only *ac-
commodated* itself to the *prejudices* and *powers of comprehension* of the Mass, as God is wont to do in his revelations to man.

"It was bound to come," Absolute Criticism informs us,
"to a breach of *Theory* with its *seeming ally.*"

But as *Criticism*, here called *Theory* for a change, comes
to *nothing*, and everything, on the contrary, comes from it;
as it develops not inside but *outside* the world, and has predestined everything in its divine immutable consciousness,
the *breach* with its former ally was a *"new turn"* only in
appearance, only for others, not in itself and not for *Criticism* itself.

"However, this turn *properly speaking* was not even new. *Theory* had continually worked on *criticism of itself*" (we know how much effort has been expended on it to force it to criticize itself); "it had never flattered the Mass (but itself all the more); "it had ever *taken care* not to get itself involved in the premises of its opponent."

The Christian theologian must tread *cautiously*. (Bruno Bauer. *Das entdeckte Christenthum*, S. 99.) How came it, then, that "cautious" Criticism nevertheless did get involved and did not already then express its "proper" meaning clearly and audibly? Why did it not speak its mind out? Why did it let the illusion of its brotherhood with the Mass persist?

"Why hast thou done this to me?" said Pharaoh to Abraham as he restored to him Sarah his wife. "Why didst thou say she was thy sister?" (*Das entdeckte Christenthum* by Bruno Bauer. P. 100.)

"Away with reason and language!" says the theologian, "for otherwise Abraham would be a liar. It would be a mortal insult to Revelation!" (Ibid.)

"Away with reason and language!" says the Critic. "For had Herr Bauer *really* and not just apparently been involved with the Mass, Absolute Criticism would not be absolute in its revelations, it would be mortally insulted.

"It is *only*," Absolute Criticism continues, "that its" (Absolute Criticism's) "*efforts have not been noticed*, and besides, *there was* a stage in criticism when it was *forced sincerely* to consider its opponent's premises and to take them seriously for an instant; a stage, in brief, when it was *not yet completely* capable of taking away from the Mass the conviction that it had the same cause and the same interest as the Mass."

"*Criticism's*" efforts were just not noticed: the Mass was to blame. On the other hand Criticism admits that its efforts *could not* have been noticed because it itself was not yet *"capable" of making them noticeable.* The *fault therefore* *appears* to be Criticism's.

God help us! *Criticism* was "forced"—violence was used against it—"sincerely to take into account its adversary's premise and to take it seriously for an instant." Lovely sincerity, truly theological sincerity which does not really take a thing seriously but only *"takes it seriously for an instant"*; which has always, therefore *every instant,* been careful not to get itself involved in its opponent's premises, and nevertheless, *for an instant* "sincerely" takes those very premises into consideration. Its "sincerity" is still greater in the next sentence. While *Criticism* "sincerely took into consideration the premises of the Mass" it "was not yet fully *capable*" of destroying the illusion as to the unity of *its* cause and the cause of the *Mass.* It was *not yet capable,* but it already had the *will* and the *thought* of it. It *could* not yet *outwardly* break with the Mass but the break was already complete *inside it,* in *its mind*—complete at the very instant at which it *sincerely* sympathized with the Mass!

In its involvement with the prejudices of the Mass, Criticism was not *really* involved in them; on the contrary, it was, *properly speaking,* free from its own limitation and was "only *not yet completely* capable" of informing the Mass of this. Hence all the limitation of "Criticism" was pure *appearance*; an appearance which without the limitation of the Mass would have been superfluous and would therefore not have existed at all. The fault is therefore *back* on the Mass.

Inasmuch as this *appearance,* however, was supported by "the inability," "the impotence" of Criticism to express its thought, Criticism itself was *imperfect.* This it admits in its own way, which is as sincere as it is apologetic.

"In spite of its" (Criticism's) "having subjected liberalism itself to devastating criticism, it could *still* be considered as a peculiar kind of liberalism, *perhaps* for its extreme implementation; *in spite of* its true and decisive arguments having gone beyond politics, it had *still* necessarily to *appear* to *engage in politics*, and this *incomplete appearance* has won it most of the friends mentioned above."

Criticism won most of its friends through its *incomplete appearance* of engaging in politics. Had it *completely appeared* to engage in politics, it would infallibly have lost its *political* friends. In its *apologetic anxiety* to wash itself of all sin, it accuses the *false appearance* of being an *incomplete false appearance*, not a *complete* one. By substituting one appearance for another, "Criticism" can console itself with the fact that if it had the "complete appearance" of wishing to engage in politics, it had not, on the other hand, even the "incomplete appearance" of anywhere or ever having abolished politics.

Not completely satisfied with the "incomplete appearance," Absolute Criticism again wonders:

How can *criticism* at that time have become involved in "massy, political" interests! How can *it—even* (!)—"*have been obliged*" (!)—"*to engage in politics*" (!).

Bauer the *theologian* takes it *as a matter of course* that *Criticism* had to indulge in unending *speculative theology* for *he*, "Criticism," is indeed a theologian *ex professo*. But to *engage in politics*? That must be motivated by very special, political, personal circumstances.

Why, then, had "Criticism" to *engage* even in *politics*? "*It was accused—that is the answer to the question.*" At least the "mystery" of "*Bauer's politics*" is thereby disclosed; at least the *appearance* which in Bruno Bauer's *Die gute Sache der Freiheit und meine eigene Angelegenheit* joins *its "own cause"* to the *massy* "cause of freedom" by means of an "*and*," cannot be called *non-political*. But if Criticism pursued not its "*own cause*" in the *interest of politics*, but *politics* in the *interest of its own cause*, it must be admitted that not Criticism was taken in by politics, but politics by Criticism.

So Bruno Bauer was to be dismissed from his chair of theology: he was *accused*; "Criticism" had to engage in politics, that is to say, to *conduct "its,"* i.e., Bruno Bauer's suit. Herr Bauer did not conduct the suit of Criticism, "Criticism" conducted Herr Bauer's suit. Why *had* "Criticism" to conduct its suit?

"In order to justify itself!" *Perhaps so*; only "Criticism" is far from limiting itself to such personal, vulgar grounds. Perhaps so; *not for that alone*, however, *"but mainly* in order to bring out the contradictions of its opponents," and, Criticism could add, in order to have bound together in a single *book* old essays against various theologians (see among other things the wordy bickering with *Plank*) that family affair between "Bauer-theology" and "Strauss-theology."

Having got a load off its heart by admitting the real interests of its *"politics,"* Absolute Criticism remembers its *"suit"* and again chews the old *Hegelian* cud (cf. the struggle between Enlightenment and faith in *Phenomenology*, cf. the whole of *Phenomenology*) that the old which resists the new is no longer really the old, that it has already chewed at length in the "good cause of freedom." Critical Criticism is a ruminant. It keeps on warming up the few crumbs dropped by Hegel, like the above-quoted sentence about the "old" and the "new" or again that of the "development of the extreme out of its opposite extreme" and the like, without ever feeling the need of dealing with *"speculative dialectics"* in any other way than by exhausting Professor Hinrichs. Hegel, on the contrary, it always got over "Critically" by repeating him. For example:

"By appearing and giving the investigation a new form, i.e., giving it the form which is *no longer susceptible* of being *transformed* into an *external limitation,"* etc.

When I *transform* something I make it something substantially different. As every form is also "an *external limitation*" *no* form is "susceptible" of being *transformed* into an "external limitation" any more than an apple of being "transformed" into an apple. Admittedly, the form which "Criticism" gives to the investigation is not susceptible for quite *another* reason of being transformed into an "external limitation." Beyond every "external limitation" it is blurred into an ash-grey dark-blue vapour of nonsense.

"It" (the struggle between the old and the new) "would, *however*, be completely *impossible even*" (to be precise, the moment Criticism "gives the investigation a new form") "if the old were to deal with the question of compatibility or incompatibility ... *theoretically.*"

But why does not the old deal with this question theoretically? Because "this *however*, is the *least* possible for it in the beginning, *since* at the *moment of surprise*" (i.e., in the beginning) it "knows neither itself nor the new," i. e., it deals *theoretically* neither with itself nor with the new. It would be quite impossible if "impossibility," unfortunately, were not impossible!

When *the "Critic"* from the theological faculty further "admits that he erred *intentionally* that he committed the mistake deliberately and after mature reflexion" (all that Criticism has endured, experienced and done *is transformed* for it into a free, pure and intentional product of its reflexion) this confession of the Critic has only an "incomplete appearance" of truth. As the *Kritik der Synoptiker*[28] is based completely on *theological* foundations, as it is through and through *theological* criticism, Herr Bauer, the docent in theology, could write and teach it "without mistake or error." On the contrary, the mistake and error were on the side of the theological faculties who did not realize how strictly Herr Bauer had kept his promise,

the promise he gave in *Kritik der Synoptiker*, Vol. I, Foreword, p. XXIII.

"Were the *negation* to seem too sharp and far-reaching
in this first volume too, we must remember that the really
positive can be born only when the negation has been
serious and general ... *In the end* it will be patent that only
devastating criticism of the world can teach us the creative
power of Jesus and his *principle*."

Herr Bauer intentionally separates the Lord "Jesus" and
his "principle" to free the *positive* meaning of his promise
from all appearance of ambiguity. And Herr Bauer has really made the "*creative*" power of the Lord Jesus and his
principle so evident that his "*infinite self-consciousness*"
and the "*Spirit*" are nothing but *creatures* of Christianity.

If Critical Criticism's dispute with the Bonn theological
faculty explained its former "politics" so well, why does
Critical Criticism continue to engage in politics after the
dispute has been settled? Listen to this:

"At this point Criticism *should have* either *remained*
where it was or immediately *proceeded further* to examine
the essence of politics and represent it as its adversary;—if
only it had been possible for it to be able to remain where
it was in the struggle at that time and if, *on the other
hand*, there had not been a far too strict historical law that
when a principle measures itself for the first time with its
opposite it must let Itself be repressed by it...."

What a delightful apologetic phrase! "Criticism *should
have* remained where it was" if only it had been possible ...
"to be able to remain where it was!" Who "*should*" remain
where he is? And who should have done "what it was not
possible ... to be able to do?" On the other hand! Criticism
should have proceeded "if *only*, on the other hand, there
had not been a far *too* strict historical law, etc." Historical
laws are also "*far too strict* with Absolute Criticism! If
only they did *not* stand on the *opposite* side to Critical

Criticism, how brilliantly the latter would proceed! But *à la guerre comme à la guerre*! In history Critical Criticism must suffer to be made a sorry "story" of!

"If criticism" (still Herr Bauer) "had to ... it will *at the same time* be *admitted* that it still felt *uncertain* when it gave in to demands of this" (political) "kind, that as a result of these demands it entered into a contradiction with its *true elements* that had *already* found its *solution* in those *elements*."

➡ Criticism was forced into political weaknesses by the far too strict laws of history, but, it entreats, *it must at the same time be admitted* that it was above those weaknesses, if not really, at least *in itself*. First of all it had overcome them "*in feeling*" for "it still felt uncertain in its demands"; it felt *ill at ease* in politics, it could not make out what was the matter with it. More than that! It entered into contradiction with its *true elements*. And finally the greatest thing of all! The contradiction with its truest *elements* into which it entered found its solution not in the course of Criticism's *development*, but "*had*" on the contrary, "already" found its solution in Criticism's true *elements* existing independently ➡ of the contradiction! These Critical elements can claim with pride: before Abraham was, we are. Before the opposite to us was produced by development it lay yet *unborn* in our chaotic womb, solved, dead, ruined. But as Criticism's contradiction of its true elements "*had already* found its solution" in the true elements of Criticism, and as a *solved* contradiction is *no longer* a contradiction, it really found itself, properly speaking, in *no* contradiction to its true elements, in no contradiction to itself, and—the general aim of self-apology seems attained.

Absolute Criticism's self-apology disposes of a whole *apologetical* dictionary:

"not even properly speaking," "only not noticed," "there was besides," "not yet complete," "although never-

theless," "not only ... but mainly," "just as much, properly
speaking, only," "Criticism should have if only it had been
possible and if on the other hand," "if ... it must *at the
same time* be admitted," "was it not natural, was it not inevitable," "neither ..." etc.

Not so very long ago Absolute Criticism gave the following opinion on apologetic phrases of this kind:

"Although" and "nevertheless," "indeed" and "but," a
heavenly "Nay," and an earthly "Yea" are the main pillars
of modern theology, the stilts on which it strides along,
the artifice to which its whole wisdom is reduced, the phrase
which occurs in all its phrases, its *alpha and omega*" (*Das
entdeckte Christenthum*, p. 102).

b) The Jewish Question No. 3

"Absolute Criticism" does not remain where it is when
it has proved by its autobiography its own singular omnipotence which "*first creates the old, properly speaking,* just
as much as the *new.*" It does not remain where it is when
it *has written in person* the apology of its past. It now sets
a third party, the rest of the profane world, the Absolute
"*Task,*" the "task which is *now* the *main one,*" the *apology*
of Bauer's deeds and "works."

Deutsch-Französische Jahrbücher published a criticism of
Herr Bauer's *Die Judenfrage*.[29] His basic error, the confusion
of "*political*" with "*human*" emancipation was revealed.
Granted, the old Jewish question was not at first given its
"*correct setting*"; the Jewish question was dealt with and
resolved in the setting which new developments have given
to *old questions* and as a result of which the latter have
become "questions" of the present instead of "questions" of
the past.

Absolute Criticism's *third* campaign, it seems, is to reply
to *Deutsch-Französische Jahrbücher*. At first Absolute
Criticism admits:

"In *Die Judenfrage* the same 'oversight' was made—the *human* and the *political* were identified."

Criticism notes:

"it would be too late to *reproach* Criticism for the stand which it still adopted partially *two* years ago." "*The question is rather to give the explanation why* Criticism ... had to engage even in politics."

"*Two* years ago?" We must reckon according to the *absolute* chronology, from the *birth* of the Critical Redeemer, Bauer's *Literatur-Zeitung*! The Critical Redeemer was born in 1843. In the same year the second enlarged edition of *Die Judenfrage* was published. The "Critical" treatise on the Jewish question in *Einundzwanzig Bogen aus der Schweiz*[30] appeared later in the same year, 1843 old style. *After the downfall* of *Deutsche Jahrbücher* and *Rheinische Zeitung*, in the same momentous year 1843 old style or *anno* 1 of the critical era, appeared Herr Bauer's fantastic-political work *Staat, Religion und Partei*, which exactly repeated his old errors on "the essence of *politics*." The apologist is forced to falsify *chronology*.

The "*explanation*" why Herr Bauer "*had to*" engage "*even*" in "politics" remains of general interest only under certain conditions. The fact is that if the infallibility, purity and absoluteness of Critical Criticism are assumed as the *basic dogma*, the facts contradicting that dogma are turned into riddles which are just as difficult, profound and mysterious as the apparently ungodly deeds of God are for theologians.

If, on the other hand, "the *Critic*" is considered as a finite individual, if he is not separated from the *limitations* of his time, one can dispense with the answer to the question *why* he *must* develop *even* within the world, because the *question* itself no longer exists.

If, notwithstanding, Absolute Criticism insists on its demand, one can offer to provide a nice little scholastic treatise dealing with the following *"questions of the times"*:

"Why had the Virgin Mary's conception by the Holy Ghost to be proved by no other than Herr Bruno Bauer?" "Why had Herr Bauer to prove that the angel that appeared to Abraham was a *real* emanation of God, an emanation which, nevertheless, lacked the consistency necessary to *digest food?"* "Why had Herr Bauer to provide an apology of the Prussian royal house and to raise the Prussian state to the rank of *absolute* state?" "Why had Herr Bauer, in his *Kritik der Synoptiker* to substitute '*infinite self-consciousness*' for *man?"* "Why had Herr Bauer in his *Das entdeckte Christenthum* to repeat the *Christian theory of creation* in a *Hegelian* form?" "Why had Herr Bauer to demand of himself and others the '*explanation*' for the wonder that he must have been mistaken?"

While waiting for proofs of these necessities which are just as "Critical" as they are "Absolute" let us listen once more to *"Criticism's* apologetic evasions."

"The Jewish question ... had ... first to be brought into its *correct* setting, as a *religious, theological* and *political* question." "As the treatment and solution of both these questions, *Criticism* is *neither religious nor political."*

The point is that *Deutsch-Französische Jahrbücher* declares Bauer's treatment of the Jewish question to be *really* theological and *fantastic*-political.

To begin with, "*Criticism*" answers the "reproach" of *theological* limitation:

"The Jewish question is a *religious* question. The *Enlightenment* claimed to solve it by describing the *religious contradiction* as *insignificant* or by denying it altogether. *Criticism*, on the contrary, had to present it in its purity."

When we get to the *political* part of the Jewish question we shall see also that in politics Herr Bauer the theologian does not deal with politics but with theology.

But when *Deutsch-Französische Jahrbücher* attacked his treatment of the Jewish question as *"purely religious"* it was concerned mainly with his article in *Einundzwanzig Bogen aus der Schweiz*, the title of which was "The Capacity of the Christians and Jews of Today to Obtain Freedom."

This article has nothing to do with the old "Enlightenment." It contains Herr Bauer's *positive* view on the ability of the Jews of today to be emancipated, that is, on the possibility of their emancipation.

"Criticism" says: "The Jewish question is a *religious* question."

The question is: "*What* is a *religious* question? and, in particular, *what* is a religious question today?

The *theologian* will judge by *appearances* and see a *religious* question in a *religious* question. But "Criticism" must remember the explanation it gave against Professor *Hinrichs* that the *political* interests of the present have *social* significance, that it is *"no longer* a question" of *political interests.*

Deutsch-Französische Jahrbücher was just as right when it said to "Criticism": *Religious* questions of the day have at the present a *social* significance. It is no longer a question of *religious* interests as *such*. Only the *theologian* can believe it is a question of religion as religion. Granted, *Deutsch-Französische Jahrbücher* committed the error of not stopping at the *word* "social." It characterized the *real* position of the Jews in civil society today. Once Jewry was laid bare of the *religious* shell in which it was disguised and released in its empirical, worldly, practical nucleus, the practical, *really social* way in which that nucleus is to be abolished could be indicated. Herr Bauer was content with a "religious question" being a "religious question."

It was by no means denied, as Herr Bauer *pretends*, that the Jewish question is also a *religious* question. It was said, on the contrary: Herr Bauer grasps *only the religious essence* of Jewry and not the *worldly, real basis* of that religious essence. He opposes *religious consciousness* as if it were an independent being. Herr Bauer therefore explains the *real* Jews by the *Jewish religion*, instead of explaining the mystery of the Jewish religion by the *real Jews*. Herr Bauer therefore understands the Jew only insofar as he is an immediate object of *theology*, or a *theologian*.

But Herr Bauer has not an inkling that real, *worldly* Jewry and hence *religious* Judaism *too*, is being continually produced by the *present civil life* and finds its final development in the *money system*. He could have no inkling of this because he did not know Jewry as a link in the real world but only as a link in *his* world, *theology*; because he, as a pious godly man, considers not the *everyday Jew* but the *Jew of the Sabbath* to be the *real Jew*. For Herr Bauer, the theologian of the *Christian faith*, the *historic* significance of Jewry must cease the *moment* Christianity is *born*. Hence he must repeat the old orthodox view that it has maintained itself *in spite of* history; he must serve up again in a *Critical-theological* form the old theological superstition that Jewry exists only as a confirmation of the divine curse, as *palpable proof* of the Christian revelation; that it exists and has existed only as a *vulgar religious doubt* of the supernatural origin of Christianity, that is, as a *palpable proof* against Christian revelation.

In *Deutsch-Französische Jahrbücher* is proved, on the contrary, that Jewry has maintained itself and developed *through* history, *in* and *with* history, and that that development is to be perceived not by the eye of the theologian, but by the eye of the man of the world, because it is to be found, not in *religious theory*, but only in *commercial* and *industrial practice*. It is explained why practical Jewry reaches perfection only in the perfection of the *Christian*

10*

world; why, indeed, it is the perfect *practice* of the *Christian world itself*. The existence of the *present-day* Jew is not explained by his religion, as though the latter were some independent being existing apart, but the survival of the Jewish religion is explained by practical factors of civil society which are *fantastically* reflected in that religion. The emancipation of the Jews to make human beings of them, or the human emancipation of Jewry, is therefore not conceived, as by Herr Bauer, as the special task of the Jews, but as the general practical task of the whole world today, which is *Jewish* to the core. It was proved that the task of abolishing the essence of Jewry is in truth the task of abolishing *Jewry in civil society*, abolishing the inhumanity of today's practice of life, the summit of which is the *money system*.

Herr Bauer, a *genuine* though *Critical theologian* or *theological critic*, could not get beyond the *religious contradiction*. In the attitude of the Jews to the Christian world he could see but the attitude of the *Jewish religion* to the *Christian religion*. He even had to restore the religious opposition *critically* in the *antithesis* between the attitudes of the Jew and the Christian to *critical* religion—*atheism*, the last stage of *theism*, the *negative* recognition of God. Finally, in his *theological fanaticism* he had to *limit* the capacity of "Jews and Christians of today," i.e., of the world of today, "to obtain freedom," to their capacity to grasp "the criticism" of theology and apply it themselves. For the orthodox theologian the world is dissolved in "religion and theology." (He could just as well dissolve it in politics, political economy, etc., and call *theology* heavenly *political economy*, for example, as it is the teaching of the production, distribution, exchange and consumption of "*spiritual wealth*" and of the treasures of heaven!) Similarly for the radical, critical theologian, the *capacity* of the world to obtain freedom, is dissolved in the *single* abstract capacity to criticize "religion and theology" as "religion and theology." The only struggle he knows is the struggle against the *religious* limitations of self-consciousness, whose critical *"purity"* and *"infinity"* is just as much a theological limitation.

Herr Bauer, therefore, dealt with *religious* and *theological* questions in the *religious* and *theological* way, if only because he saw in the "religious" question of the time a *"purely religious"* question. His *"correct setting* of the question" sets the question "correctly" only in respect of his *"own capacity"*—to answer!

Let us now go on to the political part of *Die Judenfrage*.

The *Jews* (like the Christians) are fully *politically emancipated* in various states. Both Jews and Christians are far from being *humanly* emancipated. Hence there must be a *difference* between *political* and *human* emancipation. The essence of *political* emancipation, i.e., of the developed, modern state, must therefore be studied. On the other hand, states which cannot yet *politically* emancipate the Jews must be rated by comparison with accomplished political states and must be considered as under-developed.

That was the point of view from which the *"political* emancipation" of the Jews should have been dealt with and is dealt with in *Deutsch-Französische Jahrbücher*.

Herr Bauer offers the following defence of "Criticism's" *Die Judenfrage*:

"The Jews were shown that they laboured under an illusion as to the *system* of which they demanded to be freed."

Herr Bauer *did* show that the illusion of the *German* Jews was to demand the right to take part in general political life in a land where there was no general political life and to demand *political rights* where only political privileges existed. On the other hand, Herr Bauer was shown that he himself laboured under no less "illusions" as to the "German political system" than the Jews. His illusion was that he explained the position of the Jews in the German states by the alleged inability of *"the Christian state"* to emancipate the Jews politically. He argued in the teeth of facts and construed the state of *privilege*, the **Christian-German** state, as the Absolute Christian state. It was proved to him, on the contrary, that the politically perfect, modern state that knows no religious privileges is also the perfect *Christian* state, and that hence the perfect Christian state, not only *can* emancipate the Jews but has emancipated them and by its very nature must emancipate them.

"The Jews are shown ... that they had the greatest illusions concerning themselves when they wanted to demand *freedom* and the *recognition of free humanity*, whereas for them it was only, and could only be, a question of a special *privilege*."

Freedom! Recognition of free humanity! Special privilege! Edifying words by which certain questions can be apologetically by-passed!

Freedom? It was a matter of *political* freedom. Herr Bauer was shown that if the Jew demands freedom and nevertheless will not renounce his religion, he *"is indulging in politics"* and sets no condition contrary to *political* freedom. Herr Bauer was shown that it is by no means contrary to political emancipation to *divide* man into the non-religious *citizen* and the religious *private individual*. He was shown that as the state emancipates itself from religion by emancipating itself from *state religion* and leaving religion to itself within civil society, so the individual emancipates himself *politically* from religion when his attitude to it is no longer as to a *public* but as to a *private matter*. Finally, it was shown that the *terroristic* attitude of the French *Revolution* to *religion*, far from refuting this conception, bears it out.

Instead of studying the real attitude of the *modern* state to religion. Herr Bauer thought it necessary to imagine a

Critical state, a state which is nothing else but the *critic of theology inflated to the size of a state* in Herr Bauer's imagination. Whenever Herr Bauer is in a fix in *politics* he makes politics a prisoner of his faith, *Critical* faith. Insofar as he deals with the state he always makes out of it an *argument* against "*the adversary*," *un-Critical* religion and theology. The state acts as executor of the *Critical-theological* desires.

When Herr Bauer had first freed himself from *orthodox*, un-Critical *theology*, *political authority* took for him the place of *religious authority*. His faith in Jehovah changed into faith in the Prussian state. In Bruno Bauer's treatise *Die evangelische Landeskirche Preußens und die Wissenschaft* not only the Prussian state, but, quite consistently, the Prussian royal house too, was construed as *absolute*. In reality Herr Bauer had no *political* interest in that state; its merit, in the eyes of "Criticism" was that it abolished dogmas by means of the *Unified Church* and suppressed the dissenting sects with the help of the police.

The political movement that started in the year 1840 saved Herr Bauer from his *conservative politics* and raised him for a moment to *liberal* politics. But here again politics was in reality only a *pretext* for theology. In his work *Die gute Sache der Freiheit und meine eigene Angelegenheit* the free state is the critic of the Bonn Theological Faculty and an argument against religion. In *Die Judenfrage* the antagonism between state and church is the main interest, so that the criticism of political emancipation changes into a criticism of the Jewish religion. In his last political work, *Staat, Religion und Parthei*, the most secret wish of the critic inflated to the size of a state is expressed. *Religion* is *sacrificed* to the *state*, or, more correctly, the state is only the *means* by which the opponent of *Criticism*, un-Critical religion and theology, is done to death. Finally, after Criticism has been saved, if only apparently, from all

politics by the socialist ideas which were spread in Germany
from 1843 onwards in the same way as it was saved from
its conservative politics by the political movement after
1840, it is finally able to proclaim its treatises against *un-
Critical* theology social and to indulge unhindered in its
own *Critical* theology, the contrasting of Spirit and Mass,
as the annunciation of Critical Saviour and the Redeemer
of the world.

Let us return to our subject!

Recognition of free Humanity? "Free humanity" which
the Jews did not just mean to aim at but really did aim at,
is the same "free humanity" which found *classic* recognition
in what are called the universal *Rights of Man.* Herr Bauer
himself dealt with the Jews' desire for the recognition of
their free humanity explicitly as the desire to obtain the
universal *Rights of Man.*

In *Deutsch-Französische Jahrbücher* it was expounded to
Herr Bauer that this "free humanity" and the "recognition"
of it are nothing but the recognition of the *selfish civil individual* and of the *uncurbed* movement of the spiritual and
material elements which are the content of his life situation,
the content of civil life *today*; that the *Rights of Man* do
not, therefore, free man from religion but give him *freedom
of religion*; that they do not free him from property, but
procure for him *freedom of property*; that they do not free
him from the filth of gain but give him *freedom of choice
of a livelihood.*

He was shown that the *recognition of the Rights of Man*
by the *modern state* means nothing more than did the *recognition of slavery* by the *state of old.* In the same way, in
other words, as the state of old had slavery as its *natural
basis*, the *modern state* has civil society and the *man* of
civil society, i.e., the independent man depending on other
men only by private interest and *unconscious* natural necessity, the slave of earning his living and of his own as well

as other men's *selfish* need. The modern state has recognized this as its natural basis in the *universal rights of man*. It did not create it. As it was the product of civil society driven beyond its bounds by its own development, it now recognizes the womb it was born of and its basis by the *declaration* of the *rights of man*. Hence, the *political* emancipation of the Jews and the granting to them of the "*rights of man*" is an act the two sides of which are mutually interdependent. Herr *Riesser* correctly expressed the meaning of the Jews' desire for recognition of their free humanity when he demanded, among other things, the freedom of movement, sojourn, travel, earning one's living, etc. These manifestations of "*free humanity*" are explicitly recognized as such in the French Declaration of the Rights of Man. The Jew has all the more right to the recognition of his "free humanity" as "free civil society" is thoroughly commercial and Jewish and the Jew is a necessary link in it. *Deutsch-Französische Jahrbücher* further expounds why the member of civil society is called "Man" *par excellence* and why the Rights of Man are called "inborn rights."

The only critical thing *Criticism* could say about the rights of man was that they are *not* inborn but arose in the course of history; that much *Hegel* had already told us. Finally, to its assertion that both Jews and Christians, in order to give or receive the universal rights of man, *must sacrifice the privilege of faith*—the Critical theologian supposes his *one* fixed idea at the basis of all things—was specially opposed to the fact contained in all un-Critical declarations of the rights of man that the *right* to believe what one wishes, the right to practise any religion, is explicitly recognized as a *universal right of man*. Besides, "*Criticism*" should have known that Hebert's party was defeated mainly on the grounds that it attacked the rights of man in attacking *freedom of religion*; similarly the rights of man were invoked later when freedom of worship was restored.

"As far as *political* essence is concerned, *Criticism* follows its contradictions to the point to which the *contradiction between theory and practice* had been most thoroughly elaborated for the past fifty years, to the *French representative system*, in which the freedom of theory was disavowed by practice and the freedom of practical life sought in vain its expression in theory.

"When the basic illusion had been done away with, *the contradiction* disclosed in the *debates of the French Chamber*, the contradiction between *free theory* and the *practical import of privileges*, between the legal import of privileges and a *public system* in which the *egotism of the pure individual* tries to dominate the *exclusivity of the privileged*, should have been conceived as a *general contradiction* in this sphere."

The contradiction that *Criticism* disclosed in the debates of the French Chamber was nothing but a contradiction of *constitutionalism*. Had Criticism conceived this as a *general* contradiction it would have conceived the general contradiction of constitutionalism. Had it gone still further than in its opinion it "should have" gone; had it, to be precise, gone as far as the *abolition* of this general contradiction, it would have proceeded correctly from constitutional *monarchy* to the *democratic representative state*, the perfect modern state. Far from having criticized the essence of political emancipation and proved its definite relation to the essence of man, it would have arrived only at the *fact* of political emancipation, the developed modern state, that is to say, only to the point where the existence of the modern state conforms to its essence and in which, therefore, not only the relative, but the absolute *vices*, those which constitute its very essence, could have been observed and described.

The above quoted "critical" passage is all the more valuable as it succeeds more in proving beyond any doubt that while *Criticism* sees the *"political essence"* far below itself, it is actually far below politics; it still needs to find in politics the solution of *its own* contradictions and still persists in not giving a thought to the *modern principle of statehood*.

To *"free theory" Criticism* opposes the *"practical import of privileges"*; to the *"legal import of privileges"* it opposes *"the public system."*

In order not to misinterpret the opinion of *Criticism*, let us recall the contradiction it disclosed in the debates in the French Chamber, the very contradiction which "should have been conceived" as a *general* one. One of the questions dealt with was the fixing of a day in the week on which children would not have to go to school. *Sunday* was suggested. One deputy moved that it was unconstitutional to allow Sunday to be mentioned in a law. The Minister Martin (*du Nord*) saw in that motion an attempt to assert that Christianity had ceased to exist. Monsieur Crémieux declared on behalf of the French Jews that the Jews, out of respect for the religion of the majority of Frenchmen, did not object to Sunday being mentioned. Now according to free theory Jews and Christians are equal, but according to this practice Christians have a privilege over Jews; for otherwise how could the Sunday of the Christians have a place in a law made for all Frenchmen? Should not the Jewish Sabbath have the same right, etc.? Or else the Jew is not really oppressed by Christian privileges in the practical life of the French too, but the law does not dare to express this practical equality. All the contradictions in the political essence expounded by Herr Bauer in *Die Juden-frage* are of this kind—contradictions of *constitutionalism*, that is, on the whole, the contradiction between the modern representative state and the old state of privileges.

Herr Bauer makes a very serious oversight when he thinks he is rising from the *political* to the *human* essence by conceiving and criticizing this contradiction as a "general" one. He would thus only rise from half political emancipation to full political emancipation, from the constitutional to the democratic representative state.

Herr Bauer thinks that by the abolition of *privileges* the *object* of privilege will also be abolished. Concerning the statement of Monsieur Martin (*du Nord*) he says:

"*There is no more religion* when *there is no more privileged religion*. Take away from religion its exclusive force and it no longer exists."

As *industrial activity* is not abolished by the abolition of the *privileges of the trades*, guilds and corporations, but, on the contrary, real *industry* begins only after the abolition of these privileges; as *ownership of the land* is not abolished when *privileges* of land ownership are abolished, but, on the contrary, begins its universal movement with the abolition of privileges and the free division and free alienation of land; as *trade* is not abolished by the abolition of *trade privileges* but finds its true materialization in free trade; so religion develops in its *practical* universality only where there is no *privileged* religion (cf. the North American States).

The modern "*public system*," the developed modern state, is not based, as Criticism thinks, on a society of privileges, but on a society in which *privileges are abolished* and *dissolved*; on developed *civil society* based on the vital elements which were still politically fettered in the privilege system and have been set free. Here "*no privileged exclusivity*" stands opposed either to any other exclusivity or to the public system. Free industry and free trade abolish privileged exclusivity and thereby the struggle between the privileged exclusivities. In its place they set man free from privilege—which isolates from the social whole but at the same time joins in a narrower exclusivity—man, no longer bound to other men even by the *semblance* of common ties.

Thus they produce the universal struggle of man against man, individual against individual. In the same way *civil society* as a whole is this war among themselves of all those individuals no longer isolated from the others by anything else but their *individuality*, and the universal uncurbed movement of the elementary forces of life freed from the fetters of privilege. The contradiction between the *democratic representative state* and *civil society* is the perfection of the *classic* contradiction between public *commonwealth* and *slavedom*. In the modern world each one is *at the same time* a member of slavedom and of the public commonwealth. Precisely the *slavery of civil society* is in *appearance* the greatest *freedom* because it is in appearance the perfect *independence* of the individual. Indeed, the individual considers as his *own* freedom the movement, no longer curbed or fettered by a common tie or by man, the movement of his alienated life elements, like property, industry, religion, etc.; in reality, this is the perfection of his slavery and his inhumanity. *Right* has here taken the place of *privilege*.

It is therefore only here, where we find no contradiction between free theory and the practical import of privilege, but, on the contrary, the practical abolition of privilege, *free* industry, *free* trade, etc., conforming to "free theory," where the public system is *not* faced with any privileged exclusivity, where the contradiction expounded by Criticism is *abolished*; here only do *we find the accomplished modern state*.

Here reigns the *reverse* of the law which Herr Bauer, in connection with the debates in the French Chamber, formulated in perfect agreement with Monsieur Martin (*du Nord*):

"As Monsieur Martin (*du Nord*) saw in the motion not to mention *Sunday* in the *law* a motion declaring that Christianity had ceased to exist, with the same right, and *a completely warranted right*, the declaration that the *law of the*

Sabbath is no longer binding on the Jews would be the *declaration of the dissolution of Judaism.*"

It is *just the opposite* in the developed modern state. The state declares that religion, like the other elements of civil life, only *begins* to exist in its full scope when the state declares it to be *non-political* and thus leaves it to itself. To the dissolution of the *political* existence of these elements, for example, the dissolution of *property* by the abolition of the *property* qualification for electors, the dissolution of *religion* by the abolition of the *state church*, to this very proclamation of their civil death corresponds their most vigorous life, which henceforth obeys its own laws undisturbed and develops to its full scope.

Anarchy is the law of civil society emancipated from disjointing *privileges*, and the *anarchy* of *civil society* is the basis of the modern *public system*, just as the public system is in turn the guarantee of that anarchy. To the same extent as the two are opposed to each other they also determine each other.

It is clear how capable *Criticism* is of assimilating the "new." But if we remain within the bounds of "pure Criticism" the question arises: Why did Criticism not conceive as a *universal* contradiction the contradiction that it disclosed in connection with the debates in the French Chamber, although in its own opinion that is what "*should have been*" done?

"That step *was*, however, then *impossible*—not only because ... not only because ... *but also because* without that *last remnant* of interior involvement with its opposite criticism *was impossible* and *could not have come to the point* from which it had only *one step* to make."

It was impossible ... because ... it was impossible! *Criticism* affirms moreover, that the fateful "*one step*" necessary to "come to the point from which it had only *one step* to make" was impossible. Who will dispute that? In order to come to a point from which there is only *"one step"* to make, it is absolutely impossible to make still that *"one step"* that leads beyond the point beyond which there is still *"one step."*

All's well that ends well! At the end of the encounter with the *Mass,* who is hostile to Criticism's *Die Judenfrage,* *"Criticism"* admits that *its* conception of *"the rights of man,"* its "appraisal of religion in the French Revolution," the "free political essence *it* pointed to occasionally *in concluding its* considerations," in a word, that the "whole time of the French Revolution was no more nor no less for *Criticism* than a symbol—that is to say, not the time of the revolutionary actions of the French in the exact and prosaic sense, but a symbol, only a fantastic expression of the figures which it saw at the end." We shall not deprive *Criticism* of the consolation that when it erred politically it did so only at the "conclusion" and at the "end" of its work. A well-known drunkard used to console himself with the thought that he was never drunk before midnight.

On the Jewish question *Criticism* has indisputably continually won ground from *the* enemy. In No. 1 of *Die Judenfrage* the treatise of *"Criticism"* defended by Herr Bauer was still absolute and revealed the *"true"* and *"general"* significance of the Jewish question. In No. 2 Criticism had neither the *"will"* nor the *"right"* to go beyond *Criticism.* In No. 3 it *had* still to make *"one step"* but that step was "impossible"—because it was "impossible." It was not its "will or right" but its involvement in its "opposite" that prevented it from making that *"one step."* It would have liked to clear the last obstacle, but unfortunately there was a *last remnant* of *Mass* on its Critical seven-league boots.

c) Critical Battle against the French Revolution

The *limitedness of the Mass* forced "*the* Spirit," "*Criticism*," Herr Bauer, to consider the *French Revolution* not as the time of the revolutionary endeavours of the French in the "*prosaic* sense" but "*only*" as the "*symbol* and *fantastic expression*" of the Critical figments of his own brain. *Criticism* does *penance* for its "*oversight*" by submitting the *Revolution* to a *further examination*. At the same time it punishes the seducer of its innocence—"the Mass"—by communicating to it the results of that "further examination."

"The *French Revolution* was an experiment which still belonged entirely to the eighteenth century."

The chronological truth that an experiment of the eighteenth century like the French Revolution is still entirely an experiment of the eighteenth century and not, for example, an experiment of the nineteenth seems "still entirely" to be one of those truths "which are understood of themselves from the start." But in the terminology of Criticism, which is very prejudiced against "crystal-clear" truths, a truth like that is called an "*examination*" and therefore naturally has its place in a "further examination of the revolution."

"The ideas which the French Revolution gave rise to did not, however, lead beyond the *system* that it wanted to abolish by force."

Ideas can never lead beyond an old world system but only beyond the ideas of the old world system. Ideas cannot *carry anything out* at all. In order to carry out ideas men are needed who dispose of a certain practical force. In its literal *sense* the Critical sentence is therefore another example of a truth that is understood of itself, that is, another "*examination*."

Undeterred by this examination, the French Revolution brought forth ideas which led beyond the *ideas* of the entire old world system. The revolutionary movement which began in 1789 in *Cercle social*,[31] which in the middle of its course had as its chief representatives *Leclerc* and *Roux* and which finally was temporarily defeated with *Baboeuf's* conspiracy, brought forth the *communist* idea which *Baboeuf's* friend *Buonarroti* re-introduced into France after the Revolution of 1830. This idea, consistently developed, is *the idea of the new world system*.

"After the Revolution had therefore" (!) "abolished feudal barriers in the life of the people, it was compelled to satisfy the pure egotism of the nation and to fan it itself, and, on the other hand, to curb it by its necessary complement, the recognition of a supreme being, that higher confirmation of the general state system, the function of which is to hold together the individual self-seeking atoms."

The egotism of the nation is the natural egotism of the general state system, as opposed to the egotism of the feudal estates. The supreme being is the higher confirmation of the general state system, that is, again the nation. Nevertheless, the supreme being is supposed to *curb* the egotism of the nation, that is, of the general state system! A really Critical task, to curb egotism by means of its confirmation and even of its *religious* confirmation, i.e., by recognizing that it is superhuman and therefore cannot be curbed by man! The creators of the supreme being were not aware of this, their Critical intention.

Monsieur *Buchez*, who supports national fanaticism with religious fanaticism, understands his hero *Robespierre* better.

Rome and Greece were ruined by nationalism. Criticism therefore says nothing specific about the French Revolution when it says that nationalism was its downfall, just as it says nothing about the nation when it defines its egotism

11—1192

as *pure*. This pure egotism appears rather to be very dark one, natural and adulterated with flesh and blood when compared, for example, with *Fichte's "ego."* But if, in contrast to the egotism of the feudal estates its purity is only relative, no "further examination of the revolution" was needed to see that the egotism which has a nation as its content is more general or purer than that which has as its content a particular estate or a particular corporation.

Criticism's explanations on the general state system are no less instructive. They are confined to saying that the general system must hold together the separate self-seeking atoms.

Speaking exactly and in the prosaic sense, the members of civil society are not *atoms*. The *specific property* of the atom is that it has *no* properties and is therefore not connected with beings outside it by any relations determined by its own *natural necessity*. The atom *has no needs*, it is *self-sufficient*; the world outside it is absolute *vacuum*, i.e., it is contentless, senseless, meaningless, just because the atom has *all its fulness* in itself. The egotistic individual in civil society may in his non-sensuous imagination and lifeless abstraction inflate himself to the size of an *atom*, i.e., to an unrelated, self-sufficient, wantless, *absolutely full*, blessed being. Unblessed *sensuous reality* does not bother about his imagination; each of his senses compels him to believe in the existence of the world and the individuals outside him and even his *profane* stomach reminds him every day that the world *outside* him is *not empty*, but is what really fills. Every activity and property of his being, every one of his vital urges becomes a *need*, a *necessity*, which his *self-seeking* transforms into seeking for other things and human beings outside him. But as the need of one individual has no self-understood sense for the other egotistic individual capable of satisfying that need and therefore no direct connection with its satisfaction, each in-

dividual has to create that connection; it thus becomes the
intermediary between the need of another and the object of
that need. Therefore, it is natural necessity, *essential human
properties*, however alienated they may seem to be, and
interest that hold the members of civil society together:
civil, not *political* life is their *real* tie. It is therefore not the
state that holds the *atoms* of civil society together, but the
fact that they are atoms only in *imagination*, in the *heaven*
of their fancy, but in *reality* beings tremendously different
from atoms, in other words, not *divine egoists*, but *egotistic
human beings*. Only *political superstition* today imagines
that social life must be held together by the state whereas
in reality the state, is held together by civil life.

"*Robespierre's* and *Saint Just's* tremendous idea of
making a "*free people*" which would live only according to
the laws of *justice* and *virtue*—cf. Saint Just's report of
Danton's crimes and his other report on the general police
—could be maintained for a certain time only by terror and
was a *contradiction against which* the base, self-seeking
elements of *the popular essence* reacted in the most coward-
ly and crafty way that could be expected of them."

These words of *Absolute Criticism*, which describe a "free
people" as a "*contradiction*" *against* which the elements of
"*the popular essence*" had to react is absolutely hollow, for
according to Robespierre and Saint Just *liberty, justice* and
virtue could, on the contrary, be only manifestations of the
life of the "*people*" and properties of the "popular essence."
Robespierre and Saint Just spoke explicitly only of "liberty,
justice and virtue" of *ancient times*, belonging to "*the
popular essence*." *Spartans, Athenians* and *Romans* in the
time of their greatness were "free, just and virtuous
peoples."

"Which," asks Robespierre in his speech on the principles
of public morals (sitting of the Convention on February 5,
1794), "is the *fundamental principle* of democratic or

11*

popular government? It is *virtue*. I mean *public* virtue which
worked such prodigies in *Greece* and *Rome* and which must
work still greater ones in republican France; virtue which
is nothing but love of one's country and its laws."

Robespierre then explicitly calls the *Athenians* and
Spartans "free peoples." He continually recalls the "antique
popular essence" and quotes their heroes as well as their
corrupters—Lycurgus, Demosthenes, Miltiades, Aristides,
Brutus and Catilina, Caesar, Claudius and Pisones.

In his report on Danton's arrest (referred to by Criticism)
Saint Just says explicitly:

"The world has been empty since the *Romans*, and only
their memory fills it and still prophesies *liberty*."

His attainder is composed in the ancient style and directed against *Danton* as against a *Catilina*.

In *Saint Just*'s other report, the one on the *general police*,
the *republican* is described exactly in the *ancient* comprehension, as *inflexible, modest, simple* and so on. The
police should be an institution substantially similar to the
Roman *censorship*. He does not fail to mention Codrus,
Lycurgus, Caesar, Cato, Catilina, Brutus, Anthony, or
Cassius. And concluding, *Saint Just* describes the *"liberty,
justice and virtue"* that he demands in *a single word* when
he says:

"Revolutionaries must be *Romans*."

Robespierre, Saint Just and their party fell because they
confused the ancient, *realistic* and *democratic republic*
based on *real slavery* with the *modern spiritualist democratic representative state* which is based on *emancipated
slavery*, on *bourgeois society*. What a terrible mistake it is
to have to recognize and sanction in *the Rights of Man*
modern bourgeois society, the society of industry, of universal competition, of private interest freely following its
aims, of anarchy, of the self-alienated natural and spiritual
individuality, and yet subsequently to annul the *manifesta-*

tions of the life of that society in separate individuals and at the same time to wish to model the *political head* of that society after the fashion of the *ancients*!

This mistake appears tragic when Saint Just, on the day of his execution, points to the large table of the *Rights of Man* hanging in the hall of the *Conciergerie* and says with proud dignity: "Yet it was I who made that." It was that very table that proclaimed the *right of a man* who cannot be the man of the ancient republic any more than his *economic* and *industrial* relations are those of the *ancient* times.

This is not the place to vindicate the mistake of the *Terrorists* historically.

"After the fall of Robespierre *political enlightenment* and the *movement* rushed to where they were to be the prey of *Napoleon* who, shortly after 18 Brumaire, could say: 'With my prefects, gendarmes and priests I can do what I like with France.' "

Profane history, on the other hand, reports: After the fall of Robespierre, the *political* enlightenment which formerly had wished to *overreach* itself and had been *extravagant*, began to develop *prosaically*. Under the government of the *Directorate bourgeois society*, freed by the Revolution from the trammels of feudalism and officially recognized in spite of the *Terror's* wish to sacrifice it to an ancient form of political life, broke out in powerful streams of life. A storm and stress of commercial enterprise, a passion for enrichment, the frenzy of the new bourgeois life whose first self-enjoyment is pert, light-hearted, frivolous and intoxicating; a *real* enlightening of the *land* of France the feudal structure of which had been smashed by the hammer of the revolution and which, in fever of the numerous new owners, had become the object of all-round cultivation; the first moves of industry that had now become free—these were a few of the signs of life of the newly arisen bourgeois society. *Bourgeois society* is *positively* represented by the *bourgeoisie*. The bourgeoisie, therefore, *begins* its rule. The *Rights of Man* cease to exist *merely* in *theory*.

It was not the revolutionary movement as a whole that became the prey of Napoleon on 18 Brumaire, as *Criticism* in its faith in a Herr von Rotteck or Welker believed; it was the *liberal bourgeoisie*. One only needs to read the speeches of the legislators of the time to be convinced of this. One has the impression of stepping out of the National Convention into a modern Chamber of Deputies.

Napoleon was the last act in *revolutionary terror's* struggle against *bourgeois society*, which had been equally proclaimed by the revolution, and against its policy. Granted, Napoleon already discerned the essence of the *modern state*; he understood that it is based on the unhampered development of bourgeois society, on the free movement of private interest, etc. He decided to recognize and protect that basis. He was no terrorist with his head in the clouds. Yet at the same time he still regarded the *state* as an *end in itself* and civil life only as a treasurer and his *subordinate* which must have *no will of its own*. He *perfected* the *Terror* by *substituting permanent war* for *permanent revolution*. He fed the egotism of French nationalism to complete satiety but demanded the sacrifice of bourgeois business, delights, wealth, etc. as often as it was expedient to the political aim of conquest. If he despotically oppressed the liberalism of bourgeois society—the political idealism of its daily practice—he showed no more pity for its essential *material* interests, trade and industry, whenever they conflicted with his political interests. His scorn of industrial business men was the complement to his scorn of *ideologists*. In his home policy, too, he fought bourgeois society as the opponent of the state which he still considered in his own person as the absolute aim in itself. Thus he declared in the State Council that he would not suffer the owner of extensive estates to cultivate them or not as he pleased. Thus again he conceived the plan of subordinating trade to the state by appropriation of *road haulage*. French business men prepared for the event that first shook Napoleon's power. Paris exchange brokers forced him by artificial famine to delay the opening of the Russian campaign by nearly two months and thus to carry it out too late in the year.

Just as the liberal bourgeoisie was opposed once more by revolutionary terror in the person of Napoleon so it was opposed once more by counter-revolution in the Restoration in the person of the Bourbons. Finally, in 1830 the bourgeoisie put into effect the wish it had had since 1789, with the only difference that its *political enlightenment* was now *accomplished* and that it no longer considered the constitutional representative state the ideal of the state and no longer intended to fight for the salvation of the world and for universal human aims but, on the contrary, considered it as the *official* expression of its own *exclusive* power and the *political* recognition of its own *particular* interests.

The history of the French Revolution, which started in 1789, did not end in 1830 with the victory of one of its components enriched by the consciousness of its own *social* importance.

d) Critical Battle against French Materialism

"*Spinozism* dominated the eighteenth century in its later French variety which made matter into substance, as well as in deism, which conferred on matter a more spiritual name.... *Spinoza's French school* and the supporters of deism were but two sects disputing over the true meaning of *his system*.... The simple fate of this Enlightenment was its sinking into *romanticism* after being obliged to surrender to the reaction which began after the French movement."

That is what Criticism says.

To the Critical history of French materialism we shall oppose a brief outline of its profane, massy history. We shall admit with due respect the abyss between history as it really happened and history as it happened according to the decree of *"Absolute Criticism,"* the creator equally of the old and of the new. And finally, obeying the prescriptions of *Criticism*, we shall make the "Why?", "Whence?" and "Whither?" of Critical history the "objects of a persevering study."

"Speaking *exactly* and in the *prosaic* sense," the French Enlightenment of the eighteenth century, in particular *French materialism*, was not only a struggle against the existing political institutions and the existing religion and theology; it was just as much an *open* struggle against *metaphysics* of the *seventeenth century*, and against all metaphysics, in particular that of *Descartes, Malebranche, Spinoza and Leibnitz. Philosophy* was opposed to *metaphysics* as *Feuerbach*, in his first decisive attack on *Hegel* opposed *sober philosophy* to *drunken speculation.* Seventeenth-century *metaphysics*, beaten off the field by the French Enlightenment, to be precise, by *French materialism* of the eighteenth century, was given a *victorious and solid restoration* in *German philosophy*, particularly in *speculative German philosophy* of the nineteenth century. After *Hegel* linked it in so masterly a fashion with all subsequent metaphysics and with German idealism and founded a metaphysical universal kingdom, the attack on *speculative metaphysics* and *metaphysics in general* again corresponded, as in the eighteenth century, to the attack on theology. It will be defeated for ever by *materialism* which has now been perfected by the work of *speculation* itself and coincides with *humanism.* As *Feuerbach* represented *materialism* in the *theoretical* domain, French and English *socialism* and *communism* in the *practical* field represent *materialism* which now *coincides* with *humanism*.

"Speaking *exactly* and in the *prosaic* sense," there are *two trends* in *French materialism*; one traces its origin to *Descartes*, the other to *Locke*. The latter is *mainly* a *French* development and leads direct to *socialism*. The former, *mechanical* materialism, merges with what is properly French *natural science*. The two trends cross in the course of development. We have no need here to go deep into French materialism, which comes direct from *Descartes*, any more than into the French *Newton* school or the development of French natural science in general.

We shall therefore just note the following:

Descartes in his *physics* endowed *matter* with self-creative power and conceived *mechanical* motion as the act of its life. He completely separated his *physics* from his *metaphysics*. *Within* his physics *matter* is the only *substance*, the only basis of being and of knowledge.

Mechanical French materialism followed *Descartes' physics* in opposition to his metaphysics. His followers were by profession *anti-metaphysicists*, i.e., *physicists*.

The school begins with the *physician Leroy*, reaches its zenith with the physician *Cabanis*, and the physician *Lamettrie* is its centre. Descartes was still living when Leroy, like Lamettrie in the eighteenth century, transposed the Cartesian structure of *animals* to the human soul and affirmed that the soul is a *modus of the body* and *ideas* are *mechanical motions*. Leroy even thought Descartes had kept his real opinion secret. Descartes protested. At the end of the eighteenth century *Cabanis* perfected Cartesian materialism in his treatise: *Rapport du Physique et du Moral de l'homme.*

Cartesian materialism still exists today in France. It had great success in *mechanical natural science* which, "speaking *exactly* and in the *prosaic* sense" will be least of all reproached with *romanticism*.

Metaphysics of the seventeenth century, represented in France by *Descartes*, had *materialism* as its *antagonist* from its very birth. It personally opposed Descartes in *Gassendi*, the restorer of *epicurean* materialism. French and English materialism was always closely related to *Democritus* and *Epicurus*. Cartesian metaphysics had another opponent in the *English* materialist *Hobbes*. Gassendi and Hobbes were victorious over their opponent long after their death when metaphysics was already officially dominant in all French schools.

Voltaire observed that the indifference of Frenchmen to the disputes between Jesuits and Jansenists[32] in the eighteenth century was due less to philosophy than to *Law's* financial speculation. And, in fact, the downfall of seventeenth-century metaphysics can be explained by the materialistic theory of the eighteenth century only as far as that theoretical movement itself is explained by the practical nature of French life at the time. That life was turned to the immediate present, worldly enjoyment and worldly interests, the *earthly* world. Its anti-theological, anti-metaphysical, and materialistic practice demanded corresponding anti-theological, anti-metaphysical and materialistic theories. Metaphysics had *in practice* lost all credit. Here we have only to indicate briefly the *theoretical* process.

In the seventeenth century metaphysics (cf. Descartes, Leibnitz, and others) still had an element of *positive*, profane content. It made discoveries in mathematics, physics and other exact sciences which seemed to come within its pale. This appearance was done away with as early as the beginning of the eighteenth century. The positive sciences broke off from it and determined their own separate fields. The whole wealth of metaphysics was reduced to beings of thought and heavenly things, although this was the very time when real beings and earthly things began to be the centre of all interest. Metaphysics had gone stale. In the very year in which Malebranche and Arnauld, the last great French metaphysicians of the seventeenth century, died, *Helvetius* and *Condillac* were born.

The man who deprived seventeenth-century metaphysics of all *credit* in the domain of *theory* was *Pierre Bayle*. His weapon was *scepticism* which he forged out of metaphysics' own magic formulae. He at first proceeded from Cartesian metaphysics. As *Feuerbach* was driven by the fight against speculative theology to the fight against *speculative philosophy* precisely because he recognized in speculation the last prop of theology, because he had to force theology to turn back from pretended science to *coarse*, repulsive *faith*, so Bayle too was driven by religious doubt to doubt about metaphysics which was the support of that faith. He therefore critically investigated metaphysics from its very origin. He became its historian in order to write the history of its death. He mainly refuted *Spinoza* and *Leibnitz*.

Pierre Bayle did not only prepare the reception of materialism and the philosophy of common sense in France by shattering metaphysics with his scepticism. He heralded *atheistic society*, which was soon to come to existence, by *proving* that a society consisting only of atheists is *possible*, that an atheist *can* be a respectable man and that it is not by atheism but by superstition and idolatry that man debases himself.

To quote the expression of a French writer, *Pierre Bayle* was "*the last metaphysician in the seventeenth-century sense of the word and the first philosopher in the sense of the eighteenth century.*"

Besides the negative refutation of seventeenth-century theology and metaphysics, a *positive, anti-metaphysical* system was required. A book was needed which would systematize and theoretically justify the practice of life of the time. *Locke's* treatise on the origin of human reason came from across the Channel as if in answer to a call. It was welcomed enthusiastically like a long-awaited guest.

To the question: Was *Locke* perchance a follower of *Spinoza*? "Profane" history may answer:

Materialism is the son *of Great Britain by birth.* Even Britain's scholastic *Duns Scotus* wondered: *"Can matter think?"*

In order to bring about that miracle he had recourse to God's omnipotence, i.e., he forced *theology* itself to preach *materialism.* In addition he was a *nominalist.* Nominalism is a main component of *English* materialism and is in general the *first expression* of materialism.

The real founder of *English materialism* and all *modern experimental* science was *Bacon.* For him natural science was true science and *physics* based on perception was the most excellent part of natural science. *Anaxagoras* with his *homoeomeria* and *Democritus* with his atoms are often the authorities he refers to. According to his teaching the *senses* are infallible and are the *source* of all knowledge. Science is *experimental* and consists in applying a *rational method* to the data provided by the senses. Induction, analysis, comparison, observation and experiment are the principal requisites of rational method. The first and most important of the inherent qualities of *matter* is *motion*, not only *mechanical* and *mathematical* movement, but still more *impulse, vital life-spirit, tension*, or, to use Jacob Bohme's expression, the *throes* [*Qual*] of matter. The primary forms of matter are the living, individualizing *forces of being* inherent in it and producing the distinctions between the species.

In *Bacon*, its first creator, materialism contained latent and still in a naive way the germs of all-round development. Matter smiled at man with poetical sensuous brightness. The aphoristic doctrine itself, on the other hand, was full of the inconsistencies of theology.

In its further development materialism became *one-sided*. *Hobbes* was the one who *systematized Bacon*'s materialism. Sensuousness lost its bloom and became the abstract sensuousness of the *geometrician*. *Physical* motion was sacrificed to the *mechanical* or *mathematical, geometry* was proclaimed the principal science. Materialism became *hostile* to *humanity*. In order to overcome the *anti-human incorporeal* spirit in its own field, materialism itself was obliged to mortify its flesh and become an *ascetic*. It appeared as a *being of reason*, but it also developed the implacable logic of reason.

If man's senses are the source of all his knowledge, Hobbes argues, proceeding from Bacon, then conception, thought, imagination, etc., are nothing but phantoms of the material world more or less divested of its sensuous form. Science can only give a name to these phantoms. One name can be applied to several phantoms. There can even be names of names. But it would be a contradiction to say, on the one hand, that all ideas have their origin in the world of the senses and to maintain, on the other hand, that a word is more than a word, that besides the beings represented, which are always individual, there exist also general beings. An *incorporeal substance* is just as much a nonsense as an *incorporeal body*. *Body, being, substance*, are one and the same *real* idea. One cannot separate the thought from matter *which* thinks. Matter is the subject of all changes. The word *infinite* is *meaningless* unless it means the capacity of our mind to go on adding without end. Since only what is material is perceptible, knowable, *nothing* is known of the existence of God. I am sure only of my own existence. Every human passion is a mechanical motion ending or beginning. The objects of impulses are what is called good. Man is subject to the same laws as nature; might and freedom are identical.

Hobbes systematized Bacon, but did not give a more precise proof of his basic principle that our knowledge and our ideas have their source in the world of the senses.

Locke proved the principle of Bacon and Hobbes in his essay on the origin of human reason.

Just as Hobbes did away with the *theistic* prejudices in Bacon's materialism, so Collins, Dodwall, Coward, Hartley, Priestley and others broke down the last bounds of Locke's sensualism. For materialists, at least, deism is no more than a convenient and easy way of getting rid of religion.

We have already mentioned how opportune Locke's work was for the French. Locke founded the philosophy of *bon sens*, of common sense; i.e., he said indirectly that no philosopher can be at variance with the healthy human senses and reason based on them.

Locke's *immediate* follower, *Condillac*, who also translated him into *French*, at once opposed Locke's sensualism to seventeenth-century *metaphysics*. He proved that the French had quite rightly rejected metaphysics as the mere bungling of fancy and theological prejudice. He published a refutation of the systems of *Descartes, Spinoza, Leibnitz* and *Malebranche*.

In his *Essai sur l'origine des connaissances humaines* he expounded Locke's ideas and proved that not only the soul, but the senses too, not only the art of creating ideas, but also the art of sensuous perception are matters of *experience* and *habit*. The whole development of man therefore depends on *education* and *environment*. It was only by *eclectic* philosophy that Condillac was ousted from the French schools.

The difference between *French* and *English* materialism follows from the difference between the two nations. The French imparted to English materialism wit, flesh and blood, and eloquence. They gave it the temperament and grace that it lacked. They *civilized* it.

In *Helvetius*, who also based himself on Locke, materialism became really French. Helvetius conceived it immediately in its application to social life, (Helvetius, *De l'homme, de ses facultés intellectuelles et de son éducation*). Sensuous qualities and self-love, enjoyment and correctly understood personal interests are the bases of moral. The natural equality of human intelligence, the unity of progress of reason and progress of industry, the natural goodness of man and the omnipotence of education are the main points in his system.

In *Lamettrie's* works we find a combination of Descartes' system and English materialism. He makes use of Descartes' physics in detail. His *"Man Machine"*[33] is a treatise after the model of Descartes' beast-machine. The physical part of Holbach's *Système de la nature, ou des lois du monde physique et du monde moral* is also a result of the combination of French and English materialism, while the moral part is based substantially on the moral of Helvetius. *Robinet* (*De la Nature*), the French materialist who had the most connection with metaphysics and was therefore praised by Hegel, refers explicitly to *Leibnitz*.

We need not dwell on Volney, Dupuis, Diderot and others any more than on the physiocrats, having already proved the dual origin of French materialism from Descartes' physics and English materialism, and the opposition of French materialism to seventeenth-century *metaphysics* and to the metaphysics of Descartes, Spinoza, Malebranche, and Leibnitz. The Germans could not see this opposition before they came into the same opposition with *speculative metaphysics*.

As *Cartesian* materialism merges into *natural science proper*, the other branch of French materialism leads direct to *socialism* and *communism*.

There is no need of any great penetration to see from the teaching of materialism on the original goodness and equal intellectual endowment of men, the omnipotence of experience, habit and education, and the influence of environment on man, the great significance of industry, the justification of enjoyment, etc., how necessarily materialism is connected with communism and socialism. If man draws all his knowledge, sensation, etc., from the world of the senses and the experience gained in it, the empirical world must be arranged so that in it man experiences and gets used to what is really human and that he becomes aware of himself as man. If correctly understood interest is the principle of all moral, man's private interest must be made to coincide with the interest of humanity. If man is unfree in the materialist sense, i.e., is free not through the negative power to avoid this or that, but through the positive power to assert his true individuality, crime must not be punished in the individual, but the anti-social source of crime must be destroyed, and each man must be given social scope for the vital manifestation of his being. If man is shaped by his surroundings, his surroundings must be made human. If man is social by nature, he will develop his true nature only in society, and the power of his nature must be measured not by the power of separate individuals but by the power of society.

This and similar propositions are to be found almost literally even in the oldest French materialists. This is not the place to assess them. *Fable of the Bees, or Private Vices Made Public Benefits*, by *Mandeville*, one of the early English followers of Locke, is typical of the social tendencies of materialism. He proves that in *modern* society vice is *indispensable* and *useful*. This was by no means an apology of modern society.

Fourier proceeds immediately from the teaching of the French materialists. The *Babouvists* were coarse, uncivilized materialists, but mature communism too comes *directly* from *French materialism*. The latter returned to its mother-country, *England*, in the form *Helvetius* gave it. *Bentham* based his system of *correctly understood interest* on Helvetius's moral, and *Owen* proceeded from *Bentham's* system to found English communism. Exiled to England, the Frenchman *Cabet* came under the influence of communist ideas there and on his return to France became the most popular, although the most superficial, representative of communism. Like Owen, the more scientific French communists, – Dezamy, Gay and others, developed the teaching of *materialism* as the teaching of *real humanism* and the *logical* basis of *communism.*

Where, then, did Herr Bauer of *Criticism* get the documents for the Critical history of French materialism?

1) *Hegel's History of Philosophy* represents French materialism as the *realization* of the substance of Spinoza, which at any rate is far more comprehensible than "the French Spinoza school."

2) Herr *Bauer* read French materialism out of Hegel's history as the Spinoza *school.* Then, as he found in another of Hegel's works that deism and materialism are *two parties* representing *one and the same* basic principle, he concluded that Spinoza had two *schools* which disputed over the meaning of his system. Herr Bauer could have found the supposed explanation in Hegel's *Phenomenology* where it is said: "Regarding that Absolute Being, *Enlightenment* itself falls out with itself ... and is divided between the views of *two parties* ... The one ... calls *Absolute Being* that predicateless object ... the other calls it *matter* ... Both are entirely the *same* notion—the distinction lies not in the objective fact, but purely in the diversity of starting-point adopted by the two developments" (Hegel, *Phenomenology,* pp. 420, 421, 424).

3) Finally Herr Bauer could find, again in Hegel, that when substance does not develop into a concept and self-consciousness, it merges with "romanticism." The journal *Hallische Jahrbücher* at one time developed a similar theory.

But at all costs the *"Spirit"* had to decree a *"silly destiny"* for its "adversary," *materialism.*

Note. French materialism's connection with Descartes and Locke and the opposition of eighteenth-century philosophy to seventeenth-century metaphysics are expounded in detail in most recent *French* histories of philosophy. In this respect it was a case of repeating against *Critical Criticism* what was already known. But the connection of eighteenth-century materialism with English and French *communism* of the nineteenth century still needs a detailed exposition. We confine ourselves here to quoting a few typical passages from Helvetius, Holbach and Bentham.

1) *Helvetius.* "Man is not wicked, but he is subordinate to his interests. One must not therefore complain of the wickedness of man but of the ignorance of the legislators, who have always placed private interest in opposition to the general interest."—"The moralists have so far had no success because we have to dig into legislation to pull out the roots which create vice. In New Orleans women have the right to repudiate their husbands as soon as they are tired of them. In countries like that women are not faithless, because they have no interest in being so."—"Moral is but a frivolous science when not combined with politics and legislation."—"The hypocritical moralists can be recognized on one hand by the equanimity with which they consider vices which attack the state, and on the other by the fury with which they condemn private vice."—"Human beings are born neither good nor wicked but ready to become one or the other according as social interest unites or divides them."—"If citizens could not achieve their own private good without achieving the general good, there would be no vicious people except fools" (*De l'esprit*, Paris, 1822.[31] I. 33, pp. 117, 240, 291, 299, 251, 369 and 339). As, according to Helvetius, it is education, by which he means (cf. l. c. p. 390) not only education in the ordinary sense but the totality of the individual's conditions of life, which forms man, if a reform is necessary to abolish the contradiction between private interests and those of society, a transformation of consciousness is necessary, on the other hand, to carry out such a reform: "Great reforms can be implemented only by weakening the stupid respect of the peoples for old laws and customs" (loc. cit. p. 260) or, as he says in another place, by abolishing ignorance.

2) *Holbach.* "Man can only love himself in the objects he loves: he can have affection only for himself in the other beings of his kind." "Man can never separate himself from himself for a single instant in his life; he cannot lose sight of himself." "It is always our convenience, our interest that makes us hate or love things" (*Système social, ou principes naturels de la morale et de la politique*, t. I,

Paris 1822, pp. 80, 112), but, "in his own interest man must love other men, because they are necessary to his welfare.... Moral proves to him that of all beings *the most necessary to man is man*" (p. 76). "True moral, and true politics as well, is that which seeks to bring men nearer to one another to make them work by united efforts for their common happiness. Any moral which *separates our interests from those of our associates* is false, senseless, unnatural" (p. 116). "To love others ... is to *merge our interests with those of our associates*, to work *for the common benefit.... Virtue* is but *the usefulness of men united in society*" (p. 77). "A man without desires or passions would cease to be a man.... Perfectly detached from himself, how could he be determined to attach himself to others? A man indifferent to everything and having no passions, sufficient to himself, would cease to be a social being.... Virtue is but the *communication of good*" (l. c. p. 118). "Religious moral never served to make mortals more sociable" (l. c. p. 36).

3) *Bentham*. We only quote one passage from Bentham in which he opposes "*general interest* in the political sense." "The interest of individuals ... must give way to the public interest. But .. what does that mean? Is not each individual part of the public as much as any other? This public interest that you personify is but an abstract term: it represents but the mass of individual interests.... If it were good to sacrifice the fortune of one individual to increase that of others, it would be better to sacrifice that of a second, a third, and so on *ad infinitum....* Individual interests are the only real interests" (Bentham, *Théorie des peines et des récompenses*, Paris 1826, 3 éd. II, p. 230).

e) Final Defeat of Socialism

"The French set up a series of *systems* of *how* the *mass* should be *organized*; but they had to resort to *fantasy* because they considered the mass, as it is, to be useful material."

The French and the English have, on the contrary, proved, and proved with great detail, that the present social system organizes the "mass *as it is*" and is therefore its *organization*. *Criticism* follows the example of *Allgemeine Zeitung*[35] and dispatches all socialist and communist systems with the *thorough* word "*fantasy*."

12*

Having thus shattered socialism and communism abroad, Criticism transfers its bellicose operations to Germany.

"When the *German enlighteners* suddenly found themselves disappointed in their hopes of 1842 and, in their embarrassment, did not know *what to do*, news of the latest *French* systems came in the nick of time. They were henceforth able to speak of raising the lower classes of the people and at that price they were able to dispense with the question whether they themselves belonged to the mass, which is to be looked for not only in the lowest strata."

Criticism has obviously so exhausted its provision of well-meaning motives in the apology of Bauer's literary past that it can find no other explanation for the German socialist movement than the "embarrassment" of the enlighteners in 1842. "Fortunately they received news of the latest *French* systems. Why not of the *English*? For the decisive *Critical* reason that Herr Bauer found no news of the latest English systems in *Stein's* book, *Der Communismus und Sozialismus des heutigen Frankreichs*. This is also the decisive reason why only *French systems* ever exist for *Criticism* in all its jabber about socialist systems.

The German enlighteners, Criticism goes on to explain, committed a sin against the Holy Ghost. They busied themselves with the "lower classes of the people," which already existed by 1842, in order to *get rid of* the question, which had so far *not* existed, what rank they were called to occupy in the *Critical world system* that was to be instituted in anno 1843: sheep or goat, Critical Critic or impure mass, *Spirit* or *Matter*. But first of all they should have thought seriously of the Critical *saving of their souls*, for of what profit is it to me if I gain the whole world, including the lower classes of the people, and suffer the loss of my own soul?

"But a spiritual being cannot be raised unless it is changed, and it cannot be changed before it has suffered extreme resistance."

Were *Criticism* better acquainted with the movement of the lower classes of the people it would know that the extreme resistance that they have suffered from practical life is changing them every day. Modern prose and poetry emanating in England and France from the lower classes of the people would show it that the lower classes of the people know how to raise themselves spiritually even without being directly *overshadowed by the Holy Ghost of Critical Criticism.*

"They," Absolute Criticism continues to resort to fantasy, "whose *whole wealth* is the word '*organization of the mass,*' " etc.

A lot was said about "organization of labour" although this "motto" came not from the Socialists themselves but from the politically radical party in France, which tried mediation between politics and socialism. But nobody before Critical Criticism spoke of "organization of the mass" as of a question only now to be solved. It was proved, on the contrary, that *bourgeois society,* the dissolution of the old *feudal* society, *is* that organization.

Criticism puts its discovery in quotation marks (*Gänsefüsse**). The goose that cackled to Herr Bauer the watchword to save the Capitol is none but his *own goose, Critical Criticism.* It organized the mass anew by construing it as the Absolute Opponent of the Spirit. The antithesis between spirit and mass is Critical "organization of society," in which *the* Spirit, or *Criticism* provides the organizing *work,* the mass the *raw material* and history the *product.*

After Absolute Criticism's great victories over revolution, materialism and socialism in its third campaign we may ask: What is the final result of those herculean feats? Only that those movements *perished* without any result because they were either *Criticism adulterated with mass* or *spirit*

---

* *Gänsefuss*—goose foot—is a name for quotation marks.—*Ed.*

adulterated with matter. Even in Herr Bauer's own literary past Criticism discovered manifold adulterations of *Criticism* by the mass. Here it writes an apology instead of a criticism, *"puts in safety"* instead of *surrendering;* rather than see the death of the *spirit* as well in its *adulteration* by the *flesh*, it reverses the case and finds *in the adulteration of the flesh* by the *spirit* the life even of *Bauer's flesh.* On the other hand, it is all the more ruthless and decisively *terroristic* whenever still imperfect criticism adulterated by flesh is the *work* not of Herr Bauer but of whole people and of a number of profane Frenchmen and Englishmen; whenever the imperfect criticism is not called *Die Judenfrage, Die gute Sache der Freiheit und meine eigene Angelegenheit* or *Staat, Religion und Parthei*, but revolution, materialism, socialism or communism. Criticism thus did away with the adulteration of the spirit by matter and of Criticism by the mass by sparing its own flesh and crucifying the flesh of others.

In one way or the other the "spirit adulterated by flesh" or "Criticism adulterated by mass" has been cleared out of the way. Instead of this un-Critical adulteration appears absolutely Critical *disintegration* of spirit and flesh, Criticism and mass, their pure opposition. This opposition in its *world-historic* form in which it constitutes the true historical interest of the present, is the opposition of Herr Bauer and Company or *the* Spirit to the rest of the human race or Matter.

Revolution, materialism and communism have therefore fulfilled their historic purpose. By their *downfall* they have cleared the way for the Critical *Lord*. Hosannah!

f) The Speculative Circular Motion
of Absolute Criticism and the Philosophy
of Self-Consciousness

Criticism, having supposedly attained *perfection* and purity in *one* domain, made only one *oversight*, "only" one "inconsistency," that of not being "pure" and "perfect" in *all* domains. The "one" critical domain is none other than the domain of *theology*. The *pure* area of this domain extends from the *Kritik der Synoptiker* by Bruno Bauer to *Das ent-deckte Christenthum* by Bruno Bauer, the last frontier post.

"Modern Criticism," *Allgemeine Literatur-Zeitung* tells us, "had dealt with Spinozism; it was therefore inconsistent of it naively to presuppose *Substance* in one domain, even if only in individual falsely expounded points."

Criticism's earlier admission that it had been involved in *political* prejudice was immediately followed by the attenuating circumstance that the involvement had been "*in the main so light.*" Now the admission of *inconsistency* is tempered by the parenthesis that it was committed only *in individual falsely expounded points*. It was not Herr Bauer who was to blame, but the *false points* which *ran away with Criticism* like recalcitrant mounts.

A few quotations will show that by overcoming *Spinozism* Criticism ended up in *Hegelian idealism*, that from "*Substance*" it went on to another *metaphysical monster, the "Subject*," to the "*Substance as a process,*" to "*infinite self-consciousness,*" and that the final result of "perfect" and "pure" Criticism is the *restoration of the Christian theory of creation in a speculative, Hegelian form.*

Let us first open *Kritik der Synoptiker*:

"Strauss remains true to the point of view according to which *Substance* is the Absolute. Tradition in this form of universality which has not yet attained the real and reasonable certitude of universality, that certitude which can be attained only in *self-consciousness*, in the *oneness* and *in-finity* of self-consciousness, is nothing but *Substance* which has emerged from its logical simplicity and has assumed a definite form of existence as the *power of the community*" (*Kritik der Synoptiker*, Vol. I, Preface, pp. VI-VII).

Let us leave "*the* universality which attains certitude," the "oneness and infinity" (Hegel's *Concepts*) to their fate. Instead of saying that the point of view professed in *Strauss's* theory on the "power of the community" and "tradition" has its *abstract* expression, its logical and metaphysical *hieroglyphic*, in the Spinozist conception of *substance*, Herr Bauer makes "*Substance emerge from* its *logical simplicity* and assume a definite form of existence in the power of the community." He applies the *Hegelian* miracle apparatus by which the "*metaphysical categories*"—abstractions extracted out of *reality*—break out of *logic*, where they are dissolved in the "*simplicity*" of thought, and assume "a *definite* form" of physical or human existence; he makes them become incarnate. Help, *Hinrichs*!

"Mysterious," Criticism continues its argument against Strauss, "mysterious is this view because the moment it wishes to explain and make visible the process to which the gospel history owes its origin, it can never bring out any more than the *appearance* of a process. The sentence: "The gospel history has its source and origin in tradition" states the same thing *twice*—"tradition" and the "gospel history"; though, admittedly it does state a relation between them. But it does not tell us to what *interior process of the substance* their development and exposition owe their origin."

— According to *Hegel* the *Substance* must be conceived as an *interior process*. He characterizes *development* from the point of view of the Substance as follows:

"But if we look more closely at this *expansion*, we find that it has not been reached by one and the same principle taking shape in diverse ways; it is the shapeless *repetition of one and the same idea* ... keeping up the *semblance* of diversity" (*Phenomenology*, Preface, p. 12). *Help, Hinrichs!*

"Criticism," Herr Bauer continues, "must according to this, turn against itself and find the solution of the *mysterious substantiality* ... where the *development of the substance itself* leads to, to the universality and certitude of the idea and its real existence, to *infinite self-consciousness.*"

Hegel's Criticism of the substantiality view continues:

"Philosophy ... is expected to open up the compact solidity of the substance and bring it to *self-consciousness*" (l. c. p. 7).

Bauer's *self-consciousness*, too, is *substance raised to* self-consciousness or *self-consciousness as Substance*: self-consciousness is transformed from an *attribute of man* into a *self-existing subject*. This is the *metaphysical-theological* caricature of man in his *severance* from nature. The *being* of this self-consciousness is therefore not *man*, but the *idea* of which self-consciousness is the *real existence*. It is the *idea become man*, and therefore it is *infinite*. All *human* qualities are thus transformed in a *mysterious* way into qualities of imaginary "*infinite self-consciousness*." Hence Herr Bauer says *expressly* that *everything* has its *origin*, its *explanation*, in this "infinite self-consciousness," i.e., finds in it the *basis* of its *existence*. Help, *Hinrichs!*

Herr Bauer continues: "The power of the *substantiality relation* lies in its impulse, which leads us to the concept, the idea and self-consciousness."

Hegel says: "Thus the *notion* is the *truth* of the substance." "The transition of the *substantiality relation* takes place through its own inherent necessity and consists in this only, that the concept is the truth of the substance." "The *idea* is the adequate notion." "The notion ... having achieved *free* existence ... is nothing but the "*ego*" or *pure self-consciousness*." (*Logic*, Hegel's Works, 2 ed. Vol. V, pp. 6, 9, 229, 13.) Help, *Hinrichs!*

It seems comic in the extreme when Herr Bauer still says in his *Literatur-Zeitung*: "Strauss failed because he was unable to *give a complete criticism of Hegel's system*, although he proved by his half-measure criticism the necessity for making it complete, etc."

It was not a *complete criticism* of Hegel's system that Herr Bauer himself thought he was giving in his *Kritik der Synoptiker* but at the most the *completion of Hegel's system*, at least in its application to theology.

He describes his critique *Kritik der Synoptiker*, Foreword, p. XXI) as "the last act of a definite system" which is no other than *Hegel's* system.

The dispute between *Strauss and Bauer* over *Substance* and *Self-Consciousness* is a dispute *within Hegelian* speculation. In *Hegel* there are *three* elements, *Spinoza's Substance, Fichte's Self-Consciousness and Hegel's* necessary and antagonistic *oneness* of the two, the *Absolute Spirit*. The first element is metaphysically travestied *nature severed* from man; the second is the metaphysically travestied *spirit severed* from nature; the third is the metaphysically travestied *oneness* of these two, *real man* and the real *human race.*

Strauss expounds *Hegel* from *Spinoza's point of view*, and Bauer from *Fichte's point of view* in the domain of theology, both with perfect consistence. They both *criticized* Hegel insofar as with him each of the two elements was *falsified* by the other, while they carried each of the elements to its *one-sided* and hence *consistent* development. Both of them therefore go *beyond* Hegel in their Criticism, but both of them also remain *within* his speculation and each represents *one* side of his system. *Feuerbach* was the first to *complete* and criticize *Hegel from Hegel's point of view*, by resolving the metaphysical *Absolute* Spirit into "*real man on the basis of nature*" and to complete the *Criticism of religion* by drafting in a masterly manner the *general basic features* of the *Criticism of Hegel's speculation and hence of every kind of metaphysics.*

With Herr Bauer it is, admittedly, no longer the *Holy-Ghost,* but *infinite self-consciousness* that dictates the writings of the evangelist.

"We can no longer conceal the fact that the correct conception of the gospel history also has its *philosophical basis, which is* the *philosophy of self-consciousness"* (Bruno Bauer, *Kritik der Synoptiker,* Foreword, p. XV).

This philosophy of Bauer, the *philosophy of self-consciousness,* like the *results* Herr Bauer achieved by Criticism of theology, must be characterized by a few extracts from *Das entdeckte Christenthum,* his *last* work on the philosophy of religion.

Speaking of the *French materialists* he says:

"When the *truth* of materialism, *the philosophy of self-consciousness,* is revealed and *self-consciousness* is recognized as the *All,* as the solution of the puzzle of *Spinoza's substance* and as the true *causa sui** . . . , what is the purpose of the *spirit? What is the purpose of self-consciousness?* As if *self-consciousness,* by supposing the *world* supposes *distinction* and produces *itself* in all it produces, since it does away again with *the distinction of what it produced from itself,* because it is itself only in production and in movement—as if self-consciousness had not its purpose and did not possess itself in that movement which it itself is! (*Das entdeckte Christenthum,* p. 113.)

"The French materialists did, indeed, conceive the movement of self-consciousness as the movement of the universal being, matter, but they could *not yet* see that the *movement of the universe* became *real* for itself and combined in oneness with itself *only as the movement of self-consciousness"* (1. c. pp. 114-115). Help, *Hinrichs!*

---

* Cause in itself.—*Ed.*

In plain language the *first* extract means: the truth of *materialism* is the *opposite* of materialism, *absolute*, i.e., exclusive, unmitigated *idealism*. Self-consciousness, *the Spirit*, is the *All*. Outside of it is *nothing*. "Self-consciousness," "*the Spirit*," is the almighty creator of the world, of heaven and earth. The *world* is a manifestation of the life of self-consciousness that has had to *empty itself* and take on the *form of a slave*, but the difference between the world and self-consciousness is only an *apparent difference*. Self-consciousness distinguishes *nothing real* from itself. The world is rather only a metaphysical *distinction*, a figment of the ethereal brain and an imagination of *self-consciousness*. Hence it does away again with the appearance that it had assumed for a moment that something exists outside of it and recognizes in what it has "produced" no real object, i.e., no object which in reality is distinct from self-consciousness. By this movement self-consciousness first produces itself as absolute, for the *absolute* idealist, in order to be an absolute idealist, must necessarily go constantly through the *sophistic process* of first transforming the world *outside himself* into an *apparent being*, a mere fancy of *its own* brain, and afterwards, declaring that *fantasy* to be what it really is, i.e., a pure fantasy, so as finally to be able to proclaim its sole, exclusive existence, which not even the appearance of an outside world disturbs any longer.

The second extract means: The French materialists did, admittedly, conceive the movements of matter as spiritualized movements, but they could not yet see that they are not *material*, but *ideal* movements, movements of self-consciousness, pure movements of thought. They were not yet able to see that the real movement of the universe became true and real only as the *ideal* movement of self-consciousness free and freed from *matter*, that is, from *reality*; in other words, that *material* movement as distinct from ideal brain movement exists only *in appearance*. Help, *Hinrichs*!

This speculative *theory of creation* is almost word for word in *Hegel*; it can be found in his *first* work, *Phenomenology*.

"This *estrangement of self-consciousness* itself establishes *thinghood.* . . . In this estrangement self-consciousness establishes itself as *object*, or sets up the object as *itself*. On the other hand, there is also this other moment that it has just as much *abolished* this *estrangement and objectification* and resumed them into itself. . . . This is the *movement of consciousness*" (Hegel, *Phenomenology*, pp. 574-575).

"Self-consciousness has a *content* which it distinguishes *from itself.* . . . This content in its *distinction* is the *ego*, for it is the *movement* of self-abolishment. . . . More precisely stated, this content is nothing else than the *very movement just spoken of*; for it is *the Spirit* which pervades *itself* and *for itself* as Spirit!" (Loc. cit. pp. 582, 583.)

Referring to this theory of creation of Hegel's, *Feuerbach* observes:

"Matter is the self-estrangement of the spirit. Thereby matter itself acquires spirit and reason—but at the same time it is assumed as a *nothingness*, an *unreal* being, inasmuch as only the product of this estrangement, i.e., being divesting itself of matter, of sensuousness, being in its perfection, is expressed in its true shape and form. The natural, the material, the sensuous, is therefore to be *negated* here, as *nature adulterated by original sin* is in theology" (*Grundsätze der Philosophie der Zukunft*, p. 35).

Herr Bauer is thus defending materialism against *un-Critical theology*, at the same time as he reproaches it with "not yet" being *Critical theology, theology of reason, Hegelian speculation. Hinrichs! Hinrichs!*

Herr Bauer, who carries through *his own* opposition to *substance, his own philosophy of self-consciousness* or of the *Spirit* in *all* domains, must consequently only have the *figments* of his own *brain* to deal with in all domains. In his hand *Criticism* is the instrument to sublimate into mere *appearance* and *pure thought* all that claims a *finite* material existence *outside infinite self-consciousness*. In the substance it is not the *metaphysical illusion* he combats but its *worldly* kernel, *Nature*; nature existing both *outside* man and as man's nature. Not to presume *Substance* in any domain—he still uses this language—means therefore for him not to recognize any *being* distinct from thought, any *natural energy* distinct from the *spontaneity of the spirit*, any *human power of being* distinct from *reason*, any *passivity* distinct from *activity*, any *influence* distinct from *one's own action*, any *feeling* or *willing* distinct from *knowing*, any *heart* distinct from the *head*, any *object* distinct from the *subject,* any *practice* distinct from *theory,* any *man* distinct from the *critic,* any *real universality* distinct from *abstract generality*, any *tu* distinct from the *ego*. Herr Bauer is therefore consistent when he goes on to identify *himself* with *infinite self-consciousness*, with *the Spirit,* that is, to replace these creations of his by their creator. He is just as consistent in rejecting as *stubborn mass and matter* the *rest of the world* which obstinately claims to be something *distinct* from what *he*, Herr Bauer, produced. And so he hopes:

> *It won't be long*
> *Till the end of bodies comes.*[36]

His *own* discontent that he has so far been unable to get at the something of "*this clumsy world*," he also construes quite consistently as *self-discontent* of this world; and the indignation of his Criticism over the development of mankind as *massy* indignation of mankind over *his* Criticism, over *the* Spirit, over Herr Bruno Bauer and Company.

Herr Bauer was a *theologian* from the very beginning but no ordinary one: he was a *Critical theologian* or *theological Critic*. While still the extreme representative of *old Hegelian* orthodoxy, a speculative arranger of all *religious* and *theological nonsense*, he constantly proclaimed *Criticism* his *private domain*. At that time he called Strauss's criticism *human* criticism and *expressly* vindicated the right of *divine* criticism in opposition to it. He later stripped the great *self-reliance* or *self-consciousness*, which was the hidden kernel of that divinity, of its religious shell, made it self-existing as an independent being, and raised it, under the trade-mark "*Infinite Self-Consciousness*," to the rank of principle of criticism. Then he accomplished in his *own* movement the movement that the "*Philosophy of Self-Consciousness*" goes through as the absolute act of life. He again abolished the "distinction" between "the product," *infinite self-consciousness* and the producer, *himself*, and acknowledged that infinite self-consciousness in his movement "*was only he himself*," and that therefore the movement of the universe first becomes *true* and *real* in his ideal self-movement.

Divine criticism in its *return into itself* was restored in a rational, conscious, Critical way; *being in itself* was transformed into *being in and for itself* and only at the *end* did the accomplished, realized, revealed *beginning* take place. *Divine* criticism, as *distinct* from *human* criticism, revealed itself as *Criticism, pure Criticism, Critical Criticism*. Instead of the apology of the Old and the New Testaments we got the apology of the old and new works of Herr Bauer. The *theological* antithesis of god and man, spirit and flesh, infinity and finity were transformed into the *Critical-theological antithesis of the Spirit, Criticism*, or *Herr Bauer, and matter, the mass*, or the profane world. The theological antithesis between faith and reason was resolved into the Critical-theological antithesis between *sound human reason* and pure Critical thinking. *Zeitschrift für spekulative Theologie*[37] was transformed into the Critical *Literatur-Zeitung. The religious saviour of the world* became a reality in the *Critical saviour of the world*, Herr *Bauer*.

Herr Bauer's last stage is not an anomaly in his development; it is the *return* of his development *into itself* from its
estrangement. Naturally, the moment at which *divine* Criticism estranged itself and came out of itself coincided with
the moment at which it was partly untrue to itself and created something *human*.

Returning to its starting-point, *Absolute Criticism* ended
the *speculative circular motion* and thereby its own *life's
career*. Its further movement is *pure—soaring round within
itself* above all *massy* interest and hence *void of any* further
interest for the Mass.

CHAPTER VII
CRITICAL CRITICISM'S CORRESPONDENCE

1) The Critical Mass

> Where can one feel better
> Than in the family circle?[33]

In its *Absolute* existence as Herr *Bruno, Critical Criticism* has declared the whole of un-Critical humanity, the *mass of* humanity, to be its *opposite*, its *essential object*; *essential*, because the mass exists *ad majorem gloriam dei*,* the glory of Criticism, of *the* Spirit; *its object*, because it is only the *matter* on which Critical Criticism operates. Critical Criticism proclaimed its relation to the mass as a *world-historical relation* of the present.

No *world-historic opposition* is formed however, by the statement that one is in opposition to the whole world. One can imagine that one is a stumbling block for the world because one is clumsy enough to stumble everywhere. But for a world-historic opposition it is not enough for me to declare the world *my* opposite; the *world* too must declare me to be its essential opposite, and must treat and *recognize* me as such. Critical Criticism ensures itself this recognition by its *correspondence*, which is destined to *testify* to the world of its Critical function of saviour and to the general *irritation* of the world at the Critical gospel. Critical Criticism is an object for itself as an *object of the world*. Its

---

* For the greater glory of God.—*Ed*.

13—1192

correspondence is intended to *show it as such*, as the *world interest* of the present.

Critical Criticism is in its own eyes the *Absolute Subject*. The Absolute Subject needs a cult. *Real* cult needs faithful individuals. That is why the *Holy Family of Charlottenburg* receives from its correspondents the cult due to it. The correspondents tell it *what it is* and what its adversary, the mass, *is not*.

However, Criticism falls into an inconsistency by thus having its opinion of itself represented as the opinion of the world and having its *concept* changed into *reality*. The *formation* of a sort of *mass* takes place *within Criticism* itself, the formation of a Critical mass whose simple function is untiringly to echo the oracles of Criticism. For consistency's sake this inconsistency may be forgiven. Not feeling at home in the sinful world, Critical Criticism must set up a sinful world in its own home.

The path of Critical Criticism's correspondent, the member of the Critical mass, is not a rosy one. It is difficult and thorny; it is a Critical path. Critical Criticism is a spiritualistic master, pure spontaneity, the *actus purus*, intolerant of any influence *from without*. The correspondent can therefore be a subject only *in appearance*, can only make a show of *independence* towards Critical Criticism, of wanting to communicate something new and of his own to Critical Criticism. In *reality* he is Critical Criticism's own *making*, he is the harking to its voice made for an instant *objective* and self-existing.

That is why the correspondents do not fail continually to affirm that Critical Criticism itself *knows, realizes, understands, grasps,* and *experiences* what in the same moment is communicated to it for *appearance'* sake. Thus *Zerrleder* uses the expressions: "Do you grasp it? You know. You know for the second and the third time. You have probably heard enough to be able to see for yourself."

So too the Breslau correspondent *Fleischhammer* says: "But that, etc., will be as little of a puzzle to you as to me." Or the Zurich correspondent *Hirzel*: "You will probably find out yourself." The Critical correspondent has such anxious respect for the absolute understanding of *Critical Criticism* that he attributes understanding to it even where there is absolutely nothing to understand. For example, *Fleischhammer* says:

"You will *perfectly*" (!) "*understand*" (!) "when I tell you that one can hardly go out without meeting young Catholic priests in their long black cassocks and cloaks."

Indeed, in their fear the correspondents hear Critical Criticism *saying, answering, exclaiming, deriding out loud.*

Zerrleder, for example, says: "But—you *say*. Well, then, listen." And *Fleischhammer*: "Yes, I hear what *you say*;—I *only* meant that..." and *Hirzel*: "Edelmann, you *will exclaim*!" And the Tübingen correspondent: "*Do not laugh at me!*"

The correspondents, therefore, also use expressions as though they were communicating *facts* to Critical Criticism and expect from it *spiritual interpretation*; they provide it with *premises* and leave the *conclusion* to it, or they even *apologize* for repeating things Criticism has known for a long time.

Zerrleder, for example, says:

"Your correspondent can only give a picture, a description of the facts. The *spirit* which animates these things is *certainly* not unknown to *you*." Or again: "You will surely draw the *conclusion for yourself*."

And *Hirzel* says: "I *do not presume* to take up your time with the speculative proposition that every creature proceeds out of the extreme of its opposite."

Sometimes what the correspondents *observe* is but the *accomplishment* and *confirmation* of *prophecies* of Criticism.

Fleischhammer, for instance says: "Your *prediction* has

13*

come true." And *Zerrleder*: "Far from being disastrous, the
tendencies that I described to you as gaining ever greater
scope in Switzerland, are very *fortunate*; they *only confirm*
the *thought you* so often expressed," etc.

Critical Criticism sometimes feels urged to express the
condescension that it sees in its correspondence and motivates it by the fact that the correspondent has successfully
carried out some *task*. Thus Herr Bruno writes to the Tübingen correspondent:

"It is really inconsistent on my part to answer your
letter—On the other hand, you have again made such an
apt remark that I ... *cannot refuse* the explanation you request."

Critical Criticism has letters written to it *from the
provinces*: not the provinces in the political sense, which, as
we know, do not exist anywhere in Germany, but from the
Critical provinces whose capital is Berlin, *Berlin*, the seat
of the Critical patriarchs and of the Holy Critical Family
while the provinces are where the Critical Mass resides. The
Critical provincials dare not engage the attention of the
highest Critical authority without bows and apologies.

Thus, somebody writes anonymously to Herr *Edgar*, who,
being a member of the Holy Family, is also a very respectable gentleman of superior rank:

"Honourable Sir, I hope you will *excuse* these lines on
the grounds that youth likes to join in the name of common
strivings (there is not more than two years *difference* in
our *ages*)."

This companion in years of Herr Edgar describes *himself*
incidentally as *the essence of the latest philosophy*. Is it not
quite normal for Criticism to correspond with *the essence*
of philosophy? If Herr Edgar's companion in years affirms
that he has already lost his *teeth*, it is only an allusion to
his *allegorical essence*. This "essence of the latest philosophy" "learned from *Feuerbach* to set the moment of

education in objective view." It at once gives a sample of its *education* and *views* by assuring Herr Edgar that it has acquired a "*totality view* of his tale, 'Long Live Firm _Principles!'" At the same time it openly admits that Herr Edgar's point of view is by no means clear to it and finally invalidates the assurance that it has acquired a totality view by the question: "Or have I *totally misunderstood* you?" After this sample it will be found quite normal that the essence of the latest philosophy, referring to the mass, should say: "*We* must at least once *condescend* to examine and untie the magic knot which bars access to the *infinite flood of thought* to *common human reason.*"

In order to get a complete view of the Critical mass one should read the *correspondence* of Herr *Hirzel* from Zurich. (No. V). This unfortunate man commits the oracles of Criticism to his creditable memory with really touching docility, not omitting Herr Bruno's favourite phrases about the battles he has waged and the campaigns he has planned and captained. But Herr *Hirzel* exercises his profession as member of the Critical mass especially by storming at the *profane mass* and its attitude to *Critical Criticism*.

He speaks of the mass claiming a part in history, "of the pure mass," of "pure criticism," of the "purity of this contradiction"—"a contradiction purer than any history has provided," of the "*discontented being,*" of the "perfect emptiness, bad humour, dejection, heartlessness, timidity, fury and bitterness of the Mass towards Criticism; of the Mass which only exists in order by its resistance to make Criticism sharper and more vigilant." He speaks of "creation from the extreme of the opposite," of how Criticism is above *hate* and similar profane sentiments. All Herr *Hirzel* provides *Literatur-Zeitung* with boils down to this profuseness of oracles of Criticism. While reproaching the *Mass* for being satisfied with the mere "disposition," "good will," "the phrase," "faith," etc., he himself, as a member of the *Critical mass*, is content with phrases, expressions of his "critical disposition," his "critical faith," his "critical good will" and leaves "action, work, struggle" and "works" to Herr Bruno and Company.

Despite the terrible picture of the world-historic tension between the profane world and "Critical Criticism" which the members of the "Critical mass" outline, the fact of the case, the fact of this *world-historic* tension is not even stated, at least for the non-believer. This obliging and un-Critical repetition of Criticism's "imaginations" and "pretensions" by the correspondents only proves that the fixed ideas of the master are the fixed ideas of the servant too. Granted, one of the correspondents makes an attempt at a proof based on *fact*.

"You see," he writes to the Holy Family, "that *Literatur-Zeitung* is fulfilling its purpose, i.e., that it meets with *no approval*. It could meet with approval only if it sounded in unison with thoughtlessness, if you strode before it with chimes of expressions of a whole janissary band of current categories."

Chimes of expressions of a whole janissary band of current categories! It is evident that the Critical correspondent does his best to trot along with non-"current" expressions. His explanation of the fact that *Literatur-Zeitung* meets with no approval must be rejected as purely *apologetic*. This fact could be explained in just the opposite way by saying that Critical Criticism is in *unison* with the great *mass*, to be precise, the great mass of scribblers who meet with *no approval*.

It is therefore not enough for the *Critical* correspondent to address expressions of Criticism to the Holy Family as "prayers" and at the same time to the mass as "curses." What is needed are un-"Critical" *massy* correspondents, *real* delegates of the *Mass* to Critical Criticism, to show the *real* tension between the Mass and Criticism.

That is why Critical Criticism also assigns a place to the *un-"Critical" Mass*. It makes unbiased *representatives* of the latter *correspond* with it, acknowledge opposition to itself, Criticism, as important and utter a *fearful cry* for redemption from that opposition.

2) The "Un-Critical Mass" and "Critical Criticism"

a) The "Obdurate Mass" and the "Unsatisfied Mass"

The hardness of heart, the obduracy and blind unbelief of "the Mass" has one rather determined representative. This representative speaks of the "exclusively Hegelian philosophical education of the Berlin Couleur."[39]

The "only true progress that we can make," he says, "lies in the acknowledgement of reality. But we learn from you that our knowledge was not knowledge of reality but of something unreal."

He calls "natural science" the basis of philosophy.

"A good naturalist stands in the same relation to the philosopher as the philosopher to the theologian."

Further he makes the following observation on the "Berlin Couleur:"

"I do not think it would be exaggerating to try to explain the state of these people by saying that they have had their spiritual *moult* but have not yet altogether got rid of their old skin in order to be able to absorb the elements of renovation and rejuvenation." "We must yet assimilate this" (natural-science and industrial) "knowledge." "The knowledge of the world and of man which we need most of all, cannot be acquired only by acuity of thought; all the senses must collaborate and all the aptitudes of man must be applied as indispensable instruments; otherwise contemplation and knowledge will always remain defective—and will lead to *moral death*."

But this correspondent gilds the pill that he is handing to Critical Criticism. He makes *Bauer's words* find their correct application," he has "followed *Bauer's thought*," he agrees that "*Bauer has spoken* the truth," and in the end he seems to polemize, not against *Criticism* itself, but against "Berlin Couleur" which is distinct from it.

Critical Criticism, feeling itself hit and being, besides, as sensitive as an old maid in all *matters of faith*, is not taken in by these distinctions and semi-courtings.

— "You are *mistaken*," it answers, "if you have taken the party you described at the beginning of your letter for *your opponent*. Rather *admit*" (and now comes the crushing anathema) "that you are an *opponent of Criticism itself*!" The wretch! The massy man! An opponent of Criticism *itself*! But as far as the content of his *massy* polemic is concerned, Critical Criticism declares its *respect* for its Critical attitude to *natural science* and *industry*.

"*All respect* for *natural science! All respect* for James Watt and" (a really noble turn!) "no respect at all for the millions that he made for his relatives."

All respect for the respect of Critical Criticism! In the same letter in which Critical Criticism reproaches the above-mentioned *Berlin Couleur* with too easily dispatching solid and clever works without studying them and having *finished* with a work when they have merely remarked that it is epoch-making, etc.,—in that same letter *Criticism itself dispatches* natural science and *industry* by merely declaring its respect for them. The clause on which it makes its declaration of respect for *natural science* dependent reminds one of the first fulminations of the deceased knight *Krug* against natural philosophy.

"Nature is not the only reality *because we eat and drink it in its individual products*."

Critical Criticism knows this much about the *individual*

products of nature that "we *eat and drink them.*" All respect for the natural science of Critical Criticism!

Criticism is more consistent in the way it counters the embarrassingly importunate demand to study "nature" and "industry" with the following indisputably witty rhetorical exclamation:

"Or" (!) "do you think that the knowledge of *historical* reality is *already complete?* Or" (!) "do you know of any single period in history which is already *actually* known?"

Or perhaps Critical Criticism believes that it has got even to a *beginning* of the knowledge of historical reality while it still excludes *from* the historical movement the theoretical and practical relations of man to nature, natural science and industry? Or does it think that it actually knows any period without having knowledge, for example, of the industry of that period, the immediate mode of production of life itself? Of course, spiritualistic, *theological* Critical Criticism only knows (at least it imagines it knows) the main political, literary and theological acts of history. Just as it separates thinking from the senses, the soul from the body and itself from the world, it also separates history from natural science and industry and sees the origin of history not in coarse *material* production on the earth but in vaporous clouds in the heavens.

The representative of the "obdurate" and "hard-hearted" mass with his apt reproofs and counsels is dealt with as a *massy materialist.* Another correspondent, not so malicious or massy, who places his hopes in Critical Criticism but is disappointed, is treated no better. The representative of the "*unsatisfied*" mass writes: "I must all the same admit that the first number of your paper was *by no means satisfying.* We expected something else."

The *Critical patriarch* answers in person: "I knew beforehand that it would not satisfy expectations, because I could rather easily imagine those expectations. One is so exhausted that one wishes to have *everything at once*. Everything? No! If possible everything and nothing at the same time. An everything that costs no trouble, an everything that one can absorb without going through any development, an everything that is contained all in one word."

In his vexation at the undue demands of the "Mass" who demands *something*, indeed *everything*, from Criticism, which by principle and disposition "*gives nothing*," the Critical patriarch tells an *anecdote* after the style of old men. Not long ago a Berlin *acquaintance* complained bitterly of the verbosity and profusion of detail of his works—Herr Bruno is known to make bulky works out of the tiniest pretence of a thought. He was consoled with the promise to send him the ink necessary for the printing of the book in a small pellet so that he could easily absorb it. The patriarch explained the length of his "works" by the bad spreading of the ink, as he explained the nothingness of his *Literatur-Zeitung* by the emptiness of the "profane mass" who wanted to swallow Everything and Nothing at once in order to be full.

As it is difficult to deny the importance of what has so far been related, it is also difficult to see a *world-historic contradiction* in the fact that a massy acquaintance of Critical Criticism considers Criticism hollow, while Criticism on the other hand declares him to be un-Critical; that a second acquaintance does not find *Literatur-Zeitung* up to his expectations and that a *third* acquaintance and friend of the family finds Criticism's work too bulky. However, acquaintance No. 2, who entertains expectations, and friend of the family No. 3, who wishes at least to find out the secrets of Critical Criticism, constitute the transition to a *more substantial* and tenser relation between Criticism and the "un-Critical Mass." Cruel as Criticism is to the "hard-hearted" Mass which has only "vulgar human reason," we shall find it condescendent to the Mass that is pining for *salvation* from contradiction. The mass which approaches Criticism with a contrite heart, a spirit of repentance and a humble mind will be rewarded for its honest striving with **well-weighed** and **weighty** words of *prophecy.*

b) The "Soft-Hearted" Mass "Pining for Salvation"

The representative of the *sentimental, soft-hearted Mass pining for salvation* cringes and implores Criticism for a kind word with effusions of the heart, deep bows and rolling of the eyes, as follows:

"Why am I writing this to you? Why am I justifying myself before you? Because I *respect* you and therefore *desire* your *respect*; because I am infinitely *obliged* to you for my development and therefore *love* you. *My heart* presses me to *justify myself* before you ... who have upbraided me.... *Far be it* from me to *obtrude* upon you; judging *by myself*, I thought you *might be pleased* to have proof of *sympathy* from a man whom you know little about. I *make no claim* whatsoever that you should answer my letter: I wish *neither* to take up your time, of which you can make better use, *nor* to be irksome to you, *nor* to expose myself to the mortification of seeing something that I hoped for remain *unfulfilled.* You *may* interpret my letter *as sentimentality, importunity, vanity* (!) or whatever you like; you may answer me or not, I cannot resist the *impulse* to send it and I only hope that you will realize the *"friendly feeling* which inspired it"(!!).

As God has from the beginning had mercy on the *poor in spirit*, this massy but humble correspondent who whimpers for mercy from Critical Criticism, also has his wish *fulfilled.* Critical Criticism gives him a kind answer. More than that! It gives him *most profound* explanations on the objects of his curiosity.

"Two years ago," Critical Criticism teaches, "it was opportune to remember the Enlightenment of the French in the eighteenth century in order to be able to make use of those *light troops* too in a place in the battle that was being waged. The situation is now *quite different*. Truths now change very quickly. What was *then opportuneness* is now an oversight."

Of course it was only "an oversight" too, but an "*opportune*" one, when the Absolute Critical All-high itself (cf. *Anekdota*, Book II, p. 89) [40] called those *light troops* "*our holy ones*," our "*prophets*," "*patriarchs*," etc. Who would call *light troops* a troop of "*patriarchs*"? It was an "opportune" oversight to speak with enthusiasm of the self-denial, moral energy and inspiration with which the *light* troops "thought, worked and studied their life long for the truth." It was an "oversight" when, in the preface to *Das entdeckte Christenthum*, it was stated that those "*light*" troops "seemed invincible and any one *well-informed* would have wagered that they would *pull the world to pieces*" and that "it seemed beyond doubt that they would succeed in giving *the world a new shape*." *Those light troops*?

Critical Criticism continues to teach the representative of the "*cordial mass*": "If it was a *new* historical merit of the French to attempt to set up a social theory, they are *now all the same exhausted*; their new theory was not yet *pure*, their social fantasies, their *peaceful democracy* are by no means free from the presumptions of the old system."

Criticism is talking here about *Fourierism*—if anything—and in particular of Fourierism as expounded by *Démocratie Pacifique*.[41] But this is far from being the "social theory" of the French. The French have *social theories*, but not *a* social theory; the diluted Fourierism that *Démocratie Pacifique* preaches is nothing else than the social doctrine of a section of the philanthropic bourgeoisie. The people is *communistic*, and, as a matter of fact, split into a number of different groups; the true movement and the elaboration of these different social shades is not only *not exhausted*, it is really only *beginning*. But it will not end in pure, i.e., abstract *theory* as Critical Criticism would like it to; it will end in a very *practical practice* that will not bother at all about the categorical categories of Criticism.

"No nation," Criticism chatters on, "has *as yet any* advantage over another. ...." "If one can win some spiritual superiority over another, it will be the one which is in a position to criticize itself and the others and to discover the causes of the universal decay."

Every nation has *so far some advantage over* another. But if the Critical prophesy is right, no nation *will have* any advantage over another because all the civilized peoples of Europe, the English, the Germans and the French now "*criticize* themselves and others" and "are in a position to discover the causes of the universal decay." Finally it is a high-sounding *tautology* to say that "criticizing," "discovering," i.e., *spiritual* activities, give a *spiritual superiority*; and Criticism, who in its infinitive self-consciousness places itself above the nations and expects them to kneel at its feet and implore it for englightenment, only shows by this caricaturized Christian-German idealism that it is still up to its neck in the filth of *German nationalism*.

The criticism of the French and the English is not an abstract, preternatural personality outside mankind; it is the *real human activity* of individuals who are active members of society and who suffer, feel, think and act as human beings. That is why their criticism is at the same time practical, their communism a socialism which gives practical, concrete measures and in which they do not just think but act even more, it is the living real criticism of existing society, the discovery of the causes of "the decay."

After Criticism's explanations for the inquisitive member of the mass, it is entitled to say of its *Literatur-Zeitung*:

"Here *pure*, tangible, relevant criticism that adds nothing is practised."

Here "*nothing self-existing* is given"; here *nothing at all* is given except *Criticism that gives nothing*, that is, criticism which has developed to extreme non-criticism. *Criticism* has underlined passages printed and reaches its full bloom *in excerpts*. *Wolfgang Menzel* and *Bruno Bauer* stretch a brotherly hand to each other and where the *philosophy of identity* stood at the beginning of this century, when *Schelling* protested against the massy supposition that he wanted to give something, anything except *pure entirely philosophical philosophy*, stands Critical Criticism.

c) Mercy Pours Forth on the Mass

The soft-hearted correspondent whose instruction we have just attended was in a *comfortable* relation to Criticism. In him there was only an idyllic hint of the tension between *Mass* and *Criticism*. Both sides of the *world-historic contradiction* behaved *kindly* and *politely*, and therefore *exoterically*, to each other.

Critical Criticism, in its *unhealthy* soul-shattering influence on the Mass, appears first in a correspondent who has one foot in Criticism and the other still in the profane world. He represents the "Mass" in its *interior* struggle with Criticism.

At times it seems to him "that Herr Bruno and his friends do not understand *mankind*," that they are really blinded. Then he immediately corrects himself:

"Yes, it is *as clear as daylight* to me that you are right and that your thoughts are correct; but *excuse* me, the people is *not* wrong *either*.... Of course, the people is right!... I cannot deny that you are right.... I really do not know what it will all lead to: you will say ... well, stay at home.... Ah! I just cannot.... Ah! One must *go mad* in the end....

Kindly accept.... Believe me, the knowledge one has acquired sometimes makes one feel as silly as if a mill-wheel were turning in one's head."

Another correspondent also writes that he "is *occasionally disconcerted*." One can see that *Critical Mercy is working to pour forth* in this massy correspondent. The poor wretch! The sinful Mass is tugging at him on one side and Critical Criticism on the other. It is not the knowledge he has acquired that stupefies this catechumen of Critical Criticism; it is the question: *faith* and *conscience*, Critical Christ or the people, God or the world, Bruno Bauer and his friends or the profane Mass! But as the shower of *divine* mercy is preceded by desperate perplexity on the part of the sinner, *Critical* mercy is preceded by a crushing *stupefaction*. And when Critical mercy at last breaks through, the chosen one loses not stupidity but the *consciousness of stupidity*.

3) The Un-Critically Critical Mass or "Criticism" and the "Berlin Couleur"

Critical Criticism did not succeed in presenting itself as the *essential opposite*, and hence at the same time as the *essential object*, of the mass of humanity. The representative of the *obdurate* mass reproaches Critical Criticism *for its objectlessness* and gives it to understand in the most courteous possible way that it has not yet had its spiritual "*moult*" and must first of all acquire solid knowledge. Besides him there is the *soft-hearted* correspondent. He is no *opposite* at all, but then the actual reason for his approach to Critical Criticism is a *purely personal* one. As we can see by further reading his letter, he really only wants to conciliate his devotion for Herr Arnold Ruge with his devotion to Herr *Bruno Bauer*. This attempt at conciliation does credit to his kind heart, but it in no way constitutes a *massy interest*. Finally, the last correspondent we saw was no long

er a *real* member of the Mass, he was only a catechumen of
Critical Criticism.

In general the *mass* is only an *indefinite* object and can
therefore neither carry out a definite action nor enter into
a definite relation. *The* Mass, as the object of Critical Crit·
icism, has nothing in common with the *real* masses who, in
turn, form very massy contradictions between themselves.
Critical Criticism's mass is "made" by itself, as would be
the case of a naturalist who, instead of speaking of definite
classes, contrasted *the* "Class" to himself.

Hence, in order to have a really massy contradiction,
Critical Criticism needs, besides this *abstract* mass which is
the figment of its own brain, a *definite* mass that can be
empirically proved and not just presumed. This mass must
see in Critical Criticism both its *essence* and the *annihilation
of its essence*. It must *wish* to be Critical Criticism, non-
Mass, without *being able to*. This Critically un-Critical mass
is the above-mentioned *Berlin Couleur*. The *mass* of humanity which seriously engages in Critical Criticism is confined
to a Berlin Couleur.

The "Berlin Couleur" the *"essential object"* of Critical
Criticism, of whom it is always thinking and who, Critical
Criticism imagines, is always thinking of Critical Criticism,
consists as far as we know, of a few *ci-devant* young
Hegelians* whom Critical Criticism maintains that it inspires
partly with *horror vacui*** and partly with a feeling of *nothingness*. We are not investigating actual facts, we rely on
what *Criticism* said.

The *Correspondence* is mainly intended to expound at
length to the public this *historic* relation of Criticism to the
"Berlin Couleur," to reveal its profound significance, to
show why Criticism must be cruel towards this "Mass," and

---

* Former.—*Ed.*
** Horror of emptiness.—*Ed*

finally to make it appear that *the whole world* is in fearful agitation over this contradiction and now supports, now opposes the action of Criticism. For example, *Absolute* Criticism writes to a correspondent who sides with the "Berlin Couleur":

"I have *so often* heard things *like that already* that I have made up my mind not to take any more notice of them."

The world has no idea how often it has to deal with critical things *like that*.

Let us now hear what a member of the *Critical* mass reports on the *Berlin Couleur*:

"If anybody recognizes the Bauers" (the Holy Family must always be recognized pell-mell), "he begins his answer, *I* am the one. But "*Literatur-Zeitung*! Each one his due. It was interesting for me to hear what one of those radicals, those clever men of *anno* 42, thought of you...."

The correspondent goes on to say that the unfortunate man had all sorts of reproaches to make to *Literatur-Zeitung*.

Herr Edgar's tale *The Three Good Fellows*, he thought, lacked polish and was exaggerated. He could not understand that the *censorship* is less a fight of man against man, an external fight, than an internal one. They do not take the trouble to collect themselves and to replace the *phrase the censor objects to* by a *cleverly* expressed and thoroughly developed *Critical thought*. He found Herr Edgar's essay on Béraud lacking in thoroughness. The Critical reporter thought it did not. He admitted himself: "I have *not* read Béraud's book." But he *believed* that Herr Edgar had *succeeded*, etc., and belief, we know, is bliss. "In general," the Critical believer continued, "he" (the one from the Berlin Couleur) "is *not at all satisfied* with Herr Edgar's works." He also found that "*Proudhon* is not dealt with *thoroughly* enough." And here the reporter gives credit to Herr Edgar:

14—1192

"*I admit that I know*" (!?) "Proudhon, I know that Edgar's presentation took its *characteristic* points from him and obviously put them all together."

The only reason why Herr Edgar's *excellent* criticism of Proudhon is not liked, the reporter says, must be that Herr Edgar does *not fulminate* against property. And just imagine it, the opponent finds Herr Edgar's essay on the "*Union Ouvrière*" *insignificant*.

To console Herr Edgar the reporter says: "Naturally it does not give anything *self-contained*, and these people have really gone back to *Gruppe's* point of view, which, to be sure, they have *always maintained*. *Criticism* must give, give and give!"

As though *Criticism* had not given quite new linguistical, historical, philosophical, political-economical and juridical discoveries! And it is so modest as to let it be said that it has not given anything *self-contained*! Even our Critical correspondent gave mechanics something that it had not known when he made people *go back* to the point of view which they had *always maintained*. It is clumsy to recall *Gruppe's* point of view. In his pamphlet, which is otherwise miserable and not worth mentioning, he asked Herr Bruno what criticism he could give on *speculative logic*. Herr Bruno referred him to future generations and—

"*a fool is waiting for an answer.*"[42]

As God punished the unbelieving Pharaoh by hardening his heart and did *not think him deserving* of enlightenment, so the reporter affirms: "They are therefore *not in the least worthy* to see or recognize the content of your *Literatur-Zeitung*."

And instead of advising his friend Edgar to acquire thoughts and knowledge he gives him the following advice: "Let Edgar get a *bag of phrases* and draw blindly out of it when he writes essays in the future, in order to acquire a style in harmony with the public."

Besides assurances of "a certain fury, ill-favour, emptiness, lack of thought, surmises at things they are not able to
get to the bottom of and a feeling of nullity," (all epithets
which apply, naturally, to the *Berlin Couleur*) eulogies like
the following are made of the Holy Family:

"Lightness of treatment permeating the matter, mastery
of the categories, insight acquired by study, in a word,
mastery of *its* objects. He" (of the *Berlin Couleur*) "takes it
easy with the thing, you make the thing easy." Or: "in
Literatur-Zeitung your criticism is pure, tangible and
relevant."

At the end we read: "I have written it all to you at such
length because I know that I shall cause you *pleasure* by
reporting the opinions of my friend. From this you can see
that *Literatur-Zeitung* is fulfilling its purpose."

Its purpose is opposition to the Berlin Couleur. As we have
just witnessed the *Berlin Couleur's polemic* against Critical
Criticism and the reproof it got for it, we shall now have a
double picture of its efforts to obtain mercy from Critical
Criticism.

One correspondent writes: "My acquaintances in Berlin
told me when I was there at the beginning of the year that
you repel all and keep all at a distance; that you keep to
yourself and let nobody approach you, purposely avoiding
all intercourse. I, of course, cannot tell which side is to
blame."

Absolute Criticism answers: "Criticism does *not* form any
party and will have no party of its own: it is *solitary* because
it is plunged in *its*" (!) "object and opposes itself to it. It
isolates itself from everything."

Critical Criticism thinks it rises above all dogmatic
contradictions by substituting the imaginary contradiction
between *itself* and the *world*, between the *Holy Ghost* and
the *profane Mass* for the real contradictions. In the same
way it thinks it rises above *parties* by falling *below the party*

14•

point of view, by opposing itself as a *party* to the rest of mankind and concentrating all its interest in the person of Herr Bruno and Co. The truth of Criticism's *admission* that it thrones in the solitude of *abstraction*, that even when it seems to be engaged with some *object* it does not come out of its objectless solitude into any true *social relation* to any *real object*, because *its object* is the object of *its imagination*, only an imaginary object—the truth of all this proves the whole of our argument. Just as correct is its definition of its *abstraction* as *absolute* abstraction, in the sense that "it *isolates itself* from *everything*," and in just the same way this isolation of *nothing* from *everything*, from *all* thought, contemplation, etc., is *absolute nonsense*. By the way, the solitude which it achieves by isolating and abstracting itself *from everything* is no more free from the object from which it abstracts itself than *Origenes* was from the *genital organ* that he *cut off* from himself.

⌐ Another correspondent begins by describing a member of the Berlin Couleur whom "he saw and spoke with," as "gloomy," "depressed," "no longer able to open his mouth" (although he was formerly "always ready with a quite *impudent* word"), and "despondent." This member of the Berlin Couleur related the following to the correspondent, who in turn reported it to Criticism.

"He cannot grasp how people like you two, who formerly respected the principle of humanity, can behave in such a retiring, repulsive even arrogant manner." He does not know "why there are some people who, it seems, intentionally cause a split. Have we not all the same point of view? Do we not all *do homage* to the extreme, to criticism? Are we not all capable, if not of producing, at least of grasping and applying an extreme thought?" He "finds that this split is motivated by no other principle than egotism and arrogance."

Then the correspondent puts in a good word:

"Have not at least some of our friends grasped Criticism, or perhaps *the good will of Criticism ... ut desint vires, tamen est laudanda voluntas.*"*

Criticism answers by the following *antitheses* between itself and the *Berlin Couleur*:

"There are *various* standpoints on criticism." The members of *Berlin Couleur* "thought they had criticism in their pocket," but Criticism "really knows and applies the force of criticism," i.e., does not keep it in its pocket. For the former criticism is pure form, while for Criticism it is the *"most substantial"* or rather the "only *substantial.*" As Absolute Thinking is for itself the whole of reality, *so* it is with Critical Criticism. That is why it sees no content *outside itself* and is therefore not the criticism of *real* objects lying outside the critical subject; on the contrary, it *makes* the object, it is the Absolute *Subject-Object.* Further. "The first kind of criticism gets over everything and over the investigation of things, with phrases. The second isolates itself *from everything* with phrases." The first is *"clever in its ignorance,"* the — second is *"learning."* The second, by the way, is not clever, it learns *par çà, par là,*** but only in appearance, only in order to be able to fling what it has superficially learnt from the mass back at the mass in the form of a "motto," as wisdom it has discovered itself, and to resolve it into the nonsense of Critical Criticism.

For the first, words such as "extreme," "proceed," "not go far enough" are of importance and are most revered categories; the latter *sounds the points of view* and does not apply to them the *measures* of those abstract categories.

The exclamations of Criticism No. 2 that it is no longer a question of politics, that philosophy is disposed of the way it dismisses social systems and development with words like "fantastic," "utopian," etc.—what is all that if not a *Criti-*

---

* Though strength be lacking, will is, however, praiseworthy.—*Ed.*
** Here and there. —*Ed.*

cally revised version of "proceeding" and "not going far enough"? And are not its "measures," such as "history," "criticism," "summing up of objects," "the old and the new," "criticism and mass," "investigation of standpoints"—in a word, all its mottos, *categorical measures* and abstractly categorical ones too?

"The former is theological, spiteful, envious, petty, presumptuous, the latter is the *opposite* of all that."

After thus praising itself a dozen times in one breath and ascribing to itself all that the Berlin Couleur lacks, as God *is* all that man *is not*, Criticism bears witness to itself that: "It has achieved a clarity, a thirst for learning, a tranquillity in which it is *unassailable* and *invincible*."

Hence it can "at the most treat its opposite, the *Berlin Couleur*, with *Olympic laughter*." This laughter—it explains with its usual thoroughness what it is and what it is not— "this laughter is not arrogance." Not on your life! It is the negation of the negation. It is *"only the process* that *the critic must apply* in all composure and equanimity against a *subordinate standpoint* which *thinks* itself *equal* to him" (What conceit!). When *the* Critic laughs, therefore, he is *applying a process!* And "in all equanimity" he applies the *process of laughter* not against *persons*, but *against a standpoint!* Even *laughter* is a *category* which it applies and even *must* apply!

Extramundane criticism is not an *essential activity* of the *real human subject* which, being real, lives and suffers in the society of today, sharing in its pains and pleasures. The *real* individual is only an *accidence*, an earthly vessel of Critical Criticism which reveals itself in it as the *eternal substance*. The subject is not the human individual's criticism, but the *non-human individual of Criticism*. Criticism is not a *manifestation of man, but man is an estrangement of Criticism*, and that is why the critic lives completely outside society.

"Can the critic live in the society which he criticizes?"

It should be: Must he not live in that society? Must he not himself be a manifestation of the life of that society? Why does the critic *sell* the product of his mind since by it he makes the worst law of the society of today his own law?

"*The Critic* must not even dare to mix *personally* with society."

That is why he sets up for himself a *holy family*, just as the solitary God endeavours to do away with his boring isolation from society in the Holy Family. If the critic *wants to free himself* from *bad society* he must first of all free himself from *his own society*.

"Thus the critic dispenses with *all the pleasures of society*, but *its sufferings too* are kept away from him. He knows neither *friendship*" (except Critical friendship) "nor love" (except *self-love*) "but then calumny is powerless against him; nothing can offend him; no hatred, no envy can affect him; vexation and grief are *feelings unknown* to him."

In short, the Critic is free from all *human passions*, he is a *divine person*; he can apply to himself the song of the nun

> *I think not of a lover,*
> *I think not of a spouse.*
> *I think of God the Father,*
> *For he my life endows.*[43]

Critical Criticism cannot write about a single point without contradicting itself. Thus it tells us finally that "the Philistinism that stones the critic" (he had to be stoned by analogy with the bible) "that misjudges him and ascribes *impure* motives to him"—ascribes *impure* motives to *pure* Criticism!) "to make *him equal to itself*" (the conceit of equality reproved above!) "is *not laughed at* by him, because it is not worth it; but is seen through and quietly relegated back to its own insignificant significance."

Earlier the Critic *had to* apply the *process* of *laughter* to "the subordinate standpoint that thought itself equal to him." Critical Criticism's uncertainty about the way it has to deal with the godless "Mass" seems almost to indicate interior irritation, a sort of bile for which "feelings" are not "unknown."

No mistake must be made about it. Having waged a herculean struggle *to free* itself from the un-Critical "profane Mass" and "everything," Critical Criticism has at last happily elaborated its *lonely, godly, self-satisfied, absolute* existence. If in its first pronouncements in this, its "new phase," the old world of *sinful feelings* seems still to have some power over it, we shall now see Criticism find aesthetic refreshment and *transfiguration* in an *artistic form* and complete its *penance* so that it can finally carry out the *Critical last judgement* like a second triumphant *Christ*, and, after defeating the dragon, ascend calmly to heaven.

CHAPTER VIII

THE WORLDLY PEREGRINATION AND THE TRANSFIGURATION OF CRITICAL CRITICISM,

OR

CRITICAL CRITICISM IN THE PERSON OF RUDOLPH, PRINCE OF GEROLDSTEIN

Rudolph, Prince of Geroldstein *does penance* in his *worldly peregrination* for a *double* crime: his *personal* crime and the crime of *Critical Criticism*. In a furious dialogue he drew his sword against his father; Critical Criticism, also in a furious dialogue, let itself be carried away by sinful feelings against the Mass. Critical Criticism did *not* reveal *a single* mystery. Rudolph does penance for that and reveals *all* mysteries.

Rudolph, Herr Szeliga informs us, is the *first* servant of the *state* of humanity ("The Humanity-State," by the Suabian Egidius. cf. *Konstitutionelle Jahrbücher* by Dr. Karl Weil, 1844, Vol. 2).

For *the world not to be destroyed*, Herr Szeliga affirms, it is necessary for

"men of ruthless criticism to appear ... Rudolph is a man of *that kind.* ... Rudolph grasps the thought of *pure criticism*. And that thought is more fruitful for him and all humanity than *all* the experience of humanity in its whole *history*, than *all* the knowledge that Rudolph, directed even by the most reliable teacher, could have derived from that history.—The impartial judgement by which Rudolph per-

petuates his *worldly peregrination* is, *in fact*, nothing
else than:

the revelation of the mysteries of society."
He is *"the mystery of all mysteries revealed."*

Rudolph has far more *exterior* means at his disposal than
the other men of Critical Criticism. But the latter consoles
itself:

"Unattainable for those less favoured by destiny are
Rudolph's *results"* (!), "not unattainable is his splendid
aim" (!).

That is why Criticism leaves the *realization* of its *own
thoughts* to Rudolph, who is so favoured by destiny. It sings
to him:

> *Hahnemann, Go on ahead.
> You've waders on, you won't get wet!*[44]

Let us accompany Rudolph in his Critical worldly peregrination which "is *more fruitful* for *humanity* than *all the
experience* of humanity in its whole history, than *all the
knowledge* etc., and which saves the world *twice* from *destruction.*

1) Critical Transformation of a Butcher into a Dog, or *Chourineur*

Chourineur was a butcher by trade. A concourse of
circumstances makes this mighty son of nature a murderer.
Rudolph comes across him accidentally as he is molesting
Fleur de Marie. Rudolph gives the dexterous brawler a few
impressive, masterly punches in the head, and thus wins
his respect. Later, in the criminals' tavern *Chourineur's*
kind-hearted disposition is revealed. "You still have heart
and honour," Rudolph says to him. By these words he fires
Chourineur with respect for himself. *Chourineur* amends or,
as Herr Szeliga says, is transformed into a *"moral* being."

Rudolph takes him under his protection. Let us follow the course of *Chourineur's* education under the direction of Rudolph.

1st Stage. The first lesson *Chourineur* gets is a lesson in hypocrisy, faithlessness, craft and *dissimulation.* Rudolph uses the moralized *Chourineur* in exactly the same way as *Vidocq* used the criminals he had moralized, i.e., he makes him a *mouchard* and *agent provocateur.* He advises him to "*pretend*" to the *gang leader* that he has altered his "principle of not-stealing" and to suggest a robbery so as to lure him into the trap set by Rudolph. *Chourineur* feels that he is being abused of for a "farce." He protests against the suggestion of playing the role of *mouchard* and *agent provocateur.* Rudolph easily enough convinces the son of nature by the "pure" *casuistry* of Critical Criticism that a foul trick is not foul when it is done for "*good, moral*" motives. *Chourineur*, as an agent provocateur and under the pretence of friendship and confidence, lures his former companion to destruction. For the *first time in his life* he commits an act of *infamy.*

2nd Stage. We next find *Chourineur* acting as *sick attendant* to Rudolph, whom he has saved from mortal danger.

Chourineur has become such a *decent moral being* that he rejects the Negro doctor David's suggestion to sit on the floor, for fear of dirtying the carpet. He is indeed too *shy* to sit on a chair. He first lays the chair on its back and then sits on the front legs. He never fails to apologize when he addresses Rudolph, whom he saved from a mortal danger, as "friend" or "*Monsieur*" instead of "*Monseigneur*."

What a wonderful breaking-in of a ruthless son of nature! *Chourineur* expresses the innermost secret of his Critical transformation when he admits to Rudolph that he has the same attachment for him as a *bull-dog* for its master: "*Je me sens pour vous, comme qui dirait l'attachement d'un bouledogue pour son maître.*" The former butcher is changed into a dog. Henceforth all his virtues will be resolved into the virtue of a dog, *pure "devotion"* to its master. His independence, his individuality will disappear completely. But as bad painters must label their painting to say what it is supposed to represent, Eugène Sue must put a label in *"bull-dog" Chourineur's* mouth so that he constantly affirms: "The two words, 'You still have heart and honour,' made a *man* out of me." Till his very last breath *Chourineur* will find the motives for his actions, not in his human individuality, but in that label. As a proof of his moral amendment he will often reflect on his own excellence and the wickedness of other individuals. And every time he throws about moralizing expressions, Rudolph will say to him: "I like to hear you *speak* like that." *Chourineur* has not become an ordinary *bull-dog* but *a moral one.*

3rd Stage. We have already admired the *petty-bourgeois decency* which has taken the place of *Chourineur's coarse* but *daring* unceremoniousness. We now learn that, as he becomes a *"moral being,"* he has also adopted the gait and demeanour of the *petty bourgeois.*

"To see his gait you would have taken him for the most harmless *petty bourgeois* in the world."

Still more distressing than this form is the content that Rudolph gives his Critically reformed like. He sends him to Africa "to show a living and salutary example of repentance to the unbelieving world." In future he will have to demonstrate, not his own human nature, but a Christian dogma.

4th Stage. The Critically moral transformation has made *Chourineur* a quiet, cautious man who behaves according to the rules of fear and worldly wisdom.

"Le Chourineur," reports Murph, who in his indiscreet simplicity continually tells tales out of school, *"n'a pas dit un mot de l'éxécution de maître d'école, de peur de se trouver compromis."*

So *Chourineur* knows that the execution of the leader was illegal. But he does not talk about it for fear of compromising himself. *Wise Chourineur!*

5th Stage. Chourineur has carried his moral education to such perfection that he gives his *canine* devotion to Rudolph a civilized form—becomes conscious of it. After saving *Germain* from a mortal danger he says to him: "I have a protector who is to me what *God* is to *priests*—enough to make one kneel before him."

And in imagination he kneels before his God.

"Monsieur Rudolph," he says to Germain, "protects you. I say '*Monsieur*' though I should say '*Monseigneur.*' But I am used to calling him '*Monsieur* Rudolph,' and he allows me to."

"Magnificent awakening and efflorescence!" exclaims Herr Szeliga in Critical delight.

6th Stage. Chourineur worthily ends his worldly peregrination of pure devotion, of moral bull-doggishness, by letting himself be stabbed to death in the end for his gracious lord. Just as Squelette threatens the prince with his knife, *Chourineur* stops the murderer's arm. Squelette stabs him. But, dying, *Chourineur* says to Rudolph:

"I was right when I said that a handful of earth" (a bull-dog) "like me can sometimes be useful to a *great and gracious master* like you."

To this canine utterance, which sums up the whole of *Chourineur's* Critical life like an epigram, the label put in his mouth adds:

"We are quits, Monsieur Rudolph. You told me that I had heart and honour."

Herr Szeliga cries as loud as he can:

"What a merit it was for Rudolph to have restored the *Shuriman*" (!) "to *humanity* (?)!"

2) Revelation of the Mystery of Critical Religion or *Fleur de Marie*

a) The Speculative "Daisy"

A word more about Herr Szeliga's speculative "Daisy" before we go on to *Eugène Sue's Fleur de Marie*.

The speculative "Daisy" is above all a *correction*. The fact is that the reader could conclude from Herr Szeliga's construction that *Eugène Sue* had "separated the presentation of the objective basis" (of the "world system") "from the development of the acting individual forces which can be understood only with them as a background."

Besides the task of correcting this erroneous conjecture that the reader may have made from Herr Szeliga's presentation, Daisy has also a metaphysical mission in our, or rather Herr Szeliga's "epic."

"The *world system* and epic events *would not* yet *be* artistically combined in a really *single* whole if they only intercrossed in a motley mixture—now here a bit of world system and then there some stage play. If *real unity* is to result, both things, the mysteries of this prejudiced *world* and the clarity, openness and confidence with which *Rudolph* penetrates and reveals them must clash in a *single* individual.... This is the task of Daisy."

Herr Szeliga construes Daisy by analogy with *Herr Bauer's* construction of the *Mother of God*.

One one side is the *"divine"* Rudolph to which all "power and freedom" are attributed, the only *active* principle. On the other side is the passive *"world system"* and the human beings belonging to it. The world system is the "ground for reality." If this ground is not to be "entirely abandoned" or "the last remnant of the natural situation is not to be abolished"; if the world itself is to have its own share in the "principle of development" that Rudolph, in contrast to the world, concentrates in himself; if "the human is not to be represented as unfree and inactive without qualification," Herr Szeliga must fall into the "contradiction of religious consciousness." Although he tears the world system and its activity asunder as the dualism of a dead mass and Criticism (Rudolph) he is all the same obliged to concede some attributes of divinity to the world system and the mass and to construe in Daisy the speculative unity of the two, of Rudolph and the world (cf. *Kritik der Synoptiker*, Vol. I, p. 39).

Besides the real relations of the *owner*, the active "individual force," to his *house* the "objective basis"—mystic speculation, and aesthetic speculation too, needs a third *concrete, speculative unity,* a *subject-object* which is the house and the owner *in one.* As speculation does not like natural mediations in their extensive circumstantiality, it does not understand that the same "bit of world system," the house, for example, which for one, the owner, is an "objective basis," is an "epic event" for the other, the builder, for instance. In order to get a "real single whole" and "real unity" Critical Criticism, which reproaches "romantic art" with the "dogma of unity," replaces the natural and human connection between the world system and the world events by a fantastic connection, a mystic subject-object, as *Hegel* replaces the real connection between man and nature by an absolute Subject-Object, that is at the same time the whole of nature and the whole of humanity, the Absolute Spirit.

In Critical Daisy "the universal guilt of the time, the guilt of mystery" becomes the "*mystery of guilt,*" just as the universal debt of mystery becomes the *mystery of debts* in the indebted grocer.

According to the Mother-of-God construction, Daisy should really have been *mother of Rudolph,* the saviour of the world. Herr Szeliga expressly says so:

"Logically, Rudolph should have been the *son* of Daisy."

Since, however, he is not her son, but her father, Herr

Szeliga finds in this "the new mystery that the present often bears the long departed past in its womb instead of the future." He even reveals another mystery, a still greater one, a mystery which directly contradicts massy statistics, the mystery that a "child, if it does not, in its turn, become either father or mother, but goes to its grave pure and innocent, is ... *essentially* ... a *daughter*."

Herr Szeliga faithfully follows Hegel's speculation when, "*logically*" he makes the daughter pass as the mother of her father. In Hegel's *History of Philosophy* as in his *Philosophy of Nature* the son engenders the mother, the Spirit nature, the Christian religion paganism, the result the beginning.

After proving that "*logically*" Daisy ought to have been Rudolph's mother, Herr Szeliga proves the opposite: "in order to conform fully to the *idea* she embodies in *our* epic she *must never become a mother*." This shows at least that the idea of our epic and the logic of Herr Szeliga are mutually contradictory.

Speculative Daisy is nothing but the "*embodiment of an idea*." But what idea? "She has the task of representing, *as it were*, the last tear of grief that the past sheds at its complete disappearance." She is the representation of an allegorical tear, and even the little that she is she is only "*as it were*."

We shall not follow Herr Szeliga in his further presentation of Daisy. We shall leave her the satisfaction, according to Herr Szeliga's prescription, of "constituting *the most decisive* contradiction *to every man*," a mysterious contradiction as mysterious as the attributes of God.

Neither shall we delve into the "*the true mystery*" "deposited *by God* in the breast of man" and at which Speculative Daisy "all the same as it were" hints. We shall pass from Herr Szeliga's Daisy to Eugène Sue's *Fleur de Marie* and to the Critical miraculous cure that Rudolph operates on her.

b) Fleur de Marie

We come across Marie surrounded by criminals, a prostitute, a serf to the proprietress of a criminals' tavern. In this debasement she preserves a human nobleness of soul, a human unaffectedness and a human beauty that impress those around her, raise her to the level of a poetical flower of the criminal world and win for her the name of *Fleur de Marie*.

We must observe *Fleur de Marie* attentively from her first appearance in order to be able to compare her *original form* with her *Critical transformation*.

In spite of her frailty *Fleur de Marie* shows great vitality, energy, cheerfulness, elasticity of character— qualities which alone explain her human development in her *inhuman* situation.

When *Chourineur* ill-treats her, she defends herself with her scissors. That is the situation in which we first find her. She does not appear as a defenceless lamb who surrenders without any resistance to overwhelming brutality; she is a girl that can vindicate her rights and put up a fight.

In the criminals' tavern in rue aux Fèves she tells *Chourineur* and Rudolph her life's story. As she does so she *laughs* at *Chourineur's* wit. She accuses herself of not having looked for work after her release from prison and of having spent on amusements and dresses the 300 francs she had earned. "But," she said, "I had no one to advise me." The memory of the catastrophe of her life—her selling herself to the proprietress of the criminals' tavern—rouses melancholy in her. It is the first time since her childhood that she has recalled these events. "The fact is that it grieves me when I look back ... it must be lovely to be honest." When *Chourineur* makes fun of her and tells her she must become honest, she exclaims: "Honest! My God! What do you want me to be honest with?" She insists that she is not the one "to have fits of tears" ("*je ne suis pas pleurnicheuse*"); but her position in life is sad—"*ce n'est pas gai.*" In the end, contrary to Christian *repentance*, she expresses the *stoic* and at the same time *epicurean*, human principle of a free and strong nature:

"*Enfin ce qui est fait, est fait.*"

Let us go with *Fleur de Marie* on her first outing with Rudolph.

"The consciousness of your terrible situation probably often distressed you," Rudolph says, itching to moralize. "Yes," she answers, "more than once I looked over the parapet of the Seine; but then I would gaze at the flowers and the sun and think the river would always be there and I was only seventeen years old. Who could tell? On such occasions I thought I had not deserved my fate, that I had something good in me. People have tormented me enough, I used to say to myself, but at least I have never done any harm to anybody."

Fleur de Marie considers her situation not as a free creation, not as the expression of her own person, but as a fate she has not deserved. Her bad fortune can change. She is still young.

Good and *evil*, in Marie's mind, are not the moral *abstractions* of good and evil. She is *good* because she has never caused *suffering* to anybody, she has always been *human* towards her inhuman surroundings. She is *good* because the sun and the flowers reveal to her her own sunny and blossoming nature. She is *good* because she is still *young*, full of hope and vitality. Her situation is *not good* because it does her unnatural violence, because it is not the expression of her human impulses, the fulfilment of her human desires; because it is full of torment and void of pleasure. She measures her situation in life by her *own individuality*, her *natural* essence, not by the *ideal of good*.

In *natural* surroundings the chains of bourgeois life fall

off *Fleur de Marie*; she can freely manifest her own nature
and consequently is bubbling with love of life, with a wealth
of feeling, with human joy at the beauty of nature; these
show that the bourgeois system has only grazed the surface
of her and is a mere misfortune, that she herself is neither
good nor bad, but *human*.

"Monsieur Rudolph, what happiness! ... grass, fields! If
you would only let me get out, the weather is so fine.... I
should love to run over those meadows."

Alighting from the carriage she plucks flowers for
Rudolph, "can hardly speak for joy," etc.

Rudolph tells her that he is going to take her to *Madame
Georges' farm*: There she sees dove-cotes, cowstalls and so
forth; there they have milk, butter, fruit, etc. Those are real
blessings for that child. She will *be merry*, that is her main
thought. "You just can't believe how I am longing for some
fun!" She explains to Rudolph without the least constraint
how far she was to blame for her fate. "The cause of my
whole fate was that I did not save up my money." Consequently she advises him to be thrifty and to put money in
the savings bank. Her fancy runs wild in the castles in the
air that Rudolph builds for her. She becomes sad only
because she is "forgetting the *present*" and "the contrast of
that present with the dream of a pleasant and laughing
existence reminds her of the cruelty of her situation."

So far we have seen *Fleur de Marie* in her original un-
Critical form. Eugène Sue has here risen above the horizon
of his own narrow world outlook. He has slapped bourgeois
prejudice in the face. He will hand over *Fleur de Marie* to
the hero Rudolph to make up for his own rashness and to
reap applause from all old men and women, from the whole
of the Paris police, from the current religion and from
"Critical Criticism."

Madame Georges, to whom Rudolph leaves *Fleur de Marie*,
is an unhappy, hypochondriac, religious woman. She immedi-

ately welcomes the child with the unctuous words: "*God blesses those who love and fear him, who have been unhappy and repenting.*" Rudolph, the man of "pure Criticism," has the wretched priest *Laporte*, whose hair has grayed in superstition, called in. He has the mission of accomplishing *Fleur de Marie's* Critical reform.

Joyfully and without constraint, Marie comes to the old priest. In his Christian brutality *Eugène Sue* makes a "marvellous instinct" at once whisper in her ear that "*shame ends where repentance* and *penance* begin," that is, in the church, which alone can give happiness. He forgets the unconstrained merriness of the outing, a merriness which the graces of nature and Rudolph's friendly sympathy had produced, and which was troubled only by the thought of having to go back to the proprietress of the criminals' tavern.

The priest immediately adopts a *supermundane* attitude. His first words are:

"*God's* mercy is infinite, my dear child! He has proved it to you by not abandoning you in your severe trials. ... The magnanimous man who saved you fulfilled the *word of the Scriptures*" (note—the word of the Scriptures, not a human purpose!): "Verily the Lord is nigh to those who invoke him; he will fulfil their desires ... he will hear their voice and will save them ... the Lord will accomplish *his* work."

Marie cannot yet understand the *wicked meaning* of the priest's exhortations. She answers: "I shall pray for those who pitied me and brought me back to God."

Her first thought is *not* for God, it is for her *human* saver and it is *he* that she prays for, not for her *own* absolution. She attributes to her prayer some influence on the salvation of others. Indeed, she is so naive that she supposes she has *already been brought* back to God. The priest feels it his duty to destroy this unorthodox belief.

"Soon," he says, interrupting her, " soon you will deserve absolution, absolution from your great errors ... for, to quote the prophet once more, the Lord holdeth up those who are on the brink of the abyss."

One must not fail to see the inhuman expressions the priest uses. You will soon deserve absolution. *Your sins are not yet forgiven.*

As Laporte, when he receives the girl, tries to arouse in her the *consciousness of her sins*, so Rudolph, as he leaves, presents her with a golden *cross*, the symbol of the *Christian crucifixion* awaiting her.

Marie has already been living for some time on Madame Georges' farm. Let us now listen to a dialogue between the old priest Laporte and Madame Georges. He considers "marriage" out of the question for the girl "because no man, in spite of the priest's guarantee, will have the courage to face the past that has soiled her youth." He adds: "she has great errors to atone for, she should have been sustained by a sense of moral." He proves that she could have remained good just like the commonest of bourgeois: "there are many virtuous people in Paris today." The hypocritical priest knows quite well that every hour of the day, in the busiest streets, those virtuous people of Paris go past little girls of 7 or 8 years selling matches and the like up to midnight as Marie herself used to do and who, almost without exception, will have the same fate as Marie.

The priest has decided to make Marie *repent*; inside himself he has already *condemned* her. Let us go with Marie when she is accompanying Laporte home in the evening.

"See, my child," he begins with unctuous eloquence, the boundless horizon the limits of which are not to be seen" (remember it is in the evening) "it seems to me that the calm and the vastness almost give us the idea of eternity. ... I am telling you this, Marie, because you are sensitive to the beauty of creation. ... I have often been moved by the religious fascination which they inspire you with, you who for so long were deprived of the sentiment of religion."

The priest has already succeeded in changing Marie's immediate naive pleasure in the beauties of nature into *religious* fascination. For her, *nature* has already become a devote, *christianized* nature, debased to *creation*. The transparent sea of space is desecrated and turned into a dark symbol of stagnant *eternity*. She has already learnt that all human manifestations of her being were "profane," devoid of religion, the real consecration, that they were impious and godless. The priest must soil her in her own eyes, he must trample underfoot her moral capacities and gifts to make her receptive to the supernatural grace he promises her, *baptism*.

When Marie wants to make a confession and asks him to be lenient he answers:

"The *Lord* has shown you that he is merciful." In the clemency of which she is the object Marie must not see a natural unquestioned relation of one human being to her, another human being. She must see in it a transcendent, supernatural, superhuman mercy and condescension; in *human lenience* she must see *divine mercy*. She must see all human beings and human relations in the transcendental plane of *relations to God*. The way *Fleur de Marie* in her answer accepts the priest's prattle about divine mercy shows how far she has been spoilt by religious doctrine.

As soon as she entered upon her improved situation, she said, she felt *new happiness*.

"I kept thinking of Monsieur Rudolph. I often raised my eyes to heaven, to look, not for God, but Monsieur Rudolph there and to thank him. Yes, *I confess*, Father. *I thought more* of him than of *God*; for *he* did for me what God alone could have done.... I was *happy*, as happy as anybody who has escaped a great danger for ever."

Fleur de Marie already finds it wrong that she took a new happy situation in life simply for what it *really was*, that she felt it as a new happiness, that her attitude to it was a natural, not a supernatural one. She accuses herself of seeing in the man who saved her what he *really* was, her saver, instead of supposing some imaginary saviour, *God*, in his place. She is already caught in religious hypocrisy which takes away from *another man* what he has deserved in respect of me in order to give it to God and which considers anything and everything human in man as alien to God and everything inhuman in him as *really* God's own.

Marie tells us that the *religious transformation* of her thoughts, her sentiments, her attitude towards life was effected by Madame Georges and Laporte.

"When Rudolph took me away from the city I already had a vague consciousness of my degradation.... But the education, the advice and examples I got from Madame Georges and from you made me understand ... that I had been more guilty than unfortunate. Madame Georges and you made me *realize the infinite depth of my damnation.*"

That means that she owes to the priest Laporte and Madame Georges the replacement of the human and therefore bearable consciousness of her debasement by the Christian and hence unbearable consciousness of eternal damnation. The priest and the bigot have taught her to judge herself from the *Christian point of view.*

Marie feels the depth of the moral misfortune into which she has been cast. She says:

"Since the consciousness of good and evil had to be so fatal to me, why was I not left to my wretched fate?... Had I not been snatched away from infamy, misery and blows would soon have killed me. At least I should have died in ignorance of a purity that I shall always regret not to have."

The heartless priest answers:

"The most generously gifted nature, were it to be plunged only for a day in the filth from which you have been saved would be *indelibly branded*. That is the *immutability of divine justice!*"

Deeply wounded by the *priest's* smooth honeyed *curse Fleur de Marie* exclaims: "You see yourself, I must despair!"

The gray-headed slave of religion answers:

"You must renounce all hope of effacing this desolate page from your life, but you must trust in the *infinite mercy of God. Here below*, my poor child, you will have tears, remorse and penance, but one day *on high* forgiveness and *eternal bliss!*"

Marie is not yet stupid enough to be satisfied with eternal happiness and forgiveness *on high*.

"Pity, pity my God!" she cries. "I am so young. How wretched I am!"

Then the hypocritical sophistry of the priest reaches its peak:

"Happiness for you, on the contrary, Marie; happiness for you to whom the Lord sends this bitter but saving remorse! It shows the *religious* sensibility of your soul. . . . Each of your sufferings will be marked down to you on high. Believe me, God left you a while on the path of evil only to reserve for you the *glory of repentance* and the eternal reward due to penance."

From this moment Marie is a *serf of consciousness of sin*. In her unhappy situation in life she was able to become a lovable, human individual; in her exterior debasement she was conscious that *her human* essence was *her true essence*. Now the filth of modern society which has come into exterior contact with her becomes her innermost being: continual hypochondriac self-torture because of that filth will be her duty, the task of her life appointed by God himself, the self-aim of her existence. Formerly she boasted: "I am not the one to have fits of tears" and knew that "what's done is done." Now self-torment will be her *good* and remorse will be her *glory*.

It turns out later that *Fleur de Marie* is Rudolph's daughter. We find her again as Princess of Geroldstein. We overhear a conversation she has with her father:

"It is in vain that I pray to God to deliver me from these obsessions, to fill my heart only with his pious love and his holy hopes; in a word, to take me entirely, because I wish to give myself entirely to him. . . . He does not grant my wishes, doubtless because my *earthly* preoccupations make me unworthy of intercourse with him."

When man has realized that his errings are *infinite* crimes against God he can be sure of *salvation* and *mercy* only if he gives himself *entirely* to God and dies *entirely* to the world and worldly occupations. When *Fleur de Marie* realizes that her delivery from her inhuman situation in life was a miracle of *God* she must become a *saint herself* in order to be worthy of that *miracle*. Her human love must be transformed into religious love, the desire for happiness into the striving for eternal bliss, worldly satisfaction into holy hope, intercourse with man into intercourse with God. God must take her entirely. She herself reveals to us why he does not take her entirely. She has not *given* herself entirely to him, her heart is still preoccupied and engaged with earthly affairs. This is the last blaze of her strong nature. She gives herself entirely up to God by dying entirely to the world and going into a *convent*.

> *A monastery is no place for him*
> *Who has no stock of sins laid in*
> *So numerous and great*
> *That be it early, be it late,*
> *He may not miss the sweet delight*
> *Of penance for a heart contrite.*

> (Goethe.)

In the convent *Fleur de Marie* is made abbess *through* the intrigues of Rudolph. At first she refuses to accept this appointment because she feels unworthy. The old abbess persuades her:

"I shall say more, my dear daughter: if before entering the fold your life had been as prodigal as it was pure and praiseworthy ... the *evangelical virtues* that you have given the example of since you have been here would atone for and redeem your past in the eyes of the Lord, no matter how sinful it had been."

From what the abbess says we see that *Fleur de Marie's* worldly virtues have changed into evangelical virtues, or rather that her real virtues may no longer appear otherwise than as evangelical caricatures.

Marie answers the abbess:

"Holy Mother, I now believe I can accept."

Convent life does not suit Marie's individuality—she dies. Christianity consoles her only in imagination, or rather her Christian consolation is precisely the annihilation of her real life and essence—her death.

So Rudolph changed *Fleur de Marie* first into a repentant sinner, then the repentant sinner into a nun and finally the nun into a corpse. Besides the Catholic priest, the Critical priest Szeliga also preaches a sermon over her grave.

Her *"innocent"* existence he calls her *"transient"* existence, opposing it to "eternal and unforgettable guilt." He praises the fact that her *last breath* was a "prayer for forgiveness and pardon." But as the protestant minister, after expounding the necessity of the Lord's mercy, the participation of the deceased in universal original sin and the intensity of his consciousness of sin, must praise the virtues of the departed in *worldly* terms, so, too, Herr Szeliga uses the expression:

"And yet *personally*, she has nothing to ask forgiveness for."

Finally he throws on her grave the most faded flower of pulpit eloquence:

"Inwardly pure as human beings seldom are, she has closed her eyes to this world."

Amen!

3) Revelation of the Mysteries of Law

a) The Gang Leader, or the New Penal Theory.
The Mystery of the Cell System Revealed.
Medical Mysteries

The gang leader is a criminal of herculean strength and great moral energy. He was brought up an educated and well-schooled man. This passionate athlete clashes with the laws and customs of bourgeois society whose universal yardstick is mediocrity, delicate morals and quiet trade. He becomes a murderer and abandons himself to all the excesses of a violent temperament that can nowhere find a fitting human occupation.

Rudolph captures this criminal. He wants to reform him Critically and set him as an example for the *world of law*. He quarrels with the world of law not over *"punishment"* itself, but over *kinds* and *methods* of punishment. He invents, as the Negro doctor David aptly expresses it, a penal theory worthy of the *"greatest German criminal expert"* which has since been even fortunate enough to be defended by a German criminal specialist with German earnestness and German thoroughness. Rudolph has not the slightest idea that one can rise *above* criminal experts: his ambition is to be *"the greatest criminal expert,"* *primus inter pares.** He has the gang leader *blinded* by the Negro doctor David.

At first Rudolph repeats ' all the trivial objections to

---

* The first among equals.—*Ed.*

capital punishment: that it has no effect on the criminal and
no effect on the people, for whom it seems to be an entertaining scene.

Further Rudolph establishes a difference between the gang
leader and the *soul* of the gang leader. It is not the man,
the *real* gang leader whom he wishes to save; he wants the
spiritual salvation of his *soul*.

"The salvation of a soul," he teaches, "is a holy affair. . . .
Every crime can be *atoned for and redeemed*, the Saviour
said, but only if the criminal earnestly desires to repent and
atone. The transition from the court to the scaffold is too
short. . . . You" (the gang leader) "have criminally abused
of your *strength*, I shall *paralyze* your strength . . . you will
tremble before the weakest . . . your punishment will be
equal to your crime . . . but that terrible punishment will at
least leave you the immense horizon of *penance*. . . . I shall
cut you off only from the outer world in order to plunge you
in impenetrable night, and leave you *alone* with the memory
of your ignominious deeds. . . . You will be forced to look
into yourself . . . your intelligence that you have degraded
will be roused and will lead you to penance."

As Rudolph considers the *soul* of man to be *holy* and his
body profane, as he therefore considers only the soul to be
the true essence because, in Herr Szeliga's Critical description of humanity, it belongs to heaven, the body and the
strength of the gang leader do not belong to humanity, the
manifestation of their essence cannot be given human form
or vindicated for humanity and it must not be dealt with
humanly as an essentially human thing.

The gang leader has abused of his strength, Rudolph
paralyzes, lames, destroys that strength. There is no more
Critical means of getting rid of the incorrect manifestations
of the essential force of man than to annihilate that essential
force. This is the Christian means—plucking out the eye or
cutting off the hand if it scandalizes, in a word, killing the

body if the body scandalizes; for the eye, the hand, the body are really but superfluous sinful appendages of man. Human nature must be killed in order to heal its illnesses. Massy jurisprudence too, in unison with the Critical, sees in the laming and paralyzing of human strength the antidote to the undesirable manifestations of that strength.

What Rudolph, the man of pure Criticism, objects to in profane criminal justice is the too sudden transition from the court to the scaffold. He, on the other hand, wants to link *vengeance* on the criminal with *repentance* and *consciousness of sin* in the criminal, corporal punishment with moral punishment, sensuous torture with the non-sensuous pangs of remorse. Profane punishment must at the same time be a means of Christian moral education.

This penal theory, which links *jurisprudence with theology,* this "revealed mystery of the mystery" is nothing else than the penal theory of the *Catholic* Church. *Bentham* proved this at great length in his work *Theorie des peines et des récompenses.* In that book Bentham also proved the moral futility of punishments of today. He calls legal penalties *"legal parodies."*

The punishment that Rudolph imposed on the gang leader is the same as that *Origenes* imposed on himself. It *emasculates* him, it robs him of a *productive organ,* the eye. "Your eye is the light of your body." It is a great credit to Rudolph's religious instinct that he should hit, of all things, upon the idea of *blinding.* That punishment was favoured in the thoroughly Christian empire of Byzantium and in the vigorous youth of the Christian-Germanic state in England and Franconia. Cutting man off from the perceptible outer world, pitching him back into his abstract interior in order to correct him, blinding, is the inevitable fruit of the Christian doctrine according to which the consummation of this cutting off, the pure isolation of man in his spiritual "ego" is *good itself.* If Rudolph does not shut the gang leader up in a real monastery as was the case in Byzantium and in Franconia, he at least shuts him up in an ideal monastery, in the cloister of an impenetrable night which the light of the outside world cannot pierce, the cloister of an idle conscience and consciousness of sin filled with nothing but phantoms of memory.

A certain speculative shame prevents Herr Szeliga from agreeing openly with the penal theory of his hero Rudolph that worldly punishment must be linked with Christian remorse and penance. Instead he imputes to him—naturally as a mystery which is only just being revealed to the world —the theory that punishment must make the criminal the "*judge*" of his "*own*" crime.

The mystery of this revealed mystery is *Hegel's* penal theory. Hegel holds that the criminal must as a punishment pass sentence on himself. *Gans* developed this theory at greater length. In Hegel this is the *speculative disguise* of the old *jus talionis** that *Kant* developed as the *only legal penal theory.* Hegel makes self-judgement of the criminal no more than an "*Idea*," a mere speculative interpretation of the *current empiric penal code.* He thus leaves the mode of application to the respective stages of development of the state, i.e., he leaves punishment as it is. Precisely in that he shows himself more critical than his Critical echo. A *penal* theory that at the same time sees in the criminal the *man* can do so only in *abstraction*, in imagination, precisely because *punishment, coercion* is contrary to *human* conduct. Besides, this would be impossible to carry out. Pure subjective arbitrariness would take the place of the abstract law because it would always depend on official "honest and decent" men to adapt the penalty to the individuality of the criminal. Plato admitted that the *law* must be one-sided and must *make abstraction* of the individual.

---

* The law of the talion—an eye for an eye.—*Ed.*

On the other hand, under *human* conditions punishment will *really* be nothing but the sentence passed by the culprit on himself. There will be no attempt to persuade him that *violence* from *without*, exerted on him by others, is violence exerted on himself by himself. On the contrary, he will see in *other* men his natural saviours from the sentence which he has pronounced on himself; in other words the relation will be reversed.

Rudolph expresses his innermost thought—the purpose of blinding the gang leader—when he says to him:

"Every word you say will be a prayer."

He wants to teach him *to pray.* He wants to change the herculean robber into *a monk* whose only work is prayer. How human is the ordinary penal theory that just chops a man's head off when it wants to destroy him in comparison with this Christian cruelty. Finally, it goes without saying that whenever really massy legislation seriously thought of improving the criminal it was incomparably more sensible and human than the German Harun el Rashid. The four Dutch agricultural colonies and the Ostwald penal colony in Alsace are truly human attempts in comparison with the blinding of the gang leader. As Rudolph kills *Fleur de Marie* by handing her over to a priest and consciousness of sin, as he kills *Chourineur* by robbing him of his human independence and debasing him to a bull-dog, so he kills the gang leader by having his eyes gouged out so that he can learn to *"pray."*

This is, by the way, the form in which all reality *"simply"* proceeds out of *"pure Criticism,"* to be precise, distortion and *senseless abstraction* of reality.

Immediately after the blinding of the gang leader, Herr Szeliga causes a *moral miracle* to take place.

"The terrible gang leader," he reports, *"suddenly* recognizes the power of honesty and decency and says to *Shuriman: 'Yes, I can trust you, you never stole anything.'"*

Unfortunately Eugène Sue recorded something that the gang leader said about *Chourineur*, which contains the same recognition and cannot be the effect of his having been blinded, since it was said *earlier*. In a talk to Rudolph alone he said about *Chourineur*:

"Besides, he is not capable of giving away a friend. No, there's something good in him . . . he has always had strange ideas."

This would seem to do away with Herr Szeliga's moral miracle. Now we shall see the *real* results of Rudolph's *Critical* cure.

We first come across the gang leader as he is going with a woman called *Chouette* to the estate of Bouqueval to play a foul trick on *Fleur de Marie*. The thought that dominates him is, or course, the thought of *revenge* on Rudolph. But the only way he knows of wreaking vengeance on him is metaphysically, by thinking and hatching "*evil*" to spite him. "He has taken away my sight but not the thought of evil." He tells *Chouette* why he called her.

"I was *bored* all alone with those honest people."

When Eugène Sue satisfies his monkish, bestial lust in the *self-humiliation* of man to the extent of making the gang leader implore the old hag *Chouette* and the little imp *Tortillard* on his knees not to abandon him, the great moralist forgets that that is the height of diabolical satisfaction for *Chouette*. As Rudolph, by the *violence* of having the criminal's *eyes gouged out*, proved to him the force of *physical power* which he had formerly told him was nonexistent, so Eugène Sue now teaches the gang leader really to recognize the power of *complete sensuousness*. He teaches him to understand that without it man *is unmanned* and becomes a helpless object of mockery for children. He persuades him that the world has deserved his crimes, for he only had to lose his sight to be ill-treated by it. He robs him of his last human illusion, for so far the gang leader

had believed in *Chouette's* attachment to him. He said to
Rudolph, "She would let herself be thrown into the fire for
me." Eugène Sue, on the other hand, has the satisfaction of
hearing the gang leader cry out in the depths of despair:
  "*Mon dieu! Mon dieu! Mon dieu!*"
  He has learnt to "*pray*"! In this "*spontaneous*" call for
the pity of God" Eugène Sue sees "something provi-
dential."
  The first result of Rudolph's Criticism is this *spontaneous
prayer*. It is followed immediately by *involuntary penance*
at Bouqueval farm, where the ghosts of those the gang leader
murdered appear to him in a dream.
  We shall not give a detailed description of this dream.
We find the Critically reformed gang leader fettered in the
cellar of the "Brass Rouge," half devoured by rats, half
starving and half insane as a result of being tortured by
Chouette and *Tortillard*, and roaring like a beast. *Tortillard*
has delivered *Chouette* to him. Let us watch the treatment
he inflicts on her. He *copies* the hero *Rudolph* not only
outwardly, by scratching out *Chouette's eyes*, but *morally*
too by accompanying his cruel act with a repetition of
Rudolph's hypocrisy and pious words. As soon as the gang
leader has *Chouette* in his power he shows "*a fearful joy*"
and his voice trembles with rage.
  "You realize," he says, "that I do not want to get it over
at once.... Torture for torture.... I must have a long talk
with you before killing you.... It is going to be terrible for
you. First of all, you see ... since that dream at Bouqueval
farm which brought all our crimes back before me, since
that dream which nearly drove me mad ... and which will
drive me mad ... a strange change has come over me....
I have become horrified at my past cruelty.... At first I
would not let you torture the songstress,* but that was

---

* He means *Fleur de Marie.*—*Ed.*

16—1192

nothing.... By bringing me to this cellar and making me
suffer cold and hunger you left me to the terror of my own
thoughts.... Oh, you don't know what it is to be alone....
Isolation purified me. I should not have thought it possible—
a proof that I am perhaps less of a blackguard than before.... What an infinite joy I feel to have you in my power,
you monster ... not to get my revenge ... but to avenge our
victims.... Yes, I would have done my duty if I had punished my accomplice with my own hand.... I am now horrified at my past murders, and yet ... don't you find it
strange?... it is without fear or misgivings that I am
going to commit a terrible murder on you, with terrible
refinements.... Tell me, tell me ... do you understand that?

In those few words the gang leader goes through a whole
scale of *moral casuistry*.

His first words are a *frank* expression of his desire for
vengeance. He wants to give torture for torture. He wants
to murder *Chouette* and he wants to prolong her agony by
a long sermon. And, wonderful sophistry! the speech with
which he tortures her is a *sermon on morals*. He affirms that
his dream at Bouqueval has improved him. At the same time
he reveals the real effect of the dream by admitting that it
almost drove him mad and that it will really do so. He gives
as a proof of his amendment that he prevented *Fleur de
Marie* from being tortured. Eugène Sue's personages—
earlier *Chourineur* and now the gang leader—must express
as the result of their *own* thoughts, the conscious motive of
their acts, the reason why the writer makes them behave in
a certain way and no other. They must continually say: I
have amended in this, in that, etc. As they do not really
come to a life of any content what they say must give vigorous tones to insignificant features like the protection of
Fleur de Marie.

Having reported the *salutary* effect of his Bouqueval
dream, the gang leader must explain why Eugène Sue had

him locked up in a cellar. He must find the novelist's treatment reasonable. He must say to *Chouette*: by locking me in
a cellar, letting me be gnawed by rats and suffer hunger and
thirst, you have consummated my amendment. Solitude has
purified me.

The beastly roar, the wild fury, the terrible lust for
vengeance with which the gang leader receives *Chouette* are
a rebuff to his moralizing talk. They betray what kind of
thoughts occupied him in his dungeon.

The gang leader himself seems to realize this, but as he
is a *Critical moralist*, he will know how to conciliate the
contradiction.

He declares the very "boundless pleasure" of having
Chouette in his power to be a sign of his amendment. His
lust for vengeance is not *natural* one but a *moral* one. He
wants to avenge, not his own victims, but the common
victims of *Chouette* and himself. And when he murders her, he
does not commit *murder*, he fulfils a *duty*. He does not *avenge*
himself on her, he *punishes* his accomplice like an impartial
judge. He shudders at his past murders and, all the same,
marvelling at his own casuistry, he asks *Chouette* whether
she does not find it strange that he wants to kill her without
fear or misgivings. On moral grounds that he does not
reveal he gloats at the same time over the picture of the murder that he is going to commit, because it is a *terrible
murder*, a *murder with terrible refinements*.

It fits the gang leader's character that he should murder
Chouette, especially after the cruelty with which she treated
him. But that he should commit murder on moral grounds,
that he should give a moral interpretation to the terrible
murder and the terrible refinements, that he should still
repent of his former murders when he is committing another
one, that from a simple murderer he should become a
murderer in a double sense, a *moral murderer*—all this is
the glorious result of Rudolph's Critical cure.

16*

Chouette tries to get away from the gang leader. He notices it and holds her fast.

"Keep still, *Chouette*, I must finish explaining to you how I gradually came to repentance.... It will be a horrible revelation for you ... and it will also show you how pitiless I must be in the vengeance I want to wreak on you in the name of our victims.... I must hurry.... The joy of having you here in my hands makes my blood boil.... I shall have time to make the approach of your death more terrifying by forcing you to liste to me.... I am blind ... and my thought takes a shape, a body, to present to me visibly, almost palpably, all the time ... the features of my victims.... The ideas are reflected almost materially in my brain. When repentance is accompanied by an expiation of terrifying rigour, an expiation that changes our life into a long sleep-lessness filled with avenging hallucinations or desperate reflexions ... then, perhaps, the pardon of men follows remorse and expiation."

The gang leader continues in a hypocrisy which every minute betrays itself as such. *Chouette* must hear how he came by degrees to repentance. This revelation will be horrible for her, for it will prove to her that it is his *duty* to consummate ruthless revenge, not in his own name, but in the name of their common victims. Suddenly the gang leader interrupts his didactic lecture. He must, he says, "hurry" with his lecture, for the joy of having her in his hands makes the blood pound in his veins; that is a moral ground to cut the lecture short! Then he calms his blood again. The long time that he uses to give her a moral sermon is not lost for his revenge. It will "make the approach of her death terrifying" for her. That is another moral ground to protract his sermon! And having such moral grounds he can safely resume his moral text where he left off.

The gang leader correctly describes the condition to which

isolation from the outer world reduces a man. For him who sees a *mere idea* in the *perceptible world, mere idea,* on the other hand, becomes a *perceptible being.* The figments of his brain assume corporeal form. A world of perceptible, sensible ghosts is begotten within his mind. That is the mystery of all pious visions and at the same time it is the general form of insanity. When the gang leader repeats Rudolph's words about the "power of repentance and penance associated with terrible torments," he does so in a state of half madness, thus proving in fact the connection between Christian consciousness of sin and insanity. Similarly, when the gang leader considers the transformation of *life* into a *nightmare* filled with ghosts as the real result of repentance and penance, he is expressing the true mystery of pure Criticism and of Christian amendment, which consists in changing man into a ghost and his life into a *life of dream.*

At this point Eugène Sue realizes how the *salutary thoughts* that he lets the blind robber prate away to Rudolph will be prejudiced by the gang leader's treatment of *Chouette.* That is why he makes the gang leader say:

"The salutary influence of these thoughts is such that my rage is appeased."

So the gang leader realizes that his *moral wrath* is nothing but *profane rage.*

"I lack courage ... strength ... will to kill you. . . , No, it is not I who should shed your blood ... it would be ... *murder*" (he calls things by their names) "excusable murder, perhaps, but murder all the same."

Chouette wounds the gang leader with a dagger just in time. Eugène Sue can now let him kill her without any moral casuistry.

"He uttered a cry of pain ... the fierce passion of vengeance, of rage and of bloodthirsty instinct, suddenly aroused and exasperated by this attack, had a sudden and terrible outburst in which his already badly shaken reason was shattered.... Viper! I have felt your fang ... you will be *sightless* as I am."

And he scratches her eyes out.

When the gang leader's nature, which has only been hypocritically, sophistically masked and ascetically repressed by Rudolph's cure, breaks out, the *outburst* is all the more violent and terrifying. We must be grateful to Eugène Sue for his admission that the gang leader's reason was badly shaken by the events that Rudolph had prepared.

"The last spark of his reason dies out in that cry of terror, in that cry of a damned man" (he sees the ghosts of his victims); "the gang leader rages and roars like a *frenzied beast*.... He tortures *Chouette* to death."

Herr Szeliga mutters under his breath:

"With the gang leader there cannot be such a *swift*" (!) "and *fortunate*" (!) "*transformation*" (!) "as with *Shuriman*.*"

As Rudolph sends *Fleur de Marie* to the cloister, he also sends the gang leader to the asylum, to *Bicètre*. He has paralyzed his *moral* as well as his physical strength. And rightly. For the gang leader sinned with his moral as well as his physical strength, and according to Rudolph's penal theory the *sinful forces* must be annihilated. But Eugène Sue has not yet consummated the "repentance and expiation accompanied by terrifying vengeance." The gang leader recovers his reason, but fearing to be delivered to justice he remains in Bicètre and *pretends* to be mad. Monsieur Sue forgets that "every word he said was to be a *prayer*" whereas it is much more like the inarticulate howling and raving of a madman. Or perhaps Monsieur Sue ironically puts these manifestations of life on a *footing with* praying?

The idea of the punishment that Rudolph carried out in blinding the gang leader—the isolation of the man and his soul from the outer world, the association of legal penalty

with theological torture—is decisively implemented in the
cell system. That is why Monsieur Sue glorifies that system.

"How many centuries had to pass before it was realized
that there is *only one* means of overcoming the rapidly
advancing leprosy" (i.e., the corruption of morals in prisons)
"that is threatening the body of society: isolation."

Monsieur Sue shares the opinion of respectable people
who explain the spread of crime by the organization of
prisons. To remove the criminal from bad society he is left
to his own society.

Eugène Sue says:

"I should consider myself lucky if my feeble voice could
be heard among all those who so rightly and so insistently
demand the *complete* and *absolute* application of the cell
system."

Monsieur Sue's wish has been only *partially* fulfilled. In
the debates on the cell system in the Chamber of Deputies
this year even the official supporters of that system had to
acknowledge that it leads sooner or later to insanity in the
criminal. All sentences of imprisonment for more than ten
years should therefore be converted into deportation.

Had Messieurs Toqueville and Beaumont studied Eugène
Sue's novel thoroughly they would inevitably have enforced
complete and absolute application of the cell system.

If Eugène Sue deprives criminals with a sane mind of
society in order to make them insane, he gives the insane
society to make them sane.

"Experience proves that isolation is as fatal for the insane
as it is salutary for criminals."

If Monsieur Sue and his Critical hero Rudolph have not
made *law* poorer by any mystery through the *Catholic
penance system* or the *Methodist cell system*, they have, on
the other hand, enriched medicine with *new* mysteries, and
after all, it is just as much of a service to *discover new*
mysteries as to *reveal old ones*. In its report on the blinding

of the gang leader Critical Criticism fully agrees with
Monsieur Sue:

"When he is told he is deprived of the light of his eyes he
does not even believe it."

The gang leader could not believe in the loss of his sight
because in reality he could still see. Monsieur Sue is describing a new kind of cataract and is reporting a real
mystery for massy un-Critical *ophthalmology.*

The *pupil* is *white* after the operation, so it is a case of
cataract of the crystalline lens. So far, this could, of course,
be caused by injury to the envelope of the lens without
causing much pain, though not entirely without pain. But
as doctors achieve this result only by *natural*, not by *Critical*
means, the only resort was to wait till inflammation set in
after the injury and the exudation dimmed the lens.

A still greater *miracle* and greater *mystery* befall the
gang leader in the third chapter of the third book. The man
who has been blinded *sees* again.

"*Chouette*, the gang leader and Tortillard *saw* the priest
and *Fleur de Marie.*"

If we do not interpret this seeing of the gang leader as
a kind of *author's miracle* after the method of the *Kritik der
Synoptiker* the gang leader must have had his cataract
operated. Later he is blind again. So he used his eyes too
soon and the irritation of the light caused inflammation
which ended in paralysis of the *retina* and incurable *amau-
rosis.* It is another mystery for un-Critical ophthalmology
that this could happen in a *single* second.

b) Reward and Punishment. Double Justice
(with a Table)

The hero Rudolph reveals a new theory to keep society
upright by *rewarding the good* and *punishing the wicked.*
Un-Critically considered, this theory is nothing else but the

theory of the society of today. How little it forgets to reward good and punish evil! How un-Critical the massy communist *Owen* is in comparison with this mystery revealed. In reward and punishment he only sees the consecration of the differences in social rank and the complete expression of slavish debasement.

It could be considered as a *new* revelation that Eugène Sue makes rewards the competency of justice—of a new appendix to the Penal Code—and, not satisfied with *one* jurisdiction, invents a *second*. Unfortunately this revealed mystery is also the repetition of an old doctrine expounded in detail by *Bentham* in his work already mentioned. On the other hand, we cannot dispute Monsieur Sue the honour of having justified and developed Bentham's suggestion in an incomparably more Critical way than he did. While the massy Englishman keeps his feet on solid ground, Sue's deduction rises to the Critical regions of the heavens. His argument is as follows:

"The supposed effects of heavenly wrath are materialized to terrify the wicked. Why should not the effect of the divine reward of the good be similarly materialized and anticipated on earth?"

In the *un-Critical* view it is the other way round: the heavenly criminal theory has only idealized the earthly just as divine reward is only an idealization of human wage service. It is absolutely necessary that society should not reward all good people so that divine justice will have some advantage over human.

In his presentation of his Critical rewarding justice Monsieur Sue gives "an example of the *feminine dogmatism* that must have a formula and forms it according to the categories of *what exists*" which was censured by Herr Edgar in Flora Tristan with all the "calm of knowledge." For each point of the present *penal code* which he retains, Monsieur

Sue projects an additional counterpart in a *reward code* copied from it to the last detail. To give the reader a better view of those points we shall give them and their counterparts in tabular form (see below).

TABLE OF CRITICALLY COMPLETE JUSTICE

Existing Justice	*Critically Supplementing Justice*
Name: *Criminal* Justice	Name: *Virtuous* Justice
Description: holds in its hand a *sword* to shorten the wicked by a head.	*Description*: holds in its hand a *crown* to raise the good by a head.
Purpose: Punishment of the wicked —imprisonment, infamy, privation of life.	*Purpose*: Reward of the good, free board, honour, maintenance of life.
The people is notified of the terrible chastisements for the wicked.	The people is notified of the brilliant triumphs for the good.
Means of discovering the wicked: Police spying, denouncers, to waylay the wicked.	*Means of discovering the good:* Virtue spying, denouncers, to waylay the virtuous.
Method of ascertaining whether one is wicked: Criminal assizes. The public ministry points out and denounces the crimes of the accused for public vengeance.	*Method of ascertaining whether one is good*: Virtue assizes. The public ministry points out and denounces the noble acts of the accused for public recognition.
Condition of criminal after sentence: Under supervision of supreme police. Is fed in prison. The state defrays expenses.	*Condition of virtuous after sentence*: Under supervision of supreme moral charity. Is fed at home. The state defrays expenses.
Execution: The criminal stands on the *scaffold*.	*Execution*: Immediately opposite the scaffold of the criminal a *pedestal* is erected on which the great man of good stands.—*A pillory of virtue.*

Moved by the sight of this picture, Monsieur Sue exclaims "Alas! It is a utopia! But suppose a society *organized* in this way!"

That would be *Critical organization of society.* We must defend this organization against Monsieur Sue's reproach that it is still a utopia. Sue has again forgotten the *"Virtue Prize"* that is awarded every year in Paris and which he himself mentions. This prize is even organized in duplicate: the material *Monthion Prize* for noble acts of men and women, and the Rosière Prize* for girls of good morals. There is even the *wreath* of roses demanded by Eugène Sue.

As far as spying on virtue and the supervision of supreme moral charity are concerned, they were organized long ago by the Jesuits. And besides, *Journal des Débats,*[45] *Siècle,*[46] *Petites Affiches de Paris*[47] and others point out and denounce the virtues, noble acts and merits of all the Paris stock-jobbers daily and at great cost, not counting the pointing out and denunciation of political noble acts, for which each party has its own organ.

Old Voss noted that Homer is better than his gods. The "mystery of all mysteries revealed," Rudolph, can therefore be made responsible for Eugène Sue's ideas.

In addition to this Herr *Szeliga* reports:

"Besides, there are many passages in which Eugène Sue interrupts the narration and introduces or concludes episodes, and they are all *Critical.*

c) Abolition of Degeneracy within Civilization and of Rightlessness in the State

The juridical *preventive* for the abolition of crime and hence of degeneracy within civilization consists in "protective guardianship assumed by the state over the children of

---

* *Rosière,* a virtuous girl awarded with a wreath of roses – *Ed*

executed criminals or those condemned to a life sentence."
Sue wants to organize the distribution of crimes in a
more liberal way. No family is to have the hereditary privilege of crime, free competition in crime is to triumph over
monopoly.

Monsieur Sue abolishes "rightlessness in the state" by
reforming the section of the *code pénal* on "*confidence
tricks*," and especially by the appointment of *paid lawyers
for the poor*. He finds that in countries like Piedmont and
Holland, where there are already lawyers for the poor,
rightlessness within the state has been abolished. The only
failing of French legislation is that it does not provide for
payment of the lawyers, does not foresee exclusive service
of the poor and makes the legal limits of poverty too narrow.
As if rightlessness did not begin in the very *lawsuit* itself,
and as if it had not already been known for a long time in
France that the *law* gives us nothing, but only sanctions
what we have. The already trivial differentiation between
right and *fact* seems still to be a mystery of Paris for the
novelist.

If we add to the Critical revelation of the mysteries of
law the great reforms which Eugène Sue wants to carry out
in respect of *bailiffs* we shall understand the Paris journal
Satan.[48] There we see that the residents of a district in the
city write to the "great so-much-a-line reformer" that there
is no gaslight yet in the streets. Monsieur Sue replies that he
will deal with that question in the sixth book of his
Wandering Jew. Another part of the city complains of the
shortcomings of preliminary education. Sue promises a
reform of preliminary education for that district of the city
in the tenth book of the *Wandering Jew*.

4) The Revealed "Standpoint" Mystery

"Rudolph does not maintain his lofty" (!) "*standpoint* ... he does not shirk the trouble of adopting by free choice the *standpoint* of the right and of the left, of above and below" (*Szeliga*).

One of the principal mysteries of Critical Criticism is the "*standpoint*" and *judging from the standpoint*. For Criticism every man, like every product of the spirit, is changed into a standpoint.

Nothing is easier than to see through the standpoint mystery when one has seen through the general mystery of Critical Criticism, that of warming up old speculative trash.

First of all let Criticism itself expound its "standpoint" theory in the words of its patriarch, Herr *Bruno Bauer*.

"Science ... *never* deals with a *given single individual* or a *given definite standpoint*. ... It will not fail, all the same, *to do away with the limitations of a standpoint* if it is worth the trouble and if those limitations have really general human significance; but it conceives these as a *pure category* and *determination* of *self-consciousness* and accordingly pronounces in favour only of those who have the courage to rise to the *generality of self-consciousness*, i.e., who do not wish with all their strength to remain within that limitation" (*Anekdota*, Book II, p. 27).

The *mystery* of this courage of Bauer's is *Hegel's Phenomenology*. As Hegel here puts *self-consciousness* in the place of *man*, the *most varied* human reality appears only as a *definite* form, as a *determination of self-consciousness*. But a mere determination of self-consciousness is a "*pure category*," a mere "thought" which I can consequently also abolish in "pure" thought and overcome through pure thought. In Hegel's *Phenomenology* the *material, perceptible, objective* bases of the various estranged forms of human self-consciousness are *left as they are*. Thus the whole destructive work results in the *most conservative philosophy* because it thinks it has overcome the *objective world*, the sensuously real world, by merely transforming it into a "thing of thought" a mere *determination* of *self-consciousness* and can therefore dissolve its opponent, which has become *ethereal*, in the *"ether of pure thought."* *Phenomenology* is therefore quite logical when in the end it replaces human reality by *"Absolute Knowledge"—Knowledge*, because this is the only mode of existence of self-consciousness, because self-consciousness is considered as the only mode of existence of man; *absolute* knowledge for the very reason that self-consciousness knows *itself alone* and is no more disturbed by any objective world. Hegel makes man *the man of self-consciousness* instead of making self-consciousness the *self-consciousness of man*, of real man, man living in a real objective world and determined by that world. He stands the world *on its head* and can therefore dissolve *in the head* all the limitations which naturally remain in existence for *evil sensuousness*, for *real* man. Besides, everything which *betrays the limitations of general self-consciousness*—all sensuousness, reality, individuality of men and of their world—necessarily rates for him as a limit. The whole of *Phenomenology* is intended to prove that *self-consciousness* is the *only reality* and *all reality*.

Herr Bauer recently re-christened Absolute Knowledge *Criticism* and the determination of self-consciousness *standpoint*—a name which sounds profane. In his *Anekdota* both names are to be found side by side, and standpoint is explained as determination of self-consciousness.

Since the *"religious world as such"* exists only as the world of *self-consciousness*, the Critical Critic—the theologian *ex professo*—cannot hit upon the thought that there is a world in which *consciousness* and *being* are distinct; a world which continues to exist when I do away with its existence in thought, its existence as a category or as a standpoint; i.e., when I modify my own subjective consciousness without altering the objective reality in a really objective way; in other words, without altering my own *objective* reality and that of other men. Hence the speculative *mystic identity* of *being* and *thinking* is repeated in Criticism as the equally mystic identity of *practice* and *theory*. That is why Criticism is so vexed with practice when it wishes to be something distinct from theory, and with theory when it wishes to be something else than the dissolution of a definite *category* in the "*boundless generality of self-consciousness.*" Its own theory is confined to stating that everything definite is an opposite of the boundless generality of self-consciousness and is, therefore, insignificant; for example, the state, private property, etc. It must be shown, on the contrary, how the state, private property, etc., change human beings into abstractions, or are products of the *abstract* man, instead of being the reality of individuals, of concrete human beings.

Finally, it goes without saying that if Hegel's *Phenomenology*, in spite of its speculative original sin, gives in many instances the elements of a true description of human relations, Herr Bruno and Co., on the other hand, provide only an empty caricature, a caricature which is satisfied with deriving some determination out of a product of the spirit or even out of real relations or movements, changing that determination into a determination of thought, into a *category*, and making that category the *standpoint* of the product, of the relation and the movement in order then to look down on this determination with triumphant, precocious wisdom from the standpoint of abstraction, of the general category and of general self-consciousness.

In Rudolph's opinion all men adopt the standpoint of good or bad and are judged by those two immutable conceptions.

Similarly, for Herr Bauer and Co. the standpoints are that of *Criticism* or that of the *Mass*. But both of them change *real human beings* into *abstract standpoints*.

5) Revelation of the Mystery of the Utilization of Human Impulses, or Clémence d'Harville

So far Rudolph has been unable to do more than reward the good and punish the wicked in his way. We shall now see an example of how he makes *the passions* useful and "gives the good nature of Clémence d'Harville an appropriate development."

"Rudolph," says Herr Szeliga, "draws her attention to the *entertaining* side of *charity*, a thought that testifies to a knowledge of human beings that can *only* arise in the soul of Rudolph after it has been through trial."

The expressions which Rudolph uses in his conversation with Clémence: "*to make attractive*," "*to make use of natural taste*," "*to regulate intrigue*," "*to use propensity to dissimulation and craft*," "*to change imperious, inexorable instincts into generous qualities*," etc., *betray* to no less an extent than the *very impulses* which are mostly attributed here to woman's nature, the secret source of Rudolph's wisdom—*Fourier*. He has come across some popular presentation of Fourier's doctrine.

The *application* is again just as much Rudolph's Critical own as that of Bentham's theory that we witnessed above.

It is not in charity *as such* that the young *marquise* is to find the satisfaction of her human essence, the purpose of her activity, and hence entertainment. Charity, on the contrary, offers only the exterior occasion, only the *pretext*, only the *material* for a kind of entertainment that could just as well use any other material as its content. Misery is exploited consciously to procure the charitable person "the piquancy of the novel, the satisfaction of curiosity, adventure, disguise, enjoyment of her own excellence, nervous shocks and the like."

Rudolph has thereby unconsciously expressed the mystery that was revealed long ago that human misery itself, infinite abjectness which is obliged to receive alms, must serve as a *plaything* to the aristocracy of money and education to satisfy their self-love, tickle their arrogance and amuse them.

The numerous charitable associations in Germany, the numerous charitable societies in France and the great number of charitable quixotic societies in England, the concerts, balls, plays, meals for the poor and even public subscriptions for victims of accidents have no other object. It seems then that charity has long been *organized* as entertainment.

The sudden unmotivated transformation of the marquise at the mere word "amusing" makes us doubt the durability of her cure; or rather this transformation is sudden and unmotivated only in appearance and is caused only in appearance by the description of charity as an amusement. The marquise *loves* Rudolph and Rudolph wants to disguise himself *with her*, to intrigue and to indulge in charitable adventures. Later, when the marquise pays a charity visit to the prison of Saint Lazare, her jealousy of *Fleur de Marie* becomes apparent and out of charity towards her jealousy she hides from Rudolph the fact of Marie's detention. At the best, Rudolph has succeeded in teaching an unhappy woman to play a silly comedy with unhappy beings. The mystery of the *philanthropy* he has hatched is betrayed by the Paris fop who invites his partner to supper after the dance in the following words:

"Ah, Madame, it is not enough to have danced for the benefit of these poor Poles.... Let us be philanthropic to the end.... Let us have *supper* now for the *benefit of the poor*!"

6) Revelation of the Mystery of the Emancipation of Women, or Louise Morel

On the occasion of the arrest of *Louise Morel* Rudolph indulges in reflexions which may be resumed as follows:

"The master often spoils the maid, either by fear, surprise or other use of the opportunities provided by *the nature of the condition of servants*. He reduces her to misery, shame and crime. The *law shows no concern* for this.... The criminal who has practically driven a girl to infanticide is not *punished*."

Rudolph's reflexions do not go so far as to make the *condition of servants* the object of his most gracious Criticism. Being a *petty* ruler himself, he is a *great* advocate of the condition of servants. Still less does he proceed to grasp the general condition of women in modern society as an inhuman one. Faithful in all respects to his previous theory, he objects only to the fact that there is *no law to punish* a seducer and associate remorse and penance with terrible chastisement.

He only needed to look round at legislation in other countries. *English* laws fulfil all his wishes. In their delicacy, which *Blackstone* so highly praises, they go so far as to declare it *felony* to seduce a prostitute.

Herr Szeliga exclaims with a *flourish*:

"*So*" (!) —"*thinks*" (!) —"*Rudolph*" (!) "Now compare *these thoughts* with your *fantasies* on the *emancipation of woman*. You can *almost* feel the fact of that emancipation in them with your hands, but you are too practical by upbringing, and that is why your attempts have failed so often!"

In any case, we must thank Herr Szeliga for revealing the mystery that facts can be felt in thoughts with hands. As for his amusing comparison of Rudolph with men who taught the emancipation of woman, those *thoughts* should be compared with the following "fantasies" of *Fourier's*:

"Adultery, seduction, is a credit to the seducer, it is good tone.... But, poor girl! Infanticide! What a crime! If she prizes her honour she must cut out all traces of dishonour. But if she sacrifices her child to the prejudices of the world her ignominy is all the greater and she is a victim of the prejudices of the law.... That is the *vicious circle* that all the mechanism of civilization describes."

"Is not the young daughter a ware held up for sale to the first bidder who wishes to obtain exclusive ownership of her?... Just as in grammar two negations are equal to an affirmation, we can say that *in the business of marriage two prostitutions are equal to virtue.*"

"The change in a historical epoch can always be determined by the progress of women towards freedom, because in the relation of woman to man, of the weak to the strong, the victory of human nature over brutality is most evident. The degree of emancipation of woman is the natural measure of general emancipation."

"The humiliation of the female sex is an essential feature of civilization as well as of barbarity. The only difference is that the civilized system raises to a compound, equivocal, ambiguous, hypocritical mode of existence every vice that barbarity practises in the simple form.... Nobody is punished more for keeping woman a slave than man himself" (*Fourier*).

It is superfluous to compare Rudolph's thoughts with Fourier's masterly characteristic of *marriage* or the works of the materialist section of French communism.

The most wretched offal of socialist literature, a sample of which we find in this novelist, reveal "mysteries" still unknown to Critical Criticism.

17*

7) Revelation of Political-Economic Mysteries

a) Theoretical Revelation of Political-Economic Mysteries

First revelation: Wealth often leads to waste, waste to ruin.

Second revelation: The effects of wealth that we have just seen come from a lack of education in rich youth.

Third revelation: *Heredity* and *private ownership* are and *must* be inviolable and sacred.

Fourth revelation: The rich man is *morally* obliged to give an account to the workers of the use of his fortune. A large fortune is a hereditary deposit—a *feudal fief*—confided to clever, firm, skilful and magnanimous hands, which are at the same time charged with making it fruitful and applying it in such a way that everything which has the *happiness* to be in the field of the brilliant and beneficial radiation of that fortune should be fructified, vivified and improved.

Fifth revelation: The state must give inexperienced youth the *rudiments* of *individual economy*. It must moralize fortune.

Sixth revelation: Finally, the state must tackle the vast question of *organization of labour*. It must give the beneficial example of *the association of capital and labour*, of an honest, intelligent and acceptable association guaranteeing the well-being of the *worker without* prejudice to the *fortune of the rich*; an association which will establish *links* of sympathy and recognition between these *two classes* and thus guarantee calm in the state *for ever*.

As the state does not for the time being accept this theory, *Rudolph* himself gives some practical examples. They reveal the mystery that the most widely known *economic relations* are still "mysteries" for Monsieur Sue, Herr Rudolph and Critical Criticism.

b) "The Bank for the Poor"

Rudolph institutes a *Bank for the Poor*. The statute of this Critical Bank for the Poor is as follows:

It must give support to law-abiding workers with families during periods of unemployment. It must replace alms and pawnshops. It disposes of an annual income of 12,000 francs and distributes interest-free assistance loans of 20 to 40 francs. At the beginning it extends its activity only to the *seventh arrondissement* of Paris, where most of the workers live. Working men and women applying for assistance must have a certificate from their last employer vouching for their good behaviour and giving the reason and date of the interruption of work. These loans are to be paid off in monthly instalments of one-sixth or one-twelfth of the sum as the borrower wishes, counting from the day on which he finds employment again. The loan is guaranteed by an obligation on the word of honour of the borrower; besides, it is vouched for on oath by two other workers. As the Critical purpose of the Bank for the Poor is to remedy one of the most grievous misfortunes in the life of the worker—*interruption in employment*—help can be given only to unemployed manual workers. Monsieur Germain, the manager of this institution, gets a yearly salary of 10,000 francs.

Let us now cast a massy glance at the practice of Critical political economy. The annual income is 12,000 francs. The amount loaned per person is from 20 to 40 francs, that is, 30 francs on the average. The number of workers in the seventh *arrondissement* officially recognized as "needy" is now at least 4,000. Hence, in a year only 400, or one-tenth of the neediest workers in the seventh *arrondissement* can receive relief. If we estimate the *average length* of unemployment in Paris at 4 months, i.e., 16 weeks, we shall be below the actual figure. 30 francs divided over 16 weeks gives about 37 sous and 3 centimes a week, not even 27 centimes a day. The daily expense of *one prisoner* in France is a little over 47 centimes, somewhat over 30 centimes being spent on food alone. But the worker to whom Monsieur Rudolph pays relief has a family. Let us take the average family as consisting of man, wife and two children; that means that 27 centimes must be divided among four persons. From this we must deduct rent—a minimum of 15 centimes a day—so that 12 centimes remain. The average amount of *bread*, needed by a single prisoner costs about 14 centimes. Therefore, even disregarding all other needs, the worker and his family will not be able to buy a quarter of the bread they need with the help obtained from the Critical Bank for the Poor. They will certainly starve if they do not resort to the means that the bank is intended to obviate—the pawnshop, begging, thieving and prostitution.

The manager of the Bank for the Poor, on the other hand, is all the more brilliantly provided for by the man of pitiless Criticism. The income he administers is 12,000 francs, his salary is 10,000. The management therefore costs 45% of the total, nearly three times as much as the massy poor administration in Paris, which costs only 17% of the total.

Let us suppose for a moment that the assistance that the Bank for the Poor provides is a real, not just an illusory support. In that case the institution of the revealed mystery of all mysteries rests on the illusion that only a different *distribution* of salary is necessary to enable the workers to live the whole year.

Speaking in the prosaic sense, the income of 7,500,000 French workers averages no more than 91 francs per person, that of another 7,500,000 120 francs; for at least 15,000,000 it is less than is absolutely necessary for life.

The idea of the Critical Bank for the Poor, if it is reasonably considered, comes to this: during the time the worker is employed as much will be deducted from his wage as he needs for his living during unemployment. It comes to the same thing whether I advance him a certain sum during his unemployment and he gives it back when he has employment, or he gives up a certain sum when he has employment and I give it back to him when he is unemployed. In either case he gives to me when he is working what he gets from me when he is unemployed.

Thus the "pure" *Bank for the Poor* differs from massy *savings banks* only in two very original, very Critical qualities. The first is that the bank lends money *"à fonds perdus"** on the senseless supposition that the worker could pay back if he wanted and that he would always want to pay back if he could. The second is that the bank pays no *interest* on the sum put aside by the worker. As this sum is given the form of an advance, the bank thinks it is doing the worker a favour by not charging him any interest.

The difference between the Critical Bank for the Poor and the massy savings banks is therefore that the worker loses his interest and the bank its capital.

c) Model Farm at Bouqueval

Rudolph founds a *model farm* at *Bouqueval.* The choice of the place is all the more fortunate as it still enjoys memories of the feudal times in the shape of a feudal manor.

Each of the six men employed on this farm is paid 150 *écus* or 450 francs a year, while the women get 60 *écus* or 180 francs. Moreover they get board and lodging free. The ordinary daily fare of the people at Bouqueval consists of a "formidable" plate of ham, an equally formidable plate of mutton and finally a no less massy piece of veal supplemented by two kinds of winter salad, two large cheeses, potatoes, cider, etc. Each of the six men does *twice* the work of the normal French agricultural labourer.

---

* As a sinking fund.—*Ed.*

As the total annual income produced in France when divided equally would come to no more than 93 francs per person, and as the total number of inhabitants employed directly in agriculture is two-thirds of the population of France, it will be seen what a revolution the general imitation of the German caliph's model farm would cause in the distribution, and besides, in the production of the national wealth.

According to what has been said, Rudolph achieved this enormous increase in production only by making each labourer work twice as much and eat six times as much as before.

The French peasant is very industrious; labourers who work *twice* as much must therefore be *superhuman athletes*, as the "formidable" meat dishes seem to indicate. Hence we may assume that each of the six men eats at least a pound of meat a day.

If all the meat produced in France were distributed equally there would not be even a quarter of a pound per person per day. It is therefore obvious what a revolution Rudolph's example would cause in this respect too. The agricultural population *alone* would consume more meat than is produced in France, so that as a result of this Critical reform France would be deprived of livestock altogether.

The fifth part of the gross product that Rudolph, according to the report of the manager of Bouqueval, Father Chatelain, allows the labourers in addition to a high wage and sumptuous board, is nothing else than his *ground-rent*. It is assumed according to average calculations that, after deduction of production costs and profit on the capital expended, one-fifth of the gross product remains for the French landowner, that is, that the ratio of the ground-rent to the gross product is one to five. Although it is beyond doubt that Rudolph undoubtedly decreases the profit on his expended capital beyond all proportion by increasing the expenses for the labourers beyond all proportion—according to Chaptal (*De l'industrie française*, I, 239) the average yearly income of the French agricultural labourer is 120 francs—although he gives his whole ground-rent away to the labourers, Father Chatelain reports that the prince thereby increases his revenue and thus incites un-Critical landowners to farm in the same way.

The Bouqueval model farm is nothing but a fantastic illusion; its *hidden fund* is not the *natural* land of the Bouqueval estate, it is a magic purse of Fortunatus[49] that Rudolph has!

In this connection Critical Criticism blusters out:

"You can see from the *whole plan* at a *first glance* that it is *not a utopia*."

Only Critical Criticism can see at a first glance at a *Fortunatus's purse* that it is not a utopia. The first glance of Criticism is the glance of "the evil eye"!

8) Rudolph, "the Revealed Mystery of All Mysteries"

The miraculous means by which Rudolph accomplishes all his redemptions and cures is not his fine words but his *ready money*. That is what the moralists are like, says Fourier. You must be a millionaire to be able to imitate them.

Moral is "*impotence in action*."[50] Every time it fights a vice it is defeated. And Rudolph does not even rise to the standpoint of independent moral, based at least on the consciousness of *human dignity*. On the contrary, his moral is based on the consciousness of human weakness. His is *theological* moral. We have investigated in detail the heroic feats that he accomplished with his *fixed, Christian* ideas by which he measures the world, and with his *charity, devotion, self-denial* and *repentance, his good and his wicked people, reward* and *punishment, terrible chastisement, isolation, salvation of the soul,* etc. We have proved that they are mere Eulenspiegel jokes. All we now have to deal with here is the *personal* character of Rudolph, the "revealed mystery of all mysteries" or the revealed mystery of *"pure* Criticism."

The opposition between "good" and "evil" confronts the Critical Hercules when he is still a youth in two personifications, *Murph* and *Polidori*, both of them Rudolph's teachers. The former educates him in good and is *"good."* The latter educates him in evil and is *"evil."* So that this conception should by no means be inferior in triviality to similar conceptions in other novels, Murph, the personification of *"good"* cannot be "learned" or "particularly endowed intellectually." But he is *honest, simple,* and *laconic;* he feels himself great when he applies to evil such clipped words as *"foul" or "vile,"* and has *horreur* for anything which is *base.* To use Hegel's expression, he sets the good and the true in equality of tones, i.e., in *one note.*

Polidori, on the contrary, is a prodigy of cleverness, knowledge, and education, and at the same time of the "most dangerous immorality," having, in particular, what Eugène Sue, as a member of the young devout French bourgeoisie could not forget—*"the most frightful scepticism."* We can judge of the moral energy and education of Eugène Sue and his hero by their panicky fear of *scepticism.*

"Murph," says Herr Szeliga, "is at the same time the perpetuated guilt of January 13 and the perpetual redemption of that guilt by his incomparable love and self-sacrifice for the person of Rudolph."

As Rudolph is the *deus ex machina* and the mediator of the world, Murph in turn is Rudolph's personal *deus ex machina* and mediator.

"Rudolph and the salvation of mankind, Rudolph and the realization of the essential perfections of mankind are for Murph an inseparable unity, a unity to which he dedicates himself not with the stupid canine devotion of the slave, but knowingly and independently."

So Murph is an enlightened, knowing and independent slave. Like every prince's valet, he sees in his master the salvation of mankind personified. *Graun* flatters Murph with the words: *"fearless bodyguard."* Rudolph himself calls him a *model servant* and truly he is a *model servant*. Eugène Sue tells us that Murph scrupulously addresses Rudolph as "Monseigneur" when alone with him. In the presence of others he calls him "Monsieur" with his lips to keep his incognito, but "Monseigneur" with his heart.

"Murph helps to raise the veil from the mysteries, but only for Rudolph's sake. He helps to destroy the power of mystery."

The denseness of the veil with which Murph envelopes the simplest things of this world can be seen by his conversation with the envoy Graun. From the legal right of self-defence in case of emergency he concludes that Rudolph, as *judge of the secret court*, was entitled to blind the gang leader, although the latter was in chains and "defenceless." His description of how Rudolph will tell of his "noble" actions before the assizes, what eloquence and fine phrases he will display, and how he will let his great heart pour forth could have been written by a *gymnasiast* just after reading Schiller's *Robbers*. The only "mystery" which Murph lets the world solve is whether he blacked his face with coal-dust or black paint when he played the coal man.

"The angels shall come forth and sever the wicked from among the just" (Mat. 13, 49). "Tribulation and anguish, upon every soul of man that doeth evil; but glory, honour and peace, to every man that worketh good" (Paul. Rom. 2, 9-10).

Rudolph makes himself one of those *angels*. He goes forth — into the world to separate the wicked from the just, to punish the wicked and reward the good. The conception of good and

evil has so sunk into his weak brain that he really believes
in a bodily Satan and wants to catch the devil alive, as
Professor Sack once did in Bonn. On the other hand he tries
to copy on a small scale the opposite of the devil, *God*, He
likes "to play the role of providence a little." As in *reality*
all differences melt down more and more to the difference
between *poor* and *rich*, so do *all* the aristocratic differences
dissolve in the *idea* in the opposition between *good* and *evil*.
This distinction is the last form that the aristocrat gives to
his prejudices. Rudolph rates himself as good and thinks that
the wicked exist to give him the self-satisfaction of his own
excellence. Let us consider this personification of "good"
a little more closely.

Herr Rudolph indulges in charity and dissipation like
those of the Caliph of Baghdad in the *Arabian Nights*. He
cannot lead that kind of life without sucking the blood out
of his little province in Germany to the last drop like
a vampire. As Monsieur Sue tells us, he would have been
among the German princes who were victims of mediation[51]
had he not been saved from involuntary abdication by
a French *marquis*. This gives us an idea of the size of his
territory. We can form a further idea of how *Critically*
Rudolph appraises *his own situation* by the fact that he,
a minor German *Serenissimus*, thinks it necessary to live
semi-incognito in Paris in order not to create a sensation.
He specially takes his *chancellor* with him for the Critical
purpose of being shown by him "the theatrical and childish
side of sovereign power," as though a minor German prince
needed another representative of the theatrical and childish
side of sovereign power besides himself and his mirror.
Rudolph has succeeded in plunging his suite in the same
Critical self-misunderstanding. Thus his servant *Murph* and
his envoy *Graun* do not notice how the Parisian solicitor
Monsieur *Badinot* makes fun of them when he pretends to
take their personal business as affairs of state and sarcasti-

cally chatters about the "occult relations that can exist between the most varying interests and the destinies of empires." "Yes," says Rudolph's envoy, "he has the impudence to say to me sometimes: 'How many complications there are in the government of a state that the people knows nothing about! Who would think, Herr Baron, that the notes which I deliver to you doubtless have their influence on the course of *European affairs?*' "

The envoy and Murph do not find it impudent that influence on European affairs is attributed to them, but that Badinot idealizes his base profession in such a way.

Let us first recall a scene from *Rudolph's* domestic life. Rudolph tells Murph "he was having moments of pride and bliss." Immediately afterwards he becomes furious because Murph will not answer a question of his. "I order you to speak." Murph will not be ordered. Rudolph says: "I do not like reticence." He lets himself sink to vulgarity and hints that he *pays* Murph for all his services. He will not be calmed until Murph reminds him of January 13. Murph's servile nature asserts itself after a minute's oblivion. He tears out the "hair" which he luckily has not got and is desperate at having been rude to his gracious master who called him "a model servant," "his good old faithful Murph."

After these samples of evil in him, Rudolph repeats his fixed idea on "good" and "evil" and reports the progress he is making in good. He calls alms and compassion the chaste and pious consolers of *his* wounded soul. It would be terrible, impious, a *sacrilege*, to prostitute them to rejected unworthy beings. Of course alms and compassion are the consolers of *his* soul. That is why it would be a sacrilege to desecrate them. It would be "to inspire doubt in God, and he who gives must make people believe in him." To give alms to one rejected is unthinkable!

Rudolph considers every motion of his soul as infinitely important. That is why he constantly observes and appraises them. Thus the fool consoles himself as far as Murph is concerned with the fact that he was moved by *Fleur de Marie*. "1 was moved to tears, and I am accused of being blasé, hard and inflexible!" After thus proving *his own goodness*, he waxes furious over "*evil*" and over the wickedness of Marie's unknown mother and says with the greatest possible solemnity to Murph: "You know some vengeances are very dear to me, some sufferings very precious." In speaking he makes such diabolical grimaces that his faithful servant cries out in fear: "Alas, Monseigneur!" This great lord is like the members of "*Young England*"[52] who also wish to reform the world, perform noble deeds and are subject to similar hysterical fits.

It is first in Rudolph's *adventurous nature* that we find the explanation of the adventures and situations that he finds himself in. He loves "the piquancy of novels, distractions, adventures, disguise"; his "curiousity" is "insatiable," he feels a "need for vigorous, stimulating sensations"; he is "eager for *violent nervous commotions*."

— His nature is seconded by his passion for *playing the role of providence* and arranging the world according to his fixed ideas.

His attitude to other persons is determined either by an abstract fixed idea or by quite personal fortuitous motives.

He frees the Negro doctor David and his beloved, for example, not because of the direct human sympathy that they inspire him with, not to free *them*, but to play *providence* to the slave-owner Willis and to punish him for *not believing in God*. In the same way the gang leader appears to him a godsend to whom he can *apply* the penal theory that he so long ago hatched. Murph's conversation with the envoy gives us an opportunity to search deeply from another side into the purely personal motives that determine Rudolph's noble acts.

The prince's interest in *Fleur de Marie* is based, as Murph says, "besides" the pity which the poor girl inspires him with, on the fact that the daughter whose loss caused him such bitter grief would now be of the same age as she. Rudolph's sympathy for the Marquise d'Harville has, "besides" his philanthropic idiosyncrasies, the personal ground that without the old marquis and his friendship with the Emperor Alexander, Rudolph's father would have been deleted from the line of German sovereigns.

His kindness towards Madame Georges and his interest in Germain, her son, have the same motive. Madame Georges belongs to the d'Harville family.

"It is no less to her misfortunes and her virtues than *to this relationship* that poor Madame Georges owes the ceaseless kindness of His Highness."

The apologist Murph tries to gloss over the ambiguity of Rudolph's motives by such expressions as: "above all," "besides" and "no less than."

The whole of Rudolph's character is finally resumed in the *"pure"* hypocrisy with which he manages to see and make others see in the *outbursts of his evil passions outbursts at the passions of the wicked*, in a way similar to that in which Critical Criticism represents its *own stupidities* as the *stupidities* of the *Mass*, its spiteful ill-feeling against the progress of the world outside itself as the ill-feeling of the world outside itself against progress, and finally its own egotism which thinks it has absorbed the whole spirit in itself as the egotistic opposition of the Mass to the Spirit.

We shall prove *Rudolph's* "pure" hypocrisy in his attitude to the *gang leader*, to Countess *Sarah MacGregor* and to the notary *Jacques Ferrand*.

To lure the *gang leader* into a trap and capture him, Rudolph persuades him to break into his apartment. The interest he has in this is a purely personal one, not a general human one. The fact is that the gang leader has a *portfolio* belonging to *Countess MacGregor* which Rudolph is greatly interested in gaining possession of. Speaking of Rudolph's *tête-à-tête* with the gang leader the author says explicitly:

"Rudolph was cruelly anxious: if he *let slip this opportunity of seizing the gang leader* he would probably never have another; the brigand would *carry away the secrets* that Rudolph was so keen on finding out."

With the *gang leader*, Rudolph obtains possession of Countess MacGregor's *portfolio*; he *captures* the gang leader out of purely personal interest; he has him *blinded* out of personal passion.

When *Chourineur* tells Rudolph of the gang leader's struggle with Murph and gives as the reason for his resistance the fact that he knew what was in store for him, Rudolph answers "with a sombre look, his features contracted by the almost ferocious expression of which we have spoken," "He did not know." The thought of vengeance flashes across his mind, he anticipates the savage pleasure that the barbarous punishment of the gang leader will afford him.

On the entrance of the Negro doctor David whom he intends to make the instrument of his *revenge*, Rudolph cries with *cold and concentrated fury*: "*Revenge! Revenge!*"

A cold and concentrated fury is seething in him. He then whispers his plan into the doctor's ear and when the latter shrinks away he immediately finds a "pure" theoretical motive to substitute for *personal vengeance*. It is only a case, he says, of "*applying an idea* that has often flashed across his noble brain, and he does not forget to add unctuously: "He will still have before him the boundless horizon of expiation." He follows the example of the Spanish Inquisition who, referring the victim condemned to be burnt at the stake to civil justice, added a hypocritical request for mercy for the repentant sinner.

Of course when the questioning of the gang leader takes place and when his sentence is executed, His Highness is seated in a most comfortable study in a long deep black dressing gown, his features impressively pale. In order to copy the court of justice more faithfully he is sitting at a long table on which are the exhibits of the case. He must now abandon the expression of rage and revenge which he had when he told *Chourineur* and the doctor of his plan to have the gang leader's eyes gouged out. He must show the extremely comic solemn attitude of the self-discovered judge of the world, "calm, sad and composed."

In order to leave no doubt as to the "pure" motive of the blinding, the silly *Murph* admits to the envoy Graun:

"The cruel punishment of the gang leader was intended *chiefly* to *avenge* me of the *assassin*."

In a *tête-à-tête* with Murph, Rudolph says:

"My hatred of the wicked ... has become stronger, my aversion for *Sarah* increases, doubtless, in proportion with the grief caused by the death of my daughter."

Rudolph tells us how much stronger his hatred of the wicked has become. It goes without saying that his hatred is a Critical, pure, moral hatred, hatred of the wicked *because* they are wicked. That is why he considers this hatred as his own progress in good.

At the same time, however, he betrays this growth of moral hatred as being nothing but a *hypocritical justification* by which he wishes to excuse the growth of his *personal antipathy* for Sarah. The vague moral imagination of his — increasing hatred of the wicked is only a mask for the definite, immoral fact of the growth of his aversion for Sarah. This aversion has quite a natural and quite a personal basis, his own personal distress, which is also the measure of his aversion. Doubtless!

Still more repugnant is the hypocrisy we see in Rudolph's visit to the dying Countess MacGregor.

18—1192

After the revelation of the mystery that *Fleur de Marie* is the Countess and Rudolph's daughter, Rudolph goes up to Sarah "looking threatening and ruthless." She begs for mercy.

"No mercy," he says. "Curse you, . . . you, **my** evil genius and the evil genius of my race."

So it is his "race" that he wishes to avenge. He goes on to inform the Countess how, to expiate the attempted murder of his father, he has taken upon himself a world campaign for the reward of the good and the punishment of the wicked. He tortures the Countess, he abandons himself to *his rage*, but in his *own* eyes he is only carrying out the task that he took upon himself after January 13, of "prosecuting evil."

As he is leaving, Sarah cries out: "Pity! I am dying!"

" 'Die, accursed!' replies Rudolph, terrible in his rage."

The last words "terrible in his rage" betray the pure, Critical and moral motives of his actions. It was rage that made him draw his sword against his father, his *blessed* father, as Herr Szeliga calls him. Instead of fighting this evil in himself he fights it, like a pure Critic, in others.

In the end Rudolph himself abrogates his Catholic penal theory. He wanted to abolish capital punishment, to change punishment into penance, but only as long as the murderer picked his victims and spared Rudolph's relatives. He adopts the death penalty as soon as one of his kin is murdered: he needs a double set of laws, one for his own person and one for the profane.

He learns from Sarah that Jacques Ferrand was the cause of the death of *Fleur de Marie*. He says to himself:

"No, it is not enough! . . . What a burning desire for vengeance! What a thirst for blood! . . . What calm, deliberate rage! *Until I knew* that *one* of the monster's victims was *my child* I said to myself: this man's death would be fruitless. . . . Life without money, life without the satisfaction of his furious passion will be a long and double torture.... *But it is MY daughter!* ... I will *kill* that man!"

And he rushes out to kill him, but finds him in a state which makes murder superfluous.

"Good" Rudolph! Burning with desire for revenge, thirsting for blood, with calm deliberate rage, with a hypocrisy which excuses every evil impulse with its casuistry, he has all the *evil* passions for which he gouges out the eyes of others. Only the lucky coincidence that he has money and rank in society save this "*good*" man from the *penitentiary*.

"The power of Criticism," to compensate for the otherwise complete nullity of this Don Quixote, makes him a "good lodger," a "good neighbour," a "good friend," a "good father," a "good bourgeois," a "good citizen," a "good prince," and so on, according to Herr Szeliga's gamut of eulogy. That is *more* than *all the results* that *humanity has achieved in the whole of its history.* That is enough for Rudolph to *save* "the *world*" twice from "ruin"!

Chapter IX

THE CRITICAL LAST JUDGEMENT

Through *Rudolph* Critical Criticism has twice saved the world from ruin, but only that it may now *itself* decree the *end of the world.*

And I saw and heard a mighty angel, Herr *Hirzel,* flying down from Zurich across the heavens. And he had in his hand a little book open like the fifth number of *Allgemeine Literatur-Zeitung*; and he set his right foot upon the Mass and his left foot upon Charlottenburg; and he cried with a loud voice as when a lion roareth, and his words rose like a dove—Chirp! Chirp!—to the regions of pathos and the thunder-like aspects of the *Critical Last Judgement.*

"When, in the end, *all* is united against Criticism and—*verily, verily I say unto you,**—the time is not far off when all the world in dissolution—*to it it was given to fight against the Holy*—will group around Criticism for the last onslaught; *then* will the courage of Criticism and its significance have the greatest recognition. We can have no fear for the issue. It will all end by our settling accounts with the various groups—*and we shall separate them as the shepherd separateth the sheep from the goats; and we shall set the sheep on our right hand and the goats on our left*—and give a general testimony to the misery of the hostile knights—*they are spirits of the devil, they go out into the breadth of the world and they gather to fight on the great day of God, the Almighty—and all on the earth will wonder.*"[53]

---

* The words between dashes are Marx's ironical remarks.—*Ed.*

And when the angel had cried, seven thunders uttered their voices:

Dies irae, dies illa
Solvet saeclum in favilla.
Judex ergo cum sedebit,
Quidquid latet, adparebit,
Nil inultum remanebit.
*Quid sum, miser, tunc dicturus? etc.**

Ye shall hear of wars and rumours of wars. This must first all come to pass. For there shall rise false Christs and false prophets, Messieurs Buchez and *Roux* from Paris, *Herr Friedrich Rohmer* and *Theodor Rohmer* from Zurich, *and they shall say: Here is the Christ!* But then the sign of the *Bauer* Brothers will appear in Criticism and the words of the Scripture on *Bauer's work*** will be accomplished:

With the oxen paired together,
Ploughing goes much better![54]

HISTORICAL EPILOGUE

As we later learned, it was not the world, but the Critical *Literatur-Zeitung* that had its last day.

Written by K. Marx and F. Engels in September-November 1844

Published in book form in Frankfort-on-Main in 1845

Signed: Frederick Engels and Karl Marx

The translation is made from the text of the German edition of 1845

---

* That day of wrath will reduce the world to ashes. When the judge takes his seat all that is hidden will come to light, nothing will remain concealed. What shall I, wretch, say then? (from a Catholic hymn on the Last Judgement).

** "Bauer's work" in German is *"Bauernwerk,"* which literally means "peasant's work."—*Ed.*

N O T E S

The Holy Family, or Critique of Critical Critique. Against Bruno Bauer and Co.—the first joint work of Karl Marx and Frederick Engels. It was written from September to November 1844 and published in February 1845 in Frankfurt-on-Main.

The "Holy Family" is a humorous nickname for the Bauer brothers and their followers grouped around *Allgemeine Literatur-Zeitung* (*General Literary Gazette*). Attacking Bauer and the other Young Hegelians (or Left Hegelians), Marx and Engels at the same time criticized Hegel's own idealist philosophy.

Marx gave evidence of deep divergencies with the Young Hegelians as early as summer 1842, when the club of the "Free" was formed in Berlin. When, in October 1842, Marx became editor of *Rheinische Zeitung* (*Rhine Gazette*), on the staff of which there were several Berlin Young Hegelians, he opposed the publication in the paper of insipid pretentious articles from the club, which had lost touch with reality and was absorbed in abstract philosophical disputes. During the two years following Marx's break with the "Free," the theoretical and political differences between Marx and Engels on the one hand and the Young Hegelians on the other became most profound and irreconcilable. This was due to the fact that Marx and Engels had abandoned idealism for materialism and revolutionary democratism for communism; it was also due to the evolution that the Bauer brothers and their fellow-thinkers went through during that time. Bauer and his group published in *Allgemeine Literatur-Zeitung* disavowals of the "1842 radicalism" and of its most conspicuous mouthpiece, *Rheinische Zeitung*; they slithered into the vilest vulgar subjective idealism, to propaganda of the "theory" according to which only selected individuals, vehicles of the "spirit," of "pure criticism," are the makers of history, while the mass, the people, serves as inert material, ballast, in the historical process.

Marx and Engels decided to devote their first joint work to the exposure of these pernicious reactionary ideas and to the defence of their new materialistic and communistic outlook.

During a ten days' stay of Engels in Paris the plan of the book —at first entitled *Critique of Critical Critique. Against Bruno Bauer and Co.*—was drawn up, the parts were divided between the authors and the *Foreword* was written, Engels wrote his parts before leaving Paris. Marx, to whose share the larger part of the book fell, continued to work on it until the end of November 1844. He considerably increased the intended size of the book by using in the writing of his sections part of his manuscripts on economics and philosophy on which he had been working in the spring and summer of 1844, his study of the history of the French Revolution and a number of excerpts and synopses. While the book was in the printing Marx completed the title with the words *The Holy Family.* The table of contents showed which sections had been written by Marx and which by Engels (see Contents of the present edition pp. 5-6). As the book was more than 20 signatures and of small format, it was exempted from preliminary censorship according to the regulations then in vigour in a number of German states.

Title page.

2 *Allgemeine Literatur-Zeitung* (*General Literary Gazette*), a German monthly published by the Young Hegelian B. Bauer in Charlottenburg from December 1843 to October 1844.   p. 15

3 Marx here uses the world *Mühleigner,* a literal translation of the English mill-owner, to ridicule J. Faucher, of the editorial board of *Allgemeine Literatur-Zeitung*, who applied English methods of word formation in German.   p. 21

4 The struggle for legislation limiting the working day to ten hours started in England as early as the end of the 18th century and spread by the 30's of the 19th century to the mass of the proletariat. As the landed aristocracy wanted to use this popular slogan in their fight against the industrial bourgeoisie they supported the Ten-Hour Bill in Parliament. The "Tory philanthropist" Lord Ashley headed the supporters of the bill in Parliament in 1833.   p. 23

5 These words are from Bruno Bauer's book, *Die gute Sache der Freiheit und meine eigene Angelegenheit* (*The Good Cause of Freedom and My Own Affair*), Zürich and Winterthur, 1842.   p. 26

19*

[6] The article in question here is "Herr Nauwerk and the Faculty of Philosophy" published in No. VI of *Allgemeine Literatur-Zeitung* (May 1844) and signed "J"—the first letter of Jungnitz. p. 27

[7] The reference is to the dismissal of B. Bauer whom the Prussian Government deprived temporarily in October 1841 and permanently in March 1842 of the right to lecture in Bonn University because of his writings criticizing the Bible.

[8] In this section Engels analyzes and quotes E. Bauer's review of Flora Tristan's *l'Union Ouvrière* (*The Workers' Union*), Paris, 1843, which was published in No. V of *Allgemeine Literatur-Zeitung* (April 1844). p. 29

[9] From Schiller's *Das Mädchen aus der Fremde* (*The Maid from Abroad*). p. 34

[10] The reference is to P. J. Proudhon's *Qu'est-ce que la propriété? ou Recherches sur le principe du droit et du gouvernement*, (*What is Property? or Studies on the Principle of Law and of Government*), first published in Paris in 1840. Marx quotes the Paris edition of 1841.

Qu'est-ce que la propriété? was written from the contradictory standpoint of the petty bourgeoisie. The sharp attacks it made on private property produced a profound impression. Marx gave an exhaustive critical appraisal of the book in his article "On Proudhon," published in the form of a letter to Schweitzer, editor of *Social-Demokrat*, in 1865 (see Karl Marx and Frederick Engels, *Selected Works*, two-vol. edition, Vol. I, pp. 390-398).

E. Bauer's article "Proudhon," which Marx criticizes in this section of *The Holy Family*, was published in No. V of *Allgemeine Literatur-Zeitung* (April 1844). p. 35

[11] Marx here means the political grouping formed around the Paris paper *La Réforme*, consisting of petty-bourgeois Democratic-Republicans and petty-bourgeois Socialists. p. 37

[12] *Deutsch-Französische Jahrbücher* (*German-French Year-Book*) was published in German in Paris and edited by K. Marx and A. Ruge. The only issue was a double number in February 1844, carrying Marx's articles "On the Jewish Question" and *Contribution to a Critique of Hegel's Philosophy of Law. Introduction* and Engel's works, *A Contribution to the Critique of Political Economy*, and "The Position of England. Thomas Carlyle. 'Past and Present.'" These works mark the final transition of Marx and Engels to ma-

terialism and communism. Publication of the journal was discontinued chiefly because of differences of principle between Marx and the bourgeois Radical Ruge.

13 The reference is to a review published by Szeliga in No. VII of *Allgemeine Literatur-Zeitung* (June 1844) on the French writer Eugène Sue's novel *Mystères de Paris*. The novel is written in the spirit of petty-bourgeois sentimentality and social fantasy. It was published in Paris in 1842-1843 and was popular in France and abroad.   p. 74

14 The reference is to the *Charte constitutionnelle* adopted in France after the 1830 Revolution as the basic law of the July monarchy. The expression "Charter of Truth" is an ironic allusion to the conclusive words of Louis-Philippe's proclamation on July 31, 1830: "henceforth the Charter will be the truth."   p. 77

15 Marx here paraphrases a couplet from Goethe's *Faust*, Part I, Scene 6 (*The Witches' Kitchen*).   p. 85

16 Quoted from Ch. Fourier's *Théorie de l'unité universelle*, Vol. III, Part II, Chap. 3.   p. 89

17 Here and lower quotations are made from B. Bauer's article "Latest Works on the Jewish Question" published in No. 1 of *Allgemeine Literatur-Zeitung* (December 1843); this was B. Bauer's reply to press criticism of his book *Die Judenfrage*.   p. 106

18 Bruno Bauer's book *Die Judenfrage* (*The Jewish Question*) is a reprint with a few additions of his articles on the same subject published in *Deutsche Jahrbücher* (*German Year-Book*) in November 1842. The book was published in Brunswick in 1843.   p. 106

19 The reference is to the weekly paper *Révolutions de Paris*, which appeared in Paris from July 1789 to February 1794. Until September 1790 it was edited by the revolutionary publicist Elisée Loustallot.   p. 111

20 *Doctrinaires*—a group of French bourgeois politicians during the Restoration (1815-30); they were constitutional monarchists and rabid enemies of the democratic and revolutionary movement and wished to establish in France a bloc of the bourgeoisie and gentry after the English fashion; the best known among them were the historian F. Guizot and the philosopher P. Royer-Collard.   p. 115

21 Marx has in mind B. Bauer's article "Latest Works on the Jewish Question."   p. 117

[22] The reference is to Marx's article "on the Jewish Question."   p. 118

[23] The reference is to B. Bauer's review of the first volume of a course
of lectures on law by the right Hegelian Hinrichs published in Halle
in 1843 under the title *Politische Vorlesungen*, Bd. I-II (*Political
Lectures*, Vols. I-II). Bauer's review was published in No. I of
Allgemeine Literatur-Zeitung (December 1843). Lower, in the section "Hinrichs No. 2" the reference is to B. Bauer's review on the
second volume of the lectures published in No. V (April 1844) of
the same journal.   p. 122

[24] This and the following quotations are from the second article written by B. Bauer against the critics of his book *Die Judenfrage*. This
article, entitled as the first "New Works on the Jewish Question,"
was given in No. IV of *Allgemeine Literatur-Zeitung* (March 1844).
                                                                          p. 127

[25] The title of B. Bauer's article, published in No. VIII of *Allgemeine
Literatur-Zeitung* (July 1844). Nearly all the quotations made by
Marx in *Absolute Criticism's Third Campaign* are taken from this
article.   p. 133

[26] *Deutsche Jahrbücher*—abridged title of the literary-philosophical
Young Hegelian journal *Deutsche Jahrbücher für Wissenschaft und
Kunst* (*German Year-Book on Science and Art*). The year-book was
published in Leipzig and edited by A. Ruge from July 1841. From
1838 to 1841 it appeared under the name *Hallische Jahrbücher für
deutsche Wissenschaft und Kunst* (the *Halle Year-Book on German
Science and Art*). The transfer of the editorial office from the Prussian town of Halle to Saxony and the alteration in the title of the
year-book were motivated by the threat of prohibition in Prussia
But the journal did not exist long under its new name. In January,
1843 it was closed down by the Saxonian government and prohibited in the whole of Germany by a decree of the Diet.   p. 134

[27] *Rheinische Zeitung für Politik, Handel und Gewerbe* (*Rhine Gazette of Politics, Trade and Industry*)—a daily paper which appeared in Cologne from January 1, 1842 to March 31, 1843. It
was founded by representatives of the Rhineland bourgeoisie who
were opposed to Prussian absolutism. Some young Hegelians were
also on the staff. Marx wrote for it from April 1842 and became
one of its editors in October of the same year. A number of Engels's articles were also published in *Rheinische Zeitung*. During
Marx's editorship the paper became more and more markedly

revolutionary-democratic. The government introduced a particularly strict censorship in regard to it and subsequently closed it. p. 134

27 Synoptics is the name given in the history of religion to the compilers of the first three gospels. p. 140

29 The reference is to Marx's article "On the Jewish Question." p. 143

30 The article in question is B. Bauer's "Fähigkeit der heutigen Juden und Christen, frei zu werden" ("The Capacity of the Jews and Christians of Today to Obtain Freedom"). p. 144

31 *Cercle social*—an organization established by democratic intellectuals and functioning in Paris in the first years of the French Revolution. Its place in the history of communist ideas in France is determined by the fact that its ideologist K. Foché demanded an equalitarian redivision of the land, restrictions on large fortunes and employment for all able-bodied citizens. Foché's criticism of the formal equality proclaimed in the documents of the French Revolution prepared the ground for bolder action on the question by Jacques Roux, leader of the "*Enragés.*" p. 161

32 *Jansenists*—named after the Dutch theologian Jansenius—representatives of the opposition trend among Catholics in France in the 17th and early 18th centuries. They voiced the discontent of a part of the French bourgeoisie at the feudal ideology of official Catholicism. p. 170

33 Lamettrie's book (*L'homme machine*) was published anonymously in Leyden in 1748. It was burnt and its author was banished from Holland whither he had emigrated from France in 1745. p. 175

34 The first edition of Helvetius's book, which was published anonymously in Paris in 1758, was burnt by the executioner in 1759. p. 178

35 *Allgemeine Zeitung (General Newspaper)* a reactionary German daily newspaper founded in 1798; from 1810 to 1882 it appeared in Augsburg. p. 179

36 Goethe, *Faust*, Part 1, Sc. 3 (*Faust's Study*). p. 190

37 *Zeitschrift für spekulative Theologie (Journal of Speculative Theology)*—published in Berlin from 1836 to 1838 under the editorship of B. Bauer, who then belonged to the right Hegelians. p. 191

38 From the French writer J. F. Marmontel's one-act comedy *Lucile*, Scene 4. p. 193

[39] *Berlin Couleur* was the name given by the *Allgemeine Literatur-Zeitung* correspondent to the Young Hegelians who did not belong to B. Bauer's group and who criticized *Allgemeine Literatur-Zeitung* on certain petty questions. One of them was Max Stirner.   p. 199

[40] Marx here means B. Bauer's article "Leiden und Freuden des theologischen Bewusstseins" (Suffering and Joys of Theological Consciousness") in *Anekdota zur neuesten deutschen Philosophie und Publicistik.*   p. 204

[41] *La Démocratie Pacifique*—a daily paper of the Fourierists published in Paris from 1843 to 1851 under the editorship of V. Considérant.
                                                                              p. 204

[42] Heine—*Die Nordsee* (Second cycle "Fragen")   p. 210

[43] From the German folk song *Nönnchen.*   p. 215

[44] From the German comic folk-tale *Seven Suabians.*   p. 218

[45] *Journal des Débats*, abridged title of the French bourgeois daily paper *Journal des Débats politiques et littéraires*, founded in Paris in 1789. During the July monarchy it was a government paper and the organ of the Orleanist bourgeoisie.   p. 251

[46] *Le Siècle (The Century)*—a daily newspaper appearing in Paris from 1836 to 1939. In the forties of the 19th century it reflected the views of the part of the petty bourgeoisie which confined its demands to moderate constitutional reforms.   p. 251

[47] *Petites Affiches (Short Announcements)*—an old French periodical publication founded in Paris in 1612; a sort of information sheet in which short announcements and notifications were published.
                                                                              p. 251

[48] *Satan*—a small bourgeois satirical paper appearing in Paris from 1840 to 1844.   p. 252

[49] Fortunatus, a hero of German popular legend who had a wonderful inexhaustible purse and a magic hat.   p. 265

[50] From Fourier's *Théorie des quatre mouvements et des destinées générales.*   p. 265

[51] The allusion is to the petty German princes who lost their power and whose possessions were annexed to the territories of larger German states as the result of the reshaping of the German political map during the Napoleonic Wars and at the Vienna Congress (1814-15).   p. 268

[52] "Young England"—a group of English politicians and writers belonging to the Tories, formed in the early 40's of the 19th century. They voiced the dissatisfaction of the landed gentry at the strengthening of the economic and political might of the bourgeoisie and resorted to demagogic methods in order to bring the working class under their influence and make use of it in their fight against the bourgeoisie. In the *Communist Manifesto* Marx and Engels described their views as "feudal socialism."   p. 270

[53] Marx here quotes with ironic insertions correspondence from Hirzel in Zürich published in No. V of *Allgemeine Literatur-Zeitung* (April 1844).   p. 276

[54] From a French drinking song.   p 277

INDEX OF AUTHORITIES

politique au conservatoire des arts et métiers. Sur la propriété," Paris 1841.—70.

R

R(eichardt), C(arl), "Katechismus für wahlberechtigte Bürger in Preußen. Von Dr. A. Benda. Berlin, 1843 bei Springer," in: *Allgemeine Literatur-Zeitung*, Heft 6, Mai 1844. 18, 19.

—"Preußens Beruf in der deutschen Staatsentwicklung, und die nächsten Bedingungen zu seiner Erfüllung. Von C. Brüggemann, Berlin, 1843, bei Besser," in: *Allgemeine Literatur-Zeitung*, Heft 6, Mai 1844.—18, 19.

—"Schriften über den Pauperismus. Publicistische Abhandlungen: von Wöniger, Doctor bei der Rechte und der Philosophie. 1843. Berlin bei Hermes," in: *Allgemeine Literatur-Zeitung*. Heft 1, Dezember 1843.—17, 18, 19.

—"Schriften über den Pauperismus. Die Gründe des wachsenden Pauperismus von A. T. Wöniger," in: *Allgemeine Literatur-Zeitung*, Heft 2, Januar 1844.—17.

Révolutions de Paris. Dédiées à la Nation et au District des petits Augustins, 1789-1794.—117.

Rheinische Zeitung für Politik, Handel und Gewerbe, Köln, 1. Januar 1842 bis 31. März 1843. —134, 144.

Robespierre, Maximilien, "Rapport sur les principes de morale politique qui doivent guider la Convention nationale dans l'administration intérieure de la République, fait au nom du comité de salut public, à la séance du 5 février (17 pluviôse) 1794," in: Buchez et Roux, *Histoire parlementaire de la révolution française*, T. 31, p. 271.—163, 164.

Robinet, J. B., *De la Nature* T. I-IV, 1761-1766.—175.

S

Saint-Just, Louis, "Au nom des comités de salut public et de sûreté générale. Convention nationale. Séance du 31 mars (11 germinal) 1794," in: Buchez et Roux, *Histoire parlementaire de la révolution française*, T. 32, p. 101.—164.

Saint-Just, Louis, "Rapport sur la police générale. Du 26 germinal an 2 (25 avril 1794)," in: Buchez et Roux, *Histoire parlementaire de la révolution française*," T. 32, p. 323.—164.

Satan, Le, 1842-1844.—252.

Say, J.-B., *Traité d'économie politique, ou simple exposition de la manière dont se forment, se distribuent et se consomment les richesses*, T. I/II, 3me éd., Paris 1817.—61.

Schiller, Friedrich, *Das Mädchen aus der Fremde*.—34.

Shakespeare, William, "Ende gut, alles gut," 1. Aufzug, 3 Szene.—77.

Siècle, Le, 1836-1866.—251.

Sieyès, E. J., Qu'est-ce que le tiers état?, Paris 1789.—46.

www.ingramcontent.com/pod-product-compliance
Lightning Source LLC
Chambersburg PA
CBHW072113270326
41931CB00010B/1549